BLOOD LUST

SHEILA JOHNSON

PINNACLE BOOKS
Kensington Publishing Corp.
http://www.kensingtonbooks.com

PINNACLE BOOKS are published by

Kensington Publishing Corp.
850 Third Avenue
New York, NY 10022

All Kensington Titles, Imprints, and Distributed Lines are available at special quantity discounts for bulk purchases for sales promotions, premiums, fund-raising, and educational or institutional use. Special book excerpts or customized printings can also be created to fit specific needs. For details, write or phone the office of the Kensington special sales manager: Kensington Publishing Corp., 850 Third Avenue, New York, NY 10022, attn: Special Sales Department, Phone: 1-800-221-2647.

Pinnacle and the P logo Reg. U.S. Pat. & TM Off.

ISBN-13: 978-0-7860-1852-9
ISBN-10: 0-7860-1852-6

First Printing: October 2007

10 9 8 7 6 5 4 3 2 1

Printed in the United States of America

For Lisa,
and for all those who loved her.

Acknowledgments

There are a great many people without whom this book would have not been possible. Their help has been appreciated, and hopefully, none will be omitted. But if I should fail to mention anyone who lent me a hand with their information or expertise, please know I am very grateful.

The former sheriff of Mobile County, Alabama, Jack Tillman, was extremely open and forthcoming, and I hope to be able to reciprocate someday.

Alabama attorney general Troy King and his outstanding prosecutors—Will Dill, Don Valeska, and Corey Maze—have not only my thanks for all they have done for the people of their state, but my lasting admiration for their excellent work on this case.

There is an incredible video called *Crystal Death,* and it should be shown in every school, police station, sheriff's department, district attorney's office, and church in this nation. Look for it on the Internet; you won't be sorry. Thanks to Jesse Hambrick and everyone else who was involved with *Crystal Death*'s production. You've done a great service to us all, and your work has been an inspiration that has contributed greatly to this book.

Contributions to the photo section of the book have been provided by the sheriff's departments of Carroll County, Forsyth County, and Douglas County, Georgia; Kevin Pearcey of the *Luverne Journal;* Bo Wilson, of the *Dawson News & Advertiser;* Clarice Doyle, of the *Claremore Daily Progress;* the office of the Alabama attorney general; the New Orleans Police Department; George Herrera, of the *Dawson Community News;* and Jennifer Murphy.

Jennifer, in addition to contributing many photos of her beautiful mother, Lisa Marie Nichols, has provided so much information and assistance in more areas than I can count. She has been a tremendous help, and she has become a good friend. I hope this book will serve as a tribute to her mother, and to all the other victims' families.

To the great number of other people who lent their knowledge, observations, and so much more, thank you so much. You have given me the means of creating a tool that I hope to use in encouraging families and law enforcement to never give up on their lost loved ones' cases.

Chapter 1

In mid-September 2004, emergency agencies in the cities, towns, and communities along Alabama's Gulf Coast were hurrying to prepare for a direct hit by Hurricane Ivan, a dangerous storm that had already left more than sixty people dead across the Caribbean. Cutting a trail of destruction through Jamaica and Grenada, Ivan had bypassed Cuba as it barreled its way toward the port of Mobile, Alabama, and the Florida Panhandle. Ivan was being billed by the National Hurricane Center's weather forecasters as the worst hurricane to threaten the Mobile area since Hurricane Frederic in September 1979. The potential for extreme damage was quite high, and was being predicted throughout the region. Residents of the Gulf Coast were fearful; since Ivan's path on its way through the Gulf was changing and looking unpredictable, and there was no clear indication of the storm's eventual path, evacuations had been ordered everywhere between Louisiana and the Florida Panhandle. The eye of the storm was expected to come ashore somewhere near Mobile in the early hours of Wednesday, September 15, 2004, as a Category 4 hurricane packing sustained winds of 135 miles per hour, accompanied by storm surges of ten to sixteen feet. Residents of the endangered coast rushed frantically to board up houses, secure boats and mobile homes. They quickly gathered up their prized possessions, family photos, and important paperwork, and headed inland away from the most endangered coastal communities. Shelters had been set up in local high schools, other secure locations were packed with evacuees, and Alabama's governor declared a curfew for the city of Mobile. Those few citizens who chose to ignore the curfew were warned to stay inside their homes and off the streets.

As threatening storm clouds gathered that Wednesday, Lisa Marie Nichols, her daughter Amber, and Amber's fiancé, Todd McKerchie, decided to ride out the fast-approaching hurricane in a sturdy motel on the western side of Mobile. Lisa lived by herself in a mobile home in the community of Turnerville, north of Mobile, and she felt safer in the motel with her daughter and Todd than if she had been staying alone in her home and risking Ivan's high winds.

Most of Lisa's neighbors had also evacuated their homes and could only hope that their dwellings and property would be spared serious storm damage; they knew without a doubt that they would lose their electrical service and they were sure that when they came home, their yards would be littered with fallen tree limbs and other debris. Mark and Kim Bentley, who lived next door to Lisa's home on Ann Parden Road in Turnerville, were planning to wait out the hurricane in Chickasaw, Alabama, a town north of Mobile, and Mark's cousin "Scooter" Coleman had decided to brave the storm and stay at the Bentleys' house, keeping an eye on things while they were gone.

Mark and Kim Bentley were preparing to leave, just ahead of the storm, when an unexpected visitor showed up on their doorstep. John Paul Chapman, a young man whom everyone called "Oklahoma," had worked for Mark in his construction business a few years earlier before moving to Georgia. Chapman had come down to Mobile from the Atlanta area in the hope of finding employment there after the storm. There would be much damage to be repaired, he knew, and there might be work for him in Mobile and along the Gulf Coast for weeks or even months to come. Mark and Kim left Chapman at their house to stay with Scooter, and the couple made the drive up to Chickasaw before Ivan was set to strike Mobile.

At the last minute, the storm veered slightly to the east before it made landfall in Gulf Shores, Alabama, sparing the Mobile area the worst of its fury. The Florida Panhandle, to the east of Gulf Shores, suffered the brunt of the damage, with hundreds of homes destroyed, buildings in downtown Pensacola collapsed, and extensive flooding throughout the city. But even though Mobile, and the other areas farther inland from the city, had been spared, the Turnerville community and others to the north/northwest of Mobile Bay still received some measure of damage from the high winds and heavy rain brought by Ivan. As expected, electrical service failed in much of the Mobile area and around five hundred thousand homes were left in the dark.

The hurricane soon moved out, blowing through the area as quickly as it had arrived, and Lisa, Todd, and Amber returned to Lisa's trailer the following morning, around nine-thirty, to look things over and check for damage. They found that the yard was covered with downed tree limbs and branches, as they had expected it would be, but there were also some signs that someone might have broken into the mobile home the night before, during the height of the storm. Lisa decided to go back with Todd and Amber to Amber's house for another night, since the power was out, and in the meantime, her neighbors, the Bentleys, returned home to survey the damage to their property.

Lisa Nichols left for her job at Bruno's supermarket before

6:00 A.M. on Friday, clocked out of work at 2:55 P.M., and stopped to check in with Amber on the way home. Later, while she unloaded food and supplies from her truck, Lisa talked to Amber again on her cell phone. Then Lisa called a neighbor and they compared notes about the storm damage that had been done to other homes in their community.

Sometime between seven and eight o'clock that evening, another neighbor of Lisa's heard a noise that she thought sounded like an explosion somewhere nearby in the area. A short time later, Mark Bentley returned home from a trip he had made to a nearby town to buy hamburgers, and as he walked into the house, he found John Paul Chapman just stepping out of the shower. With the electricity restored to the Bentley trailer, Chapman, Mark, and Scooter ate the hamburgers while they watched a hunting video; then Mark went to bed around 8:30 or 9:00 P.M. Around an hour later, Mark heard Chapman fumbling around outside with some gasoline cans, and told him to come back inside; it was too late at night to go riding on four-wheelers, Mark told him, assuming that was what Chapman was planning to do. Around twenty minutes later, Mark got up to check on Chapman and found him lying on the living-room couch.

The next day, Amber and her sister, Jennifer Murphy, tried several times to contact Lisa Nichols by phone, but were unable to reach her. This was highly unusual, since Lisa always answered the girls' phone calls promptly. As it began to grow later in the day, with no word from Lisa, the girls became very worried for their mother's safety. It wasn't like her not to answer the phone at all, especially for an entire day. Jennifer, Amber, and Todd decided to make the forty-five-minute drive from their homes to Turnerville that Saturday night, to find out what was the matter and why Lisa wasn't picking up the phone.

When they arrived in the neighborhood that evening, Todd McKerchie and the two girls got the flashlights they had brought along and walked up the driveway to the back door of Lisa's still-darkened house. The door was open, which was highly unusual; because she lived by herself, Lisa was always very careful to keep the door locked. They went inside, alarmed and fearful, calling their mother's name, and immediately noticed that the trailer smelled strongly of smoke.

Moments later, next door at the Bentleys' home, Scooter Coleman heard Lisa's daughters frantically screaming for help. Like all the other neighbors who heard the commotion, he rushed outside to see what had happened. Scooter found everyone else in the neighborhood running to the aid of McKerchie and the two hysterical girls, but later that evening, he realized there was one person who didn't come outside at all, and never even showed any interest in whatever was going on at the home next door. Despite all the screaming and frantic cries for help, which came from the trailer only one hundred yards away from where he sat watching television, Oklahoma never even looked outside to see what had happened next door.

There was no need; he already knew very well why Lisa Nichols's daughters were screaming for help. And a few days later, when Chapman was arrested for breaking in on Lisa, raping her, shooting her, then setting her body on fire in the bathroom of her trailer, Scooter Coleman and the Bentleys understood why Chapman had sat indoors, unconcerned, while the rest of the neighborhood ran to help Lisa's family. Chapman's dismayed hosts also learned that the man they had known for several years as John Paul "Oklahoma" Chapman was actually a fugitive named Jeremy Bryan Jones, who would soon be christened by the national media as "the next big serial killer."

Chapter 2

In January 1990, a Miami, Oklahoma, woman went to pick up her young son from school one afternoon, as she did every day. When she arrived, the boy wasn't waiting for her at his usual location. The woman looked around the school's parking area, hoping to find her son, and was shocked when she spotted him a short distance away, fighting in the school yard with another boy. When the mother rushed over to break up the fight, the other boy, Jeremy Bryan Jones, turned viciously on the woman, assaulting her, and threw her to the ground.

That incident was the first documented brush with the law for Jeremy, who was charged as a juvenile with assaulting the boy and his mother. No one had been seriously injured, and no weapons of any kind had been involved in the altercation, but that school-yard scuffle presented a good example of the apparent anger and aggression toward women and authority figures that was beginning to build up inside Jeremy Jones. The anger and aggression he showed during that incident would continue to escalate as time passed.

Because of his persistent behavior problems, Jeremy later transferred to nearby Quapaw High School from the school at Miami. There, he quickly developed a reputation for back talk and disrespect for his teachers, but nothing of a violent nature marked his record during his time at the school. He was mainly considered to be "mouthy." However, some staff members noted Jeremy's considerable ability to manipulate his friends into doing whatever he wanted them to do, and they also noted his skill at "sucking up" to those he wanted to impress. For the most part, though, Jeremy's problems at Quapaw were mostly due to his aversion to following orders and obeying the rules. After his transfer, he had taken up with a rough crowd at the school, cultivated a "bad boy" image, and began his early involvement with drugs, drinking, and delinquency.

Jeremy Jones also cultivated another image during his high-school years, one that was not noted anywhere in his school records. Jeremy earned a reputation as a "ladies' man" and developed the ability to make close friends among the girls he knew. He enjoyed good relationships with the girls he dated, and was able to retain their friendship for years to come.

One woman recalled the crush she had on Jeremy when she was a young teenager, calling him her "first puppy love," and said they were very close during their time in school. He was her prom date, and he spent a lot of time visiting in her home, during which time he made a point of endearing himself to the girl's mother.

"My mother just loved him," she said of Jeremy. "She wanted me to marry him."

Other girls, who didn't date Jeremy Jones but said they "ran around together" as good friends, also fondly remembered him many years after they had been in school together.

"We used to just hang out and do things and have fun," one

girl said. "We used to race our cars, and stuff like that. We were real buddies."

She said Jones was well-liked by everyone in their circle, and mentioned his ability to charm the girls with his outgoing personality and the attention that he paid to them, making them feel special and attractive.

On May 11, 1992, when Jeremy Jones was eighteen years old and out of high school, a young newlywed in Baxter Springs, Kansas, left her duplex apartment that morning to run errands and go to an appointment at a tanning salon in nearby Cardin, Oklahoma. Jennifer Judd was a strikingly beautiful, dark-haired, twenty-year-old bride who worked nights as a cashier at a convenience store in her hometown of Picher, Oklahoma. She had been married to her husband, Justin, for only ten days and recently had moved into the apartment where Justin already lived. Justin had called her that morning from his job at a chemical plant in nearby Riverton, Kansas, asking Jennifer to bring his lunch by the plant for him while she was on the way to the tanning salon.

Jennifer left for her appointment at the salon, taking along a bag containing Justin's lunch, which she planned to drop off on her way. The authorities believed that shortly after she drove away from the apartment, she remembered that she had left behind a rented movie, which she needed to return to the video store. Jennifer went back to the apartment and ran in to get the movie.

Later that day, Justin Judd and a friend, who had been his best man at the wedding, came home to find the body of Justin's beautiful new bride lying on the blood-spattered kitchen floor of their apartment. She had been viciously attacked and stabbed to death.

* * *

In November 1995, Jeremy Jones was charged in his first rape case; only two months later, he was charged again for a second rape and the unlawful possession of methamphetamine, the drug that would hold sway over his life during the coming decade. On the day following his arrest for rape and drug possession, yet another woman came forward to report that Jones had held a pistol to her vagina and threatened to kill her. He was arrested for that incident and charged with sexual battery.

Soon after this series of arrests, Jones received an incredibly lucky break when the court placed him in a program for delayed sentencing, which had been designed for young adult offenders. The court officials sent him to Hominy, Oklahoma, where he was held at the Dick Conner Correctional Center to be evaluated, and hopefully rehabilitated, by the court services unit in preparation for his sentencing. There, the staff experienced some of Jones's first efforts at skillfully manipulating the authorities and telling them exactly what they wanted to hear.

Jones convinced his evaluators that he had realized drugs had destroyed his life, told them that he "used to have" a drug problem, and said that he was filled with regret for the things that he had done. He blamed the incidents of sexual battery on his methamphetamine use, and swore that he had reformed. His mother, Jeanne Beard, also did her best to tell the court services officers what she thought they wanted to hear. She tried to convince them that her boy came from a loving, upstanding family that was a stellar example of closeness and stability, and assured the officers that Jones was a cooperative, productive member of that family.

There were some problems, however, with some of the statements that Jones made to his evaluators. He claimed that he had graduated from high school in Miami, Oklahoma, and he wouldn't admit to having had any problems with the law as a juvenile. Even though the claims he made about his high-school attendance were untrue, and his juvenile problems couldn't be verified by the correctional authorities due to sealed juvenile records, Jones was judged to be a good candidate for rehabilitation.

Chapter 3

There was little to get excited about in the small, quiet Delaware County community of Grove, Oklahoma, but on February 21, 1996, things changed dramatically. Emergency vehicles were called out and then rushed to the rural trailer of Daniel Oakley and Doris Harris to find it in flames. Oakley and Harris were found inside the trailer by firefighters, once the fire was extinguished. The couple had been shot to death, and between the fire and the water from the firemen's hoses, any clues at the scene that might have remained about the identity of their murderer had been quickly and permanently erased.

After receiving a fairly positive report from the correctional center, Jeremy Jones was sentenced in early March 1997 to five years of probation for the three charges of sexual battery, to which he had entered pleas of nolo contendere, or no contest. The court ordered Jones to report for DNA testing, and Jones was also ordered to attend special classes for sex offenders. Those classes, however, didn't work out quite as well as had his stint at the correctional center. Jones caused a number of problems during his sex offender classes, and he told his mother that he didn't like sitting there during group therapy and listening to what the others in the class—whom he referred to as "a bunch of perverts"—had to say. Totally unable to see himself as being in need of the classes, Jones was finally kicked out of a therapy session after losing his temper and making a scene, disrupting the session.

Authorities believed that Justin Hutchings, a clean-cut, handsome, young Oklahoma man, had died of an apparent drug overdose when paramedics got to the scene of his death on September 11, 1999. Justin's family members believed that foul play of some sort had been involved in his death, but the authorities didn't believe them. No evidence had turned up to indicate such a thing, they claimed, and drugs had been found in Justin's system. The ruling of a drug overdose remained, and the uncertainty about the events surrounding the death of Justin Hutchings would haunt his loved ones and remain a mystery for years to come.

Ashley Freeman and Lauria Bible, two teenage girls who lived near Welch, Oklahoma, were spending the night at Ashley's trailer home on December 30, 1999. Both girls were excellent students, well-liked by teachers and their fellow students. Ashley was a member of the National Honor Society and a member of the Welch High School basketball team, and Lauria was a very popular cheerleader. The two girls had been inseparable friends for years and spent much time together, usually at Lauria's house.

Ashley's family took pride in living "off the grid," hauling their own water and cutting firewood to heat their trailer. Ashley, like her parents, enjoyed hunting and the outdoors, and she had bagged a buck with a single shot only days earlier. Lauria liked makeup and hairstyling, and she was making plans to go to cosmetology school after graduation. Both girls had been members of the 4-H club, and Lauria was in the Blue-jacket High School Future Farmers of America chapter. The two best friends were known by everyone, both in the schools and the community, as being good kids.

The day before, December 29, had been Ashley's sixteenth birthday, and Kathy Freeman, Ashley's mother, took the two girls out to eat. They also stopped at a feed store and at the local Wal-Mart, and dropped by Kathy's mother's home to get water to take back to the Freeman trailer. Ashley's boyfriend, Jeremy Hurst, came to the Freemans' home around 7:30 P.M. and gave Ashley a birthday gift, a silver chain with Ashley's birthstone mounted on a heart-shaped pendant. Jeremy stayed and visited for a couple of hours, then said good night to the Freemans and the two girls, and went home.

Ashley and Kathy planned to get up early and go to the courthouse the first thing the following morning so that Ashley could take her driver's license test. Ashley could hardly wait to get her license; she had saved her money to buy a used car as soon as she turned sixteen, and she had already picked one out at a local car dealership. The money for the car, according to Jeremy Hurst, was kept in a plastic box, which Ashley had hidden in the freezer, crammed in between the packages of frozen venison. Lauria had to get up early, too; she had a dentist's appointment the next morning and knew that she needed to head back home in time to get to the dentist's office. Lauria's mother, Lorene Bible, had re-minded her daughter about the appointment as she left home to spend the night with Ashley, and Lauria promised she wouldn't forget to be home on time.

Early the next morning, a fire was reported in the area of the

Freeman home by a neighbor passing by on the way to work, and emergency personnel quickly responded to the alarm. To their shock, they arrived to find that the Freemans' trailer had already been reduced to a smoking heap of charred rubble. Kathy Freeman's nude body was found in the front bedroom. She had been shot in the head, and the firemen began looking for other victims inside the burned trailer. They knew there should have been other people there. The remains of the Freemans' home were still very hot, and the firemen carefully searched the smoking wreckage the best they could, but Danny Freeman and the two young girls, Ashley Freeman and Lauria Bible, were nowhere to be found. Lauria's car was still parked nearby with the keys in the ignition, and her purse was later found inside the trailer by her mother, but there was no sign of Danny Freeman or the girls. They had all disappeared at some time during the night, vanishing without a trace.

Lauria's parents, Jay and Lorene Bible, had been contacted by the authorities and were devastated when they were told there had been a fire at the Freemans' home, where their daughter had been spending the night. They were frantic to find out what had happened to their daughter, but when they got to the trailer, they were told that everything had been searched and there had been no other bodies inside, except for the body of Kathy Freeman. But when the Bibles came back the following day to search the smoking pile of rubble themselves, looking for any trace of evidence that might help them find out what had happened to their daughter, they made a horrifying discovery. The body of Danny Freeman was also in the bedroom of the trailer, where it had been completely covered by a thick layer of debris from the fire. The authorities, thinking they had thoroughly searched the trailer, had overlooked the remains. A great deal could not be determined due to the condition of the body, but it was apparent that, like his wife, Danny Freeman had been shot to death before the fire began.

Jay and Lorene Bible spent a devastating New Year's Eve, 1999, at the burned trailer, hoping to find something, anything, that would provide them with any clues about what might have happened to their daughter and her best friend. As the hours passed, groups of volunteers from all over the community started coming to the Freeman property offering to help the Bibles, searching the area with horses and four-wheelers, and walking the grid on foot. There was a crowd of over five hundred people helping with the search for the two missing girls by New Year's Day, but it was a useless effort.

Ashley Freeman and Lauria Bible were gone, without one single trace of evidence remaining behind.

For quite some time, Jeremy Jones had continued to refuse to cooperate with the court's instructions, failing to complete his therapy sessions as he had been ordered to do. His drug use had apparently escalated to an alarming level in both amount and frequency, and he'd had several run-ins with the law during that time. The court's repeated requests for mandatory DNA tests had also been ignored; so on October 19, 2000, a probation revocation arrest warrant for Jeremy Jones was issued by the court. He had been given a great chance to straighten out his life when he had received the order of the delayed sentencing, but he had failed to take advantage of it. As a result, Jeremy Bryan Jones had become a fugitive from the law.

Chapter 4

In December 2000, Jeremy Jones grew tired of constantly having to look over his shoulder, worrying about dodging the law in order to avoid being picked up and arrested for his revoked probation. He considered himself generally to be a lucky fellow, but he knew that sooner or later, his luck was going to run out. When it did, he would find himself landing back in jail—this time without the great degree of leniency he had been shown by the court previously. Jones felt like he'd pushed his luck about as far as he could, deciding that his best bet was going to be hitting the road, heading for someplace where he was less likely to be arrested. He very quietly left Oklahoma and got on board a bus headed south, on the way to Tuscaloosa, Alabama, where he hoped to stay with some family friends who lived there. Jones had sold his truck and collected a small stash of money, and his luck seemed to not only be holding, but improving. He had been given the Social Security number and other personal information of a man whose mother had met Jones in a bar. Her son was in prison in Missouri, she said, and she was charmed by the sweet-talking Jones and was sympathetic to his claims that he had been framed by the legal system.

To help Jones continue evading arrest, the woman readily offered him her son's identity, and his name: John Paul Chapman.

Others later claimed that it was Jeremy Jones's own mother, Jeanne Beard, who had obtained the Social Security number of John Paul Chapman for her son and engineered his new identity. However it had been obtained, Jones now had everything he needed to become someone else, and had the resources and the connections ready and waiting to establish himself in a new location with a new identity.

Armed with the means of continuing to give Oklahoma law enforcement the slip, Jones spent his time on the bus en route to Tuscaloosa memorizing his identity as John Paul Chapman. By the time he arrived at his destination, he knew his new birth date and Social Security number by heart, and he stepped off the bus into a new life—or so he thought. Despite his new identity, all of his old familiar demons had ridden the Greyhound south, right along with him. They held Jeremy Jones in an unbreakable grip, and they weren't about to let John Paul Chapman get away from them, either.

Chapman wasn't in Tuscaloosa for very long before he had to quickly get out of town and on the move again. He had found out that a bounty hunter from Oklahoma was hot on the trail of his Jeremy Jones persona, so he quickly moved on to Mobile, Alabama, where he went to work for a well-respected man named Mark Bentley, in Bentley's flourishing construction business. As he would do again a few years later, Chapman was allowed to stay at Bentley's home for a time. Bentley was adamantly opposed to drug use, Chapman knew, and he tried to walk the straight and narrow, working hard to make a good impression on Bentley, cultivating new friends among his coworkers, and trying to fit in with the other people he met when he went out to socialize. From all appearances, he was succeeding; his fellow employees liked him, considering him to be a stand-up kind of guy, and women were charmed by him, just as they had always been. John Paul Chapman seemed to have an almost uncanny ability to tell the ladies exactly what they liked to hear, and they were won over by his winning smile and his sweet-talking flattery.

Back in Oklahoma, Jeanne Beard was relieved that her wayward eldest son had found a good job and a place to stay. She believed that Jones, now known by all of his new acquaintances as John Paul "Oklahoma" Chapman, would be able to rebuild his life through the good influence of his honest and upstanding employer, Mark Bentley. But eventually, methamphetamine once again became more of a temptation than Chapman could withstand. He resumed his old drug habits, using meth as frequently as he could, and it had its usual destructive effects on him physically, also taking its toll on both his work and his relationship with the Bentleys, who finally had to tell him to move out of their house.

Dejected and depressed, Chapman left the Bentley home in disgrace and checked himself into a Mobile motel. Also staying there at the motel was Craig Baxter, a man from Douglasville, Georgia, who was working a temporary job in Mobile at the time. When he left Mobile to return home to Douglasville, Craig casually told Chapman to give him a call if he was ever in Georgia. That was all the encouragement he needed; within a couple of months, Chapman was in Douglasville, living in Craig Baxter's basement. Craig had wired some money to Chapman in Mobile after the young man contacted him to ask him for his help and told him he'd been mugged. Shortly after he received the money from Craig, Chapman showed up unannounced at the Baxter home. He was allowed to stay in the basement, since he said that he had no other place to go. Craig Baxter felt sympathy toward the young fellow who seemed so eager to fit in and tried so hard to be liked. He was willing to help Chapman get himself reestablished and helped him find work.

Before long, Chapman's old patterns began to reemerge and he was yet again sent packing, this time from the Baxter home, for his continuous drug use. He had not paid any rent for his basement accommodations while he'd been living there, and his drug use had escalated to an alarming level. Craig Baxter's wife, Jan, later said that she had felt very uneasy around Chapman, and that during his time in their home, she had been very worried that his drug habit would lead to a lot of serious trouble for her family.

After his eviction from the Baxter home, a kindly neighbor, John McIntosh, let Chapman stay at his home and got him a job as a welder at the Young Refinery in Douglasville. Using his fictional identity, Chapman easily passed the refinery's background check. John McIntosh, like Craig Baxter, felt sorry for the young man who had come to him for help, upset and uncertain about where to go and what to do. Since John and his wife, Kerry, were in a rough patch and were right on the verge of breaking up their marriage, John let Chapman move into their house. Chapman worked at the refinery, played with the McIntoshes' young son, and made Kerry McIntosh just as uneasy and uncomfortable as he had made Jan Baxter.

For a while, at least, things seemed to be rocking along on a fairly even keel and Chapman was successfully working to establish himself with his coworkers as a likable guy, one that they would want to be friends with. But Kerry McIntosh later said that when she and her husband would have arguments, she always had the feeling that Chapman was right there on the sidelines, campaigning against her, doing and saying to John McIntosh whatever he could to make matters worse between the troubled couple.

On the night of Halloween, 2002, Chapman helped his

young buddy, twelve-year-old Matt McIntosh, with the boy's
Halloween preparations, painting the faces of Matt and another boy so that they could roam the neighborhood in search
of candy and treats. Inspired by the rock group Kiss, he
painted the boys' faces black and white in a quite good imi-
tation of the rockers' distinctive makeup. Then, after the boys
left to go trick-or-treating, pleased with the cool way that
their grown-up friend had made them look, Chapman left the
McIntosh home and went out in search of some Halloween
entertainment of his own.

Gipson's, a popular bar and restaurant in Douglasville,
which Chapman frequented on a regular basis, was throwing
a costume party for their customers on October 31, 2002. The
club was full to capacity and the party was in full swing until,
at about midnight, a popular, attractive young woman named
Tina Mayberry was found collapsed outside the front entrance of the bar, bleeding from multiple stab wounds. She
had left the party only a few moments before to go out to her
car, and investigators believed that Tina had been attacked in
Gipson's parking lot. Two hours later, the beautiful young
woman was pronounced dead in an Atlanta hospital. There
were no immediately apparent clues left at the scene by Tina's
assailant, and the authorities were mystified. They had no
leads as to who could have assaulted Tina so near to the bar's
busy front entrance without being seen or heard by anyone at
all, and officials said that there were no immediate suspects
in her murder.

Chapman's popularity among his coworkers at the refinery
continued to grow—until Kerry McIntosh became aggravated

with the situation. She resented the fact that the man who had intentionally caused so many problems for her marriage was turning out to be so well-liked by his new friends. He continued to work hard to present himself as a "good guy," someone they could call on when they needed him, and there were no obvious reasons for his new acquaintances to see him any differently. But Chapman's drug use was once again beginning to quickly escalate, and John McIntosh started to see a very different, quite disturbing side to the young man that he had befriended. Chapman's indulgence in drugs seemed as though it fueled his increasing search for sexual satisfaction, and he stayed constantly on the lookout for women who, he thought, might be easily picked up from the bars he frequented. When there was an insufficient number of women who were drunk enough to leave the bars and go with Chapman, he went out and prowled the streets in search of whatever hookers were on the stroll that night.

One night, Chapman went trolling for available women in one of his favorite bars and he immediately got lucky, hitting pay dirt early on in the evening. He brought the woman back to his room at the McIntosh home, but she stayed only a short time. John McIntosh heard her flee from Chapman's room and leave the house hurriedly. In the early hours of the morning, police arrived and summoned Chapman down to the station for questioning. The woman had contacted the authorities and reported that he had attacked her, tried to choke her, and attempted to rape her. John McIntosh went along with Chapman to the police station, where John put in a good word for him with the authorities. Since the woman had been quite drunk at the time of Chapman's alleged attack and attempted rape, her story just wasn't credible enough to warrant the pressing of any charges, and Chapman and John left the station and went home with no further questioning about the incident.

Chapter 5

John Paul Chapman's increasing use of methamphetamine and his constant obsession with sex were becoming increasingly disturbing to his friend, John McIntosh. Chapman tried to convince his benefactor that he sincerely wanted to mend his ways and change his life, wanted to straighten himself out, and hoped to find a good woman and build a lasting relationship, complete with a home and family. When he met a woman at Gipson's one night, Chapman felt that he might finally have a shot at achieving his goal.

Vicki Freeman and a girlfriend were having dinner that evening at Gipson's, and Vicki would later tell interviewers that she noticed the handsome John Paul Chapman as soon as the two women walked in. Both women were charmed when the smiling, personable young man walked up to them and told them he thought they were beautiful, saying he'd been admiring them "from afar." He left the table then, but in a very short time, he returned to charm them even further, and Vicki was so smitten that later, when asked, she would be unable to remember just exactly what it was they talked about on that first evening.

"I was just lost in him," she said of the smooth-talking young man, who was around fifteen years her junior.

It wasn't long until Chapman and Vicki were sitting at an Olive Garden restaurant, out together for their first official date. And not long after that, in September 2003, they moved in together, living in an apartment in Villa Rica, Georgia.

A little over a month later, Chapman was arrested for indecent exposure and public indecency, and was processed through the Douglas County Jail. As is the case with every such arrest, he was fingerprinted and those prints were run through Georgia's Criminal Justice Information System (CJIS). Thanks to the care he had taken to firmly establish his identity, John Paul Chapman was not discovered by the Georgia authorities to actually be Jeremy Bryan Jones, and for some reason, the fingerprinting system failed to match his prints to those that were already on file for Jeremy Bryan Jones, the fugitive from justice with outstanding arrest warrants in Oklahoma. Because there were no apparent charges on his record for his new identity, Chapman had no problem making his bond and was soon released from jail.

The arrest that had landed Chapman in jail for indecent exposure and public indecency had come as a result of a very scary episode involving a neighbor of Chapman's, a teenage girl who lived in the apartment complex with her parents. Chapman had met the Godfreys by walking up and introducing himself a short time after he and Vicki had moved in, and he quickly developed an obsession with their attractive eighteen-year-old daughter, Brittney. She was frightened of Chapman because he had started coming around her family's apartment when he knew she was at home alone, going from the front door to the back entrance, attempting to make entry into the Godfrey apartment. When Chapman's obsession with Brittney escalated beyond control and he exposed himself to her, the police were immediately called, and he was arrested. Later that day, after Chapman had been taken away to jail, the Godfreys made a chilling discovery: On the ground outside Brittney's bedroom window, they found a box that held a "break-in kit." It contained a pair of binoculars, a length of rope, and a roll of tape. Brittney Godfrey had managed to narrowly escape what might have turned out to be a fatal encounter.

On January 22, Chapman was charged in another incident, this time with two counts of criminal trespassing, by the Carroll County Sheriff's Department. When his fingerprints were checked out through the system, they once again failed to raise any red flags as to his true identity and to the fact that he was a wanted sex offender in Oklahoma.

New Orleans police received an anonymous 911 tip on Valentine's Day, 2004, that sent them to an overgrown vacant lot located near the intersection of St. Thomas and St. James Streets, not far from one of the entrances to the Port of New Orleans, which was used primarily by truck drivers. There, as the tipster had said they would, they discovered the decomposing body of a white female who had been raped, stabbed, and beaten to death with a tire iron. Efforts to identify the woman were unsuccessful; the officers knew of no one who had been reported missing, and since the woman was believed to have been a prostitute in the French Quarter, it was unlikely anyone was going to come forward to claim her body. The case bore a great deal of resemblance to others in the New Orleans area and in other states, where at least four women who were suspected to have been prostitutes had been raped, then beaten to death with a tire iron. Detectives believed all the women had been picked up at truck stops, and since the unidentified New Orleans woman's body was found near the truckers' entrance to the port, they felt the murder might be linked to those other killings. Two officers, Sergeant Jeffrey Walls and Detective Armando Asaro, became especially determined to learn the name of the woman that no one seemed to be able to identify. They knew that, somewhere, she had a family and friends that surely had noticed she was missing and were searching for her. The two officers spent countless hours of their own time checking out similar crimes and poring over missing-persons reports from authorities in other states, but their efforts to identify the unknown woman continued from day to day without any success.

In early March 2004, much to the relief of his uneasy Villa Rica neighbors, Chapman and Vicki Freeman moved out of the apartment complex and into the Arbor Village trailer park near Douglasville, Georgia, where they set up housekeeping together in a mobile home. Chapman had been arrested a total of three times in Carroll and Douglas Counties, and each time CJIS had failed to recognize his fingerprints as being those of anyone other than John Paul Chapman. He had gotten lucky and had managed to escape detection several times already, but he continually worried that sooner or later he'd get arrested in Georgia and his true identity would surface. However, each time he'd been jailed since he came south on that Greyhound bus, the FBI's high-tech, foolproof computerized fingerprint system had failed to detect the fact that Chapman was actually a wanted fugitive from Oklahoma named Jeremy Bryan Jones.

Sixteen-year-old Amanda Greenwell was a real beauty, with a captivating smile and long, dark, lustrous hair. When Amanda left her family's trailer in Arbor Village on March 12, 2004, she was headed for a nearby pay phone to place a call. After a great deal of time had passed and Amanda hadn't returned, her father, Rick Greenwell, began to grow very concerned for his daughter. There was no sign of her near the phone booth, or anywhere else where he looked. He called the police and, along with the officers and other residents of the trailer park, a frantic search was begun. The authorities initially had thought that Amanda might be a runaway, but they soon discounted that possibility and began to believe that she had been abducted. Amanda was nowhere to be found—not by her father, not by friends, neighbors, and family members, and not by the local authorities who tirelessly searched for her for weeks with no success.

Beautiful, young Amanda Greenwell had disappeared without a trace.

John Paul Chapman was questioned by the police following Amanda Greenwell's disappearance, as were almost all of the other residents of the Arbor Village trailer park. The investigators found that there was no indication that Chapman had been involved in any way, nor was there any evidence found at the scene when Amanda's remains were discovered on April 20, 2004, widely scattered in a wooded area near the trailer park. She had been stabbed, and her neck had been snapped.

None of the initial forensics from the site where Amanda's body was recovered provided any information that incriminated Chapman or anyone else. Although the police continued to investigate the case as intently as if Amanda were one of their own children, no leads were produced, no evidence was found, and no witnesses were located. The case was, for the time being, at a complete dead end.

Chapter 6

On April 15, 2004, only a few days after the discovery of Amanda Greenwell's body, a well-known, well-liked hairdresser from a close-knit community in Forsyth County, Georgia, also vanished without a trace.

For eight years, Patrice Tamber Endres had owned and operated Tamber's Trim-n-Tan, a small, rural beauty salon located on Matt Highway, on State Route 369 in Cumming, Georgia. The salon, a small, neat gray building with dark shutters and window boxes, did a brisk business, and there were usually clients and visitors coming and going at all times of the day. The interior of the shop, done entirely in different shades of purple, Patrice's favorite color, was bright and cheery. Open shelves of hair products filled one section of the shop, and the atmosphere was welcoming and friendly. Clients often spent time talking and laughing with Patrice after their appointments were through, and others came in early just so they could visit with her and the other customers for a while before their turn came. Patrice's last customer before lunchtime on that date was finished at around 11:38 A.M., and as the customer left the shop, Patrice headed for the back room to warm up a quick lunch in the microwave oven before her next scheduled appointment arrived for a haircut at noon.

Patrice's food was sitting at the microwave, which had been paused with forty-five seconds still showing on the timer, when the noontime customer walked into the empty shop at 12:03 P.M. Patrice was nowhere to be seen, but her car sat parked outside the building and her purse was still lying there in the shop, although it looked as if it had been hurriedly rummaged through. The client immediately suspected that something had gone very wrong, and the police were called to investigate the suspicious situation.

When the officers arrived, they found that Patrice's wallet, which contained her cash and credit cards, had been pulled out from her purse and the cash had been taken, but all of Patrice's credit cards had been left behind. And whatever money had been accumulated in the shop's cash register after a busy morning's work was also missing, and the cash drawer had been left pulled out. The police immediately assumed that the beauty shop had been robbed, and that Patrice had been taken by the robber. They believed that she had been abducted as little as ten minutes before the noon customer arrived at the shop, but there were no signs of a struggle and no other evidence left at the scene that might provide any clues as to what had happened. The rifled purse and the open cash drawer were the only signs something bad might have taken place at the shop.

Patrice's description was immediately sent out to law enforcement agencies—petite, with long, dark hair, dark eyes, very attractive—a description that was eerily like that of Amanda Greenwell, Tina Mayberry, and the beautiful young newlywed who had been murdered in Oklahoma so many years earlier, Jennifer Judd.

After Patrice's disappearance, a woman who claimed to

have been an eyewitness to some suspicious activities outside the shop came forward to offer some information about what she had seen. She told the investigators that she had been driving past the salon right around the time Patrice was believed to have disappeared. The eyewitness said that she had seen a fairly late-model white Chevrolet or GMC cargo van sitting parked in front of the salon. Patrice always parked her vehicle, a new Chevy Tahoe, at the side entrance of the shop, with Patrice coming and going through the side entrance as a rule, but the witness said she saw Patrice's SUV sitting in front of the salon door that day, parked nose to nose with the white van.

Michelle Lee Grant, of Jasper, Georgia, told the authorities that she had seen a white man standing next to the van. He might have been in his mid-thirties, she said, with brown hair and eyes, medium height and weight, and was wearing a dark sweatshirt-style jacket and pants and a camouflage hat. A composite sketch was quickly made up and distributed nationwide, to police agencies and to Internet sites, showing a scruffy-looking man with a mustache and unruly hair sticking out beneath his camouflage-print baseball cap. Since this seemed to be a solid lead from someone who had apparently been an eyewitness, the investigators concentrated on the information Grant had provided, and an intensive search for the suspect began.

The entire north Forsyth County community united in an effort to help find Patrice, with large numbers of volunteers helping with the search efforts and raising reward money to be offered for information in the case. Car washes and other benefits were held, with the volunteers meeting regularly at the Zion Hill Baptist Church to plan and organize their efforts. Several local high-school girls, who had been regulars at the hair salon and who adored Patrice, the woman that they considered to be their "fairy godmother," spent their own money printing and distributing thousands of posters with her name, photo, and contact numbers to call with any possible tips. The girls played hooky from school to go out and tell people about the search for Patrice and to put up the flyers they'd made. Other posters, made up by several other friends and customers who loved Patrice, were plastered in almost every business in North Georgia, showing the possible suspect's composite sketch and a photo of a van similar to the one that had reportedly been seen by the eyewitness.

Forsyth County sheriff Ted Paxton ordered a number of ground and air searches of the area near the salon and assigned ten of his investigators to the case full-time. The officers worked long hours checking out over seven hundred possible leads and tips that came in to the sheriff's office regarding Patrice's disappearance. The detectives left absolutely nothing to chance; they identified and interviewed every significant person in Patrice's life, past and present, and tried to find out everything about her. Each of the interviews led the officers to other people they wanted to question, and those people, when interviewed, provided other leads. The investigation mushroomed, but so far, there was nothing significant to be found.

Captain Ron Freeman, of the sheriff's office, told reporters that the investigators wanted to know who Patrice's friends were, who she didn't like, who did she talk on the phone and go shopping with—everything about her life and her daily habits.

"That one thing we find out may yield the person who's involved in this," Freeman told reporters.

After authorities received information that someone had reported seeing a woman who, they thought, might be Patrice working as a dancer at a South Carolina club, there was some minor speculation that Patrice might have run away. But that tip, when checked out, amounted to nothing. Besides, Sheriff

Paxton told reporters, Patrice was so dedicated to her teenage son, D. W., or "Pistol," that running away would have been inconceivable for her. There was also money that had been left in a hidden compartment in her wallet and more money in her bank accounts, and she had made an additional deposit into one of the bank accounts the day before she disappeared—hardly the behavior of someone who was collecting cash because she planned to skip the country.

"It was money she could have bought a plane ticket with," Paxton said.

Some of Patrice's family members believed that Paxton and his investigators needed to look for the person responsible for Patrice's disappearance closer to home—much closer. They told the media they thought that Patrice's husband, Rob Endres, was involved in some manner in his wife's disappearance, but Paxton stated publicly that his detectives believed that Rob Endres was not a suspect. There was a great deal of division and lack of communication between Rob and his wife's family, and it would continue during the coming months as they all waited and hoped for some news of Patrice.

A number of regional and national missing-persons organizations took up Patrice's cause and sought to develop other leads concerning her disappearance. She was made a part of the Adopt a Missing Person program, featured on the Truckingboards.com missing-persons Web site, and Desert Thunder MotorSports owner Roger LaMoure placed Patrice's likeness on the hood of a stock car driven by Darrell LaMoure. The Napa Auto Parts Chevy was driven in NASCAR's Elite Division Auto Zone Southwest Series at the Stockton 99 Speedway in Stockton, California, on July 31, 2004. As a result, Patrice's face was seen by everyone at the race. Her story became known to thousands of race fans nationwide due to the thoughtful and generous help of the LaMoures.

Another missing-persons organization, Project Jason, announced on its Web site that Patrice would be featured in the 18 Wheel Angels campaign, a national missing-persons locator program, which had a network of truck drivers and business travelers, who were assisting with the program, placing posters of a specific featured missing person along their route. Patrice's case became familiar to hundreds of thousands of television viewers nationwide when it was featured on *America's Most Wanted* and on *Closing Arguments,* Nancy Grace's Court TV program. A reenactment of Patrice's possible abduction was filmed on-site at Tamber's Trim-n-Tan for *America's Most Wanted,* although it was never aired.

Rob Endres continued to spearhead the fund-raising events, saying that he was hopeful that someone who knew what had happened to Patrice would be tempted by a large amount of money as a reward and would come forward with some information about his missing wife. Rob, who was always ready to speak to the press as much as possible, told reporters he was trying to get the amount of the reward raised high enough to be a sufficient enticement to someone who had knowledge of the case. A large reward, he felt, might turn out to be something that would produce results. The reward fund grew from its $700 beginnings to $12,400, and then on to $17,000, thanks to a host of volunteers who raised money continually for months. Despite the reward and the veritable flood of nationwide publicity about the case, there was no trace of the missing hairdresser to be found. Patrice's disappearance remained an unsolved mystery.

John McIntosh had become seriously concerned about John Paul Chapman, who had made numerous late-night phone calls to McIntosh during the early months of 2004.

Chapman would tell John McIntosh that he had "screwed up again," and John felt that the man was referring to the serious problems he was having because of his escalating and uncontrollable use of methamphetamine and his dangerous obsession with sex. Later, John McIntosh would have good reason to wonder if the troubled young man might have been referring to problems that were far more serious than drug use.

Chapman had been arrested again on June 15 for possession of methamphetamine, possession of marijuana, obstruction, and possession of drug paraphernalia. On that occasion, he spent an entire week in the Douglas County Jail and, once again, was fingerprinted when he was booked into the jail. Those fingerprints, along with the details of Chapman's personal history, were checked out again through CJIS. As before, they failed to uncover Chapman's true identity and criminal history. If Georgia authorities would have had any reason to run the prints through the national database, and if Chapman had not firmly established his identity with an Alabama driver's license, a Social Security number, and other "foolproof" means of identification, things might have gone very differently for him during 2003 and 2004.

Over the past several years he'd spent in the southeastern states, Chapman had learned to keep a close eye on the weather along the Gulf Coast, not because of any particular interest in meteorology, but due to his knowledge that hurricanes always meant a lot of very well-paid cleanup and construction work. When Hurricane Ivan headed toward Mobile in mid-September 2004, Chapman knew there would be an unending opportunity for work along the coast for quite a while, cleaning up fallen trees and other debris and rebuilding scores of damaged homes and businesses in the storm's aftermath. He left Georgia and headed down to Mobile to find Mark Bentley and ask him for a job, hoping he could persuade his former boss to give him another chance and let him work for him once again.

When Chapman showed up on Mark Bentley's doorstep unannounced, just hours before the storm was expected to make landfall, Mark hurriedly agreed to let Chapman stay at his home with his cousin, Scooter Coleman, while Mark Bentley and Kim sat out the storm in a safer inland location.

Back in Georgia, Vicki Freeman got a phone call from Chapman on Friday, September 17, saying that he was going to work for Mark Bentley. She was thrilled to hear that he had successfully reconnected with Mark and would be working with him again, and she told Chapman to find them a place to live and she would move down to Mobile to be with him. Authorities would later learn that the phone call that had been placed to Vicki Freeman had been made with a phone belonging to a neighbor of the Bentleys, Lisa Nichols.

Lisa's worried daughters, Jennifer and Amber, came looking for her on Saturday evening, after they had been unable to get in touch with their mother for an entire day. When the girls and Amber's boyfriend entered Lisa's smoke-filled trailer, they found that she was dead. Their mother had been raped, shot, and set on fire in the bathroom of the mobile home. As the two girls began to scream for help, everyone in the neighborhood came rushing to their aid—everyone except the Bentleys' new houseguest, John Paul Chapman. His conspicuous absence would soon become a matter of great interest to the investigators who were quickly assigned to the murder case.

Chapter 7

Detectives Paul Burch and Mitch McRae, of the Mobile County Sheriff's Office, were both old hands at murder investigations. However, the crime they had just responded to—a homicide that had taken place at a mobile home on Ann Parden Road in Turnerville—was highly disturbing, even to the two seasoned veterans. When they saw the crime scene, the men said that they immediately had a hunch that it was not the killer's first time to commit such a murder. They knew that they might possibly have only a short time to identify and arrest the killer before he had a chance to strike again. The men organized all the other officers at the scene and they all immediately fanned out and began going door to door, canvassing the entire neighborhood for any possible leads. What Paul Burch later described as their "good, old-fashioned police work" began to pay off almost immediately, with information quickly coming to them from several sources that provided them with a potential suspect.

The neighbors of Lisa Nichols were shocked by the terrible crime, and they were deeply hurt by the loss of the vivacious, youthful woman who had been so well-liked by everyone in the community. They were all anxious to do anything they could do to help the authorities with the investigation of her murder. As it turned out, there were quite a few of them who had noticed the appearance of someone new in the area, someone who had shown up on September 15, just hours before Hurricane Ivan's winds and rain struck the community. Bits and pieces of information began to come together for Burch and McRae; one person recalled seeing a strange vehicle that had been sitting outside Lisa's mobile home, and the witness was able to give a good description. Someone else was able to provide a partial tag number for that same vehicle. Others remembered hearing someone mention the stranger's nickname: Oklahoma.

The most crucial information came from Mark Bentley, who, as a former employer, was able to supply Burch and McRae with the name, birth date, and Social Security number of the man who had worked for him, the man who was known by everyone as Oklahoma, and as John Paul Chapman.

Police agencies throughout the area began an immediate, all-out search for Chapman, who was now the prime suspect in the murder of Lisa Nichols, and who had slipped away from the Bentleys' home without any explanation on the day following the discovery of Lisa's body. An exhaustive, nonstop effort began to locate Chapman and take him into custody for some intense questioning.

Four days after the murder, on September 21, Detective Burch was in his office, busily coordinating the search for Chapman, when he was interrupted by a call on his cell phone. To his total astonishment, the caller was Chapman himself. Burch began to stall, stretching out the conversation as much as he possibly could by talking with Chapman about anything and everything that came to mind, whatever it took to keep him on the line. Burch managed to keep his prime murder suspect on the phone, talking long enough for Mitch McRae to begin tracing the call. In less than twenty minutes, with Burch still on the phone with him, John Paul Chapman found himself surrounded by Mobile County deputies. According to some reports, he was sitting inside a house only a block away from Lisa Nichols's trailer. Other reports claimed he was sitting inside a parked car, making his preparations to leave right away for the bus station and skip town before he was apprehended. Chapman was immediately placed under arrest by the Mobile County sheriff's deputies, taken to the Mobile Metro Jail, and was named as the suspect believed to be guilty of capital murder, rape, burglary, and kidnapping.

Lisa Nichols's two daughters, Jennifer and Amber, knew that Burch, McRae, and the other officers assigned to find their mother's killer had worked literally around the clock with very little time for food, sleep, or even a change of clothing. All the officers helping to work the case had been determined to take the suspect called Oklahoma into custody as quickly as they could, ending his chances of killing again.

"They worked, twenty-four/seven, without ever stopping to rest until the arrest was made," Jennifer Murphy said. "Words just can't express how much gratitude and admiration we feel for what they have done for us. I'll never forget it, and they'll always have a place in our hearts."

Detectives Burch and McRae believed that with their suspect safely locked up in the Mobile Metro Jail, the most immediately urgent part of their job was done. Now it was time for them to begin the painstaking and thorough collection of additional evidence. According to their usual procedures, they sent out a routine Teletype nationwide to check for any other pending charges against John Paul Chapman in other states, and to determine if he might have been involved in any similar crimes that had been committed elsewhere in the nation.

The Teletype included Chapman's Social Security number, birth date, driver's license number, and physical description.

Burch also ran Chapman's fingerprints through the Federal Bureau of Investigation's (FBI) Integrated Automated Fingerprint Identification System (IAFIS), holding over 200 million sets of fingerprints. The report on the prints came back identifying them as those of John Paul Chapman. On three occasions after arrests in Georgia, Chapman's identity had been confirmed when checked through IAFIS. For the fourth time, the Chapman alias had continued to hold up, this time against the scrutiny of the most reliable identification system that national law enforcement had to offer. The Mobile County authorities, however, were in for a real shock.

When officials from the state of Missouri received the routine police Teletype about the arrest of a subject named John Paul Chapman, they immediately contacted the Mobile County Sheriff's Department. They informed a very surprised Detective Burch that an alert clerk at one of their prisons had noticed the Teletype and had recognized that John Paul Chapman had been in Missouri's custody, doing time for robbery in one of their state prisons, since 2000. They sent a photo and fingerprints of "their" John Paul Chapman for comparison with the man who was currently being held in the Mobile Metro Jail. Neither the prints nor the photo matched Oklahoma, the murder suspect who currently sat in one of the jail's cells.

"That's when I said, 'Oh, we have a problem,'" Burch told reporters. "We knew we had to look more closely at this suspect."

For the next several days, the Mobile detectives searched every avenue they could think of, looking for any possible clues that could tell them who their suspect actually was. Then they received some unexpected assistance from the prisoner himself, when they traced some of the phone calls he had been making from the jail's pay phone. Several times since his arrest, he had called the number of a woman living in Miami, Oklahoma, named Jeanne Beard. When Burch contacted the Miami Police Department, a detective there, John Koch, told Burch he was familiar with Jeanne Beard, and said that he knew there were several outstanding warrants on one of her sons, who had left the area several years earlier.

Jeanne Beard's son's name was Jeremy Bryan Jones.

Detective Koch immediately sent his department's information on Jones, including photos, fingerprints, and the outstanding warrants, to Mobile authorities. The prints and mug shots were a match to the man who was in custody in the Metro Jail, the man who had successfully lived for the past several years as John Paul Chapman, fooling not only law enforcement but also his friends, coworkers, and lovers. But the game was over—much to the amazement of Jeremy Bryan Jones. He was served with the outstanding warrants from Oklahoma as he sat in jail in Mobile, believing his John Paul Chapman persona was still intact and hoping against hope that he would not be found out.

Chapter 8

Of all the people who were shocked and surprised to learn that John Paul Chapman was actually a man named Jeremy Bryan Jones—on the run from various charges of sexual assault in Oklahoma—perhaps no one was more shaken by the news than Vicki Freeman. Her relationship with the man she thought she had known was turbulent, and often abusive. But as victims of abuse consistently do, Vicki forgave each instance of domestic violence and continued to stay in the relationship. Initially she reportedly told the authorities about the abuse, and her friends verified her stories of physical and sexual assaults. One of her girlfriends said that Vicki had "a stack of 'I'm sorry' cards from over a year," and said that she thought that many of the incidents stemmed from the fact that Jones was continually using drugs.

When she was first contacted by law enforcement authorities, Vicki was informed that the man she had lived with for eighteen months, knowing him for all that time as John Paul Chapman, was actually Jeremy Bryan Jones, a fugitive from justice in Oklahoma. That bombshell was followed by the shocking news that Jones was now sitting in the Mobile Metro Jail charged with the murder of Lisa Nichols. Vicki Freeman was dumbfounded. She had heard from her boyfriend, she said, only days before, when he had called and told her that he'd secured a good job with Mark Bentley and said that he would soon be finding a place for the two of them to live so that she could come and join him in Mobile.

"Never in my wildest dreams would I imagine he would be capable of this until they called and told me he wasn't even who he said he was," she told Atlanta's *11Alive News*.

But despite her initial shock at learning her live-in lover's real name and identity, Vicki quickly rebounded and began defending him, denying that he'd ever abused her and telling interviewers that whatever had happened between the two of them was no one else's business. She had forgiven Jones for lying to her, she said, claiming that she loved him for the person he was, not for the name he had used. She quickly began proclaiming his innocence to anyone who would listen, believing him when he called her from the jail and told her that he had done nothing wrong and certainly hadn't murdered anyone. He was being framed by the authorities, he told her.

Even as more and more disturbing information began to mount up concerning Jones's activities during the time he had lived with Vicki in Georgia, she continued to defend him. For some time to come, she would staunchly stand by the man she had thought she loved. Even if she didn't know his real name, he just simply couldn't have done all the terrible things that the authorities in several states were beginning to suspect him of.

"He always put me first," Vicki said, regularly giving her little presents and cards. He was very loving, she said, kind and gentle. She seemed to have conveniently forgotten that she'd had to call the police on one occasion, telling them that she was afraid Chapman was going to "hurt her real bad." But she didn't press charges against him; her thoughtful, considerate boyfriend must have presented her with another one of his many "I'm sorry" cards.

Jones's mother, Jeanne Beard, made the trip to Mobile from Oklahoma to visit her son following his arrest, and Beard went along with Vicki Freeman to the Mobile Metro Jail. But Jeanne Beard later accused jail officials of refusing to allow her to see her son. Jeanne was told by a deputy, Beard claimed, that she was asked to leave because family members of one of her son's alleged victims had learned she would be at the jail and the deputy had supposedly told her she would be in danger.

Christina Bowersox, spokeswoman for the sheriff's office, said that it was Jeanne Beard's own choice not to visit her son at that time, and said that all inmates can have thirty-minute visits if the visitors sign up twenty-four hours ahead of time. Jeanne was never told she could *not* visit her son, Bowersox said.

Jeanne Beard held the local media responsible for causing her to miss the visit with Jones, and she said that the people from whom she was supposedly in danger had learned from news reports that she and Vicki Freeman planned to go to the jail the following day.

"My life might be in danger," she said.

Jeanne went on to claim that she had received a dire threat in a greeting card that was supposedly mailed from a Mobile address, which turned out to be nonexistent. Inside the card, she said, someone had drawn a sketch of Alabama's infamous electric chair, which was nicknamed "Yellow Mama," and wrote, "The only mother he will ever see on Christmas is Yellow Mama in Alabama."

The note, she also claimed, said, "Do not come to Mobile because you will regret it."

While Jeanne Beard sat in a motel room, ranting to the

media about her mistreatment by the jailers and the danger she was in from irate family members of victims, Vicki Freeman sat in a small visiting room in the Metro Jail, talking to Jeremy Jones by phone and staring at him through layers of shatterproof glass and reinforcing wire mesh. Shortly after the end of the thirty-minute visit, Vicki boarded a bus back to Georgia. Jones had worked his sweet-talking magic on his gullible girlfriend once again, and she later told the media, "He is an innocent man," claiming she believed the things that he had told her. She steadfastly claimed that she was certain that someone else was involved with Lisa Nichols's murder, and said she believed that Jones was being "set up."

Chapter 9

With Jeremy Jones in custody—his John Paul Chapman persona shattered and his real identity finally exposed—the Mobile County authorities busied themselves gathering evidence and preparing to prosecute him for the murder of Lisa Nichols. But as word of his arrest and his true identity began to spread among law enforcement agencies nationwide, Detectives Burch and McRae found themselves fielding a flood of inquiries from other departments across the country. It was beginning to look like Jeremy Jones might turn out to be a prime suspect in countless numbers of other murders and cold cases stretching all the way from the Midwest to several locations throughout the Southeast and in other parts of the nation. Law enforcement officials from Alabama, Georgia, Missouri, Oklahoma, and Arizona were busily going through unsolved case files of the women who had been raped and murdered in their jurisdictions, and Jeremy Jones began to drop tantalizing hints to the detectives about his involvement with other cases during his questioning sessions about the murder of Lisa Nichols. As the weeks passed and their suspicions grew while Jones continued to talk, the

Mobile authorities began to wonder if they just might have a serial killer in their custody.

Jones began to confirm those suspicions with a rambling series of confessions, which he made over the period of several months, beginning by providing the investigators with details about some of the various murders of which he claimed to have firsthand knowledge. As his questioning continued, he gave the detectives more and more information about the crimes, telling them some of the details that only the person who had actually committed the murders would have known. It had become apparent, soon after Jones's arrest for the murder of Lisa Nichols, that he was a habitual liar and a master manipulator. However, the things that he was telling Detectives Burch and McRae about the string of homicides, scattered throughout several states from Oklahoma to Georgia, were beginning to ring all too true.

One of the first departments to weigh in with a statement that Jones was a suspect in their jurisdiction was the Douglas County Sheriff's Office. Sheriff Phil Miller announced that two of the county's murder cases might possibly be linked to Jones. The sheriff said his investigators were hard at work going back over the evidence in the murders of Amanda Greenwell and Tina Mayberry, of Georgia, trying to corroborate the claims that Jones was making about the two deaths.

Tina, thirty-eight, was stabbed on the night of Halloween, 2002, while she was attending a costume party at Gipson's in Douglasville, the same bar and restaurant that Jeremy Jones had regularly visited, and the place where he first met Vicki Freeman. Tina's striking good looks—with her long, dark hair and a dazzling smile—were accentuated that night by an adorable Betty Boop costume she was wearing. When Tina left the party to go to her car, outside in the restaurant's parking lot, she was viciously attacked and stabbed. She managed to make it back to the door of the restaurant before she collapsed. Emergency medical technicians (EMTs) quickly responded to the frantic calls from Gipson's, and Tina was transported to an Atlanta hospital. Her injuries, though, were too severe; she died of her wounds two hours later.

When they learned of Jones's true identity and heard the details of the crime he was believed to have committed in Mobile, Sheriff Miller's investigators began backtracking. They questioned one more time everyone that regularly frequented Gipson's. With both Tina Mayberry and Jeremy Jones/John Paul Chapman visiting Gipson's on a continuing basis for some time, it was very likely that the two might have met at some point and could have known one another, Miller believed.

Amanda Greenwell, the beautiful sixteen-year-old with long, dark hair, like Tina Mayberry's, had left her home on March 12, 2004, to make a call at a nearby pay phone, and then disappeared without a trace. Amanda lived in the same Douglasville trailer park, Arbor Village, that Jones and Vicki Freeman had moved to. Jones, along with many other residents of the trailer park, had been questioned by Sheriff Miller's investigators at the time of Amanda's disappearance. They initially believed her to be a runaway, which was sometimes the case with teenagers who disappeared from home, but that possibility was discounted quickly and an intensive search began to take place. Amanda's remains were not found until April 20, 2004, scattered over a two-acre wooded area not far from Arbor Village. She had been stabbed to death, and her neck had been snapped.

Jeremy Jones had a knife collection, and photographs of him taken around that time showed him standing, smiling, with a large hunting knife hanging in its sheath on the wall behind him. Similar knives had been used in the assaults on both Amanda and Tina. Jones lived near Amanda in the same trailer park, and he was a regular at Gipson's bar, as was Tina. There were connections in both cases that began to look like much more than just mere coincidence. Jones was also giving more and more details of these and many other crimes that were very accurate, and the Mobile investigators, Paul Burch in particular, felt that he was, in most instances, telling the truth.

Sheriff Miller's officers, led by Investigators John Sweat and JoAnn Adams, began an immediate and intensive reinvestigation of those two cases in their jurisdiction, after Jeremy Jones continued to make statements that further implicated himself in the murders of both Amanda Greenwell and Tina Mayberry. Detectives Burch and McRae decided they would make a trip up to Georgia to compare notes with the Douglas County authorities, and consequently the Mobile investigators were able to provide the Douglas County officers with a great deal of help. Burch and McRae had obtained some information from Jones that led to the discovery of a storage building that he had rented in Douglas County. Miller's chief deputy, Stan Copeland, told the media that a warrant was quickly obtained and the contents of the storage building had been thoroughly searched. Some very disturbing items had been found inside the shed, Copeland said.

Among the things the investigators discovered in the storage building were photos of eight women, many of whom had marked similarities to Amanda Greenwell and Tina Mayberry. All were very attractive, and some had long, dark hair and bright smiles. The Douglas County authorities circulated the photos nationwide, from law enforcement agencies to the news media, and soon the photos were posted on the *America's Most Wanted* Web site. In the hope that the public might be able to help the authorities in identifying the eight women, Copeland said, "We want to locate these women and make sure they are not missing." And if they weren't missing,

Copeland added, his department was certainly very interested in having a talk with them about what their connection was to Jones and whatever the women might know about him.

"We have no idea if they are alive or dead," Sheriff Miller told the news media about the eight women. "They may be his friends, but we definitely want to identify them."

A Georgia woman got in touch with the Douglas County authorities very quickly to let them know she was one of the women in the photos, and she said that she was a relative of Jones's. She was fine, she said. One by one, the other women in the photographs began to come forward or were identified by their friends or relatives, and eventually it was determined that none of the eight women were missing. Most of the photographs, officers said, had been taken by Jones himself, and were of some of the women he had met at bars and clubs.

The most important piece of evidence found by the investigators during their search of Jones's storage building, however, had nothing to do with the eight women in the photographs. It was a woman's ring, a distinctive design that local jewelers told the investigators they believed had been custom-made. The ring was later identified by Amanda Greenwell's distraught boyfriend, who told the officers that the ring had belonged to Amanda.

When investigators initially questioned Vicki Freeman following Jones's arrest for Lisa Nichols's murder, they, at that time, did not know anything about Amanda Greenwell's murder. Vicki unwittingly offered them some priceless information when she told them that on the same day that Amanda had disappeared from the trailer park, Jones had come home scratched and bleeding, covered with mud. He had offered her no explanation, she said, but she told the officers that he had been returning that day from one of his frequent methamphetamine binges. She asked the officers why Jones had found it necessary to steal the identity of John Paul Chapman. Mitch McRae then told her that Jones was wanted in Oklahoma on rape charges, and that he had fled the state to live under a new name.

"She said, 'Oh no, he did it, he did it,'" McRae told reporters. "'I always wondered if he did it; now I know he has.'"

Vicki Freeman would later call Detective McRae a liar, and vehemently deny that she had ever told him anything of the kind. However, in her surprise and shock at hearing of her boyfriend's arrest, she had very likely blurted out what was really on her mind.

Douglas County sheriff Phil Miller told the media that he believed Jeremy Jones would be proven to be a serial killer and a serial rapist, in light of the evidence and the facts that he expected would be made public a short time later.

"If you're asking me what my belief is," Miller told reporters, "then yes, I believe he is a serial killer."

Considering what Miller and many other agencies from several states were beginning to learn about the man they now knew to be Jeremy Bryan Jones, everyone considered the eight women in the photos found in the storage building to be very lucky indeed.

Chapter 10

Almost immediately after Jeremy Jones was arrested for the murder of Lisa Nichols, rumors and speculation had begun to spread among law enforcement agencies in all the many jurisdictions in which Jones was beginning to claim that he had committed murders. It had come as a great shock to the Georgia authorities when they learned that the man they had arrested on several occasions as John Paul Chapman was actually a fugitive from justice in Oklahoma.

Chapman had been run through the FBI's IAFIS several times, and each time he had somehow managed to escape detection. Jones was arrested in October 2003 in Carroll County, Georgia, on suspicion of public indecency, and in January, 2004, he had been picked up by the police in Georgia on a trespassing charge. On both occasions, he had given his identity as John Paul Chapman, and that identity had held up when his fingerprints were sent to the FBI and checked against their national database.

The system failed to identify him as the same man who was wanted in Oklahoma for probation violation after three rape charges. Instead, since no match had turned up under Jones's newly assumed identity, a new record had been created for his fingerprints by the FBI, and the name that had been placed on that new record was that of John Paul Chapman.

Later that January, Katherine Collins had been reported missing in New Orleans by her son. In February, her body, initially unidentified, was found in a vacant lot. Days later, in March, Amanda Greenwell disappeared from her home in the same Douglasville, Georgia, trailer park where Jones and Vicki Freeman lived. In April, Patrice Endres was kidnapped from her hair salon in Cumming, Georgia. The disturbing truth was that all of these women had been killed *after* Jones's January arrest, the arrest that failed to identify him as a fugitive rapist.

The FBI fingerprint database once again failed to correctly identify Jones when he was arrested in June for methamphetamine possession. He was released from jail when his identity came up yet again under the name John Paul Chapman. A fingerprint scan made a positive "hit" on the new record that had been created for Jeremy Bryan Jones, the record that did not bear his real name, but, instead, bore the name of the man whose identity he had successfully used for several years.

When the failure of IAFIS came fully to light in early May 2005, the news of that failure caused the Jeremy Jones cases to receive even more nationwide attention. Newspapers around the country trumpeted headlines like, FBI MISTAKE LET SUSPECTED SERIAL KILLER GO FREE, and, FUGITIVE FREED BY FBI COMPUTER ERROR WENT ON TO KILL 2, FBI SAYS.

The Georgia Bureau of Investigations (GBI) criminal database is supervised by GBI assistant deputy director Terry Gibbons, who told the news media that it was very infrequent for the bureau to have such errors with their fingerprint identification system that was currently in use. She said it was quite surprising to her to learn about the errors that had kept "John Paul Chapman" a free man. Sheriff Phil Miller, of Douglas

County, Georgia, had called her, Gibbons said, and was very worried that his office might have done something that had caused the fingerprint errors, but that, she said, had not been the case at all. Gibbons said that she had been told by FBI officials that neither Sheriff Miller's office nor the Carroll County, Georgia, office of Sheriff Terry Langley were responsible for the foul-ups. Instead, the FBI told Gibbons, letters would be sent to both sheriffs acknowledging the FBI's full responsibility for the mistaken identifications.

When informed that he would be receiving such a letter, Sheriff Miller felt vindicated that his office had been cleared of any carelessness or wrongdoing in the mix-up, but Miller said he hoped that there would not be any repercussions for the FBI because of its mistake.

"I hope they tell the truth," he said, "and let the chips fall where they may."

Miller said that if Jones's prints had been properly matched, he would never have been released on bond, but, instead, he would have been held in custody in jail and the Oklahoma authorities would have been notified of his arrest.

GBI spokesman John Bankhead told the press that local authorities had always relied greatly on the accuracy of the IAFIS system to provide them with information about fugitives from other parts of the country. Sheriff Miller's chief deputy, Stan Copeland, said that he'd seen the system work properly far more times than it had ever failed, but Copeland went on to add that the incident had unfortunately occurred "with someone of the caliber of Jeremy Jones, who may be a serial killer." Copeland said he'd seen the fingerprint database previously catch fugitives on a weekly basis.

On Tuesday, May 3, 2005, an official statement about the failure by IAFIS to correctly identify Jones's fingerprints was released by the FBI through the offices of Thomas E. Bush III, assistant director of the bureau's CJIS Division.

"The FBI regrets this incident," Bush said. "Law enforcement lost an opportunity to prevent further criminal activity by this individual."

FBI spokesman Paul Bresson was a bit more specific in his assessment of the situation.

"This is obviously a worst-case scenario for us," Bresson said. He said the IAFIS was able to identify thousands of fugitives every month, but there were going to be instances—however few and far between—where the system just didn't catch everything.

"And in this case," he said, "it was the most tragic of all consequences."

FBI assistant director Bush, while acknowledging the computer error, added that the bureau had already begun rechecking fingerprints from countless numbers of fugitives wanted for serious crimes.

"We continue to improve our procedures and examine new technologies to upgrade and enhance the reliability and accuracy of IAFIS," Bush said.

An official review of the incident was said to be ongoing, but FBI supervisory special agent Joe Parris, when asked about the process, declined to comment further on the review itself. Parris said IAFIS makes fifty thousand fingerprint comparisons a day with a 95 percent accuracy rate.

"Nobody did anything wrong," Parris said, adding that most systems of any type couldn't be made to work accurately 100 percent of the time.

"There was no lapse; there was no inattention," he said. "It's just that the system missed it."

Chapter 11

While both local authorities and the FBI stated their sincere regrets that Jeremy Jones/John Paul Chapman had been missed by IAFIS on three occasions—during which time he was claiming that he had murdered from three to five women—another group of people were absolutely infuriated by the failure of the system to identify Jones on those several missed opportunities. The families and friends of Lisa Nichols, Amanda Greenwell, Katherine Collins, Patrice Endres, and Tina Mayberry were growing more and more vocal about the tragic consequences of the FBI computer glitch. Lisa Nichols and her ex-husband, Gene, had been divorced for over ten years, but they had maintained a good relationship and had remained close. Gene Nichols expressed his anger and frustration at the system itself, not at law enforcement. He said Lisa's murder could not be taken back, and said that he felt nothing could be done about the IAFIS failure except for the FBI to try to work toward the system's improvement.

"You can only blame one man," Gene said, "and that's the man that did this to Lisa."

Lisa Nichols's daughter Jennifer Murphy was astounded to

realize that her mother might have not been killed if only the system had recognized Jones in time to take him off the streets before Lisa's murder occurred.

"We just couldn't believe something like that could happen," Jennifer said, adding that the family wanted some straight answers as to how Jones had been able to slip through the system, unnoticed and unstopped.

Amanda Greenwell's father, Rick, lost his beautiful, young daughter only six weeks after Jones was let out of jail in Carroll County, Georgia, after a criminal trespassing arrest. Rick Greenwell was shocked to learn that Amanda's death had happened after Jones was released from jail due to what was being termed by the FBI as a technical malfunction. He told the media it was "just one blow after another," and said that the whole situation was highly disturbing to him, adding that he hoped the flaw in the system would be fixed.

Patrice Endres's husband, Rob, said that he hoped whatever had happened to his wife wouldn't be in vain.

"I don't want her to be just another statistic," he said, adding that he hoped the tragedy could somehow be used to get the FBI's system upgraded to avoid the occurrence of another such incredibly costly mistake.

Dr. Sue Kascher, a veterinarian at the Coal Mountain Animal Hospital, and a good friend of Patrice Endres, said she knew there was such a thing as human error, but she also told the press that she was shocked that Jones's identification had been mishandled in such a manner on multiple occasions.

"They could have saved a lot of lives," she said.

The most surprising statement of anger about the FBI's admitted identification mistake came from Jeremy Jones himself. Upon hearing of the FBI's statement, he immediately began telling the media that he wished that his prints had been correctly identified at the time of his first Georgia arrest. If they had been, he said, then he would have been extradited back to Oklahoma, and instead of sitting in jail in Mobile, facing a charge of capital murder, he would likely have only faced charges in Oklahoma for rape.

"It would have been nothing," he said.

Jones was angriest because the failure in the fingerprinting system had caused him to be labeled a serial killer. He used the opportunity to deny ever having said that he'd killed anyone, or that he'd confessed to any of the murders.

"I get blamed for every unsolved murder now," he whined. "I ain't no Ted Bundy." He went to great lengths to recant all his confessions to the media, while simultaneously continuing to give investigators more and more information, telling them further details of the long string of murders he claimed to have committed.

Paul Burch told the media that Jones fit the profile of a typical serial killer, according to the standards recognized by the FBI.

"I hate to just throw someone in a category like that," Burch said, adding that Jones was intelligent and "very personable to talk to."

Jeremy Jones laid the blame for the mix-up in identifying his fingerprints on technology; in Oklahoma, years earlier, he said, law enforcement had recorded his fingerprints on cards using ink pads. But in Georgia, when he was arrested, he said the authorities there used IAFIS and scanned his fingerprints to store in the nationwide files.

Clint Van Zandt, an MSNBC analyst and former FBI profiler, summed up the situation most accurately in a June 13, 2005, commentary. He said that in the case of Jeremy Jones, an apparent serial killer had been allowed to keep killing, while a computer tried and failed to link two names and multiple sets of fingerprints together.

"'Sorry' or 'computer error' is simply not good enough for the families of the victims," Van Zandt said.

When Cable News Network/Court TV's Nancy Grace featured the story of the FBI's failure to identify the man known as John Paul Chapman as actually being Jeremy Bryan Jones, Lisa Nichols's daughters, Jennifer and Amber, appeared on the program. They brought along several photos of their mother and talked with Grace about what had happened to Lisa and how their lives had subsequently been impacted by her loss.

Grace began the segment by asking her audience if a clerical error had allowed a suspected serial killer to walk free and add four more victims to his list. Grace then went to CNN correspondent Sara Dorsey for details.

Dorsey told viewers that the FBI had basically admitted that their national database had failed, and that it had not been able to match the prints of John Paul Chapman to those of Oklahoma fugitive Jeremy Jones. Dorsey added that Jones had been arrested three times in Georgia without a match being made.

"The significance of this," she said, "is that he was wanted in Oklahoma on a sexual assault charge."

Jones had been allowed out of jail after each of the Georgia arrests because of the fingerprint matches never being made, Dorsey said, and since that time he had been charged with three murders and was being looked at for several others. It was very clear that if the IAFIS system had come through with a positive identification, as many as four women might still be alive.

Chapter 12

Gradually, a little at a time during the months following his arrest for Lisa Nichols's death, Jeremy Jones had kept continually dropping tantalizing hints to Detectives Burch and McRae about more than a dozen other murders that he at first claimed responsibility for, then later recanted. Burch told the media that Jones would give him and his partner a little bit of information; then they would have to dig back into old files of cold cases from the states involved, check out the cases, and go back to question Jones further to see what else he might be willing to tell them about the more specific details of the murders. Jones finally ended up implicating himself in thirteen murders in six states. He also gave the investigators additional details about even more alleged murders he said that he'd also committed, the killing of a number of prostitutes. Mostly, he claimed, these were in the metro Atlanta area, and some from Mobile.

The problem with his confessions, investigators soon learned, was being able to turn up enough corroborating evidence to bring murder charges against Jones. Thanks to the successful collaboration between law enforcement in Mobile County, Alabama, and Douglas County, Georgia, sufficient evidence was quickly discovered to take decisive action on one of the Douglas County cases. A murder warrant was issued, and Jones was officially charged with the kidnapping and murder of young Amanda Greenwell.

Investigators believed that Jones had abducted Amanda from the phone booth in the trailer park where both she and Jones lived, then took her into the nearby woods and killed her. Douglas County authorities hoped that, following Jones's murder trial in Alabama, they would then be able to extradite him to Georgia to stand trial there for Amanda's murder.

Soon after that warrant was issued, following some lengthy questioning and investigation by Burch and McRae's team in conjunction with a group of New Orleans police detectives, Jeremy Jones was also charged with the rape, stabbing, and beating death of New Orleans prostitute Katherine Collins.

Collins, forty-seven, whose body had been found on Valentine's Day, 2004, in an overgrown lot near the truckers' entrance to the Port of New Orleans, had gone unidentified for some time after her murder. She had earlier been reported missing by her son, but the identity of her body was not confirmed until the following October, when a friend recognized a photo of a facial reconstruction that was released to the media and realized that it was Katherine Collins.

Following the discovery of Katherine Collins's badly decomposed body, her skull had been sent to the FACES Laboratory at Louisiana State University, where famed forensic anthropologist Mary H. Manheim led one of the nation's foremost forensic facial reconstruction facilities. Manheim, known among law enforcement circles as "the bone lady," had over nineteen years of experience in forensic cases, and was internationally known for her ability to approximate likenesses from skeletal remains. Manheim went to work supervising the careful crafting of a three-dimensional facial reconstruction of the skull, creating a likeness that could be photographed and used by investigators to attempt identification.

The technicians at the FACES Laboratory began by mounting the skull on a stand that could be turned in all directions during the reconstruction process. Tissue markers were then glued to the skull, indicating the proper tissue depth for each particular area of the face, then artificial eyes were placed into the eye sockets and centered at the correct depth. Modeling clay was then applied onto the skull at the depths which were indicated by the tissue markers.

Measurements of the skull had enabled the technicians to determine the size and placement of the nose and mouth, noting the likely length and width of those features, and the appropriate skin tone was applied and a wig was placed on the clay reconstruction. Other finishing details like clothing or accessories were added; then the reconstruction was photographed.

Forensic reconstructions normally have a very high identification success rate. When the photos of the FACES Laboratory's reconstruction of the face of the unidentified New Orleans woman were shown on television and in newspapers, someone soon came forward and told the authorities that they recognized the person in the photos as looking very much like a friend of theirs who had been missing for some time. Finally, after months of frustration, law enforcement officers Jeffrey Walls and Armando Asaro were able to positively identify their unknown murder victim as Katherine Collins.

At first, Detective Paul Burch wasn't convinced that Jones could have roamed as far afield as New Orleans to have committed that particular crime, and he just didn't believe that the man currently charged with the murder of Lisa Nichols could also have gone to New Orleans and killed Katherine Collins, despite Jones's claims that he had indeed murdered her.

"Nothing we had in our time line placed him in that area,"

Burch told the New Orleans *Times-Picayune.* "This came as a complete surprise."

Burch told reporters he would have "bet his paycheck" that Jones wasn't involved in the Katherine Collins case. But Burch was present and heard for himself when Jones began talking about the murder to Walls and Asaro and began to give a detailed confession of his guilt.

In his first questioning session with the New Orleans detectives, Jones had given them enough details about the case to convince Walls and Asaro's supervisor, New Orleans police captain Anthony Cannatella, to tell the media, "We're either going to eliminate him or make him the suspect, one of the two."

DNA samples, taken from underneath the fingernails of Katherine's body, proved to be insufficient for conclusive testing. And Jones, despite his earlier confession, soon changed his story yet again and began to claim that he really wasn't guilty, and even went on to deny that he'd ever been to New Orleans.

"Always wanted to, though," he casually told the two officers.

But Detective Armando Asaro and Sergeant Jeffrey Walls were convinced that Jeremy Jones was their suspect. They made two trips to Mobile to talk to Jones about Katherine Collins's murder. The first session had failed to provide anything concrete, only a strong hunch that they were on the right track with Jones. Determined to learn more, they returned later for a second try. Then they kept on questioning him for hours at a time, while they probed for any scrap of evidence that might reinforce his initial confession and shake his later claim of innocence.

When Jones was confronted with a string of Mardi Gras beads with a Bud Light logo—which had been found in his Douglasville trailer—the information that the officers needed about the case finally began to surface, one bit at a time. The detectives had also managed to come up with a traffic ticket that Jones had received in Louisiana near the time of Collins's murder, and they had located an eyewitness who was able to place Jones at a New Orleans truck stop on Elysian Fields Avenue during the proper time frame.

During a marathon questioning session that lasted for almost ten hours, Jones talked to the New Orleans detectives about every subject imaginable, except the murder of Katherine Collins. When the questioning continued on the following day, the officers stopped chatting about hunting, fishing, and the weather, and went straight to the point, talking to Jones about Katherine's family members and their need to know what had really happened to her. Finally, after eight more hours of beating around the bush, Jones suddenly decided to open up and tell the officers what he claimed had really happened.

Asaro and Walls said later that Jones had given them, step by step, details of the crime that only the killer could have known, specific information about the injuries that had been inflicted on Katherine Collins. He told of stabbing her in the right eye, knocking some of her teeth out with the butt of his knife, then strangling her. And then, he told them, he mutilated her vagina.

Detective Asaro would later tell the *Times-Picayune* that Jones's confession was the most chilling he'd ever heard in the twenty-two years that he'd been a police officer. He said that Jones, who was described by the two officers as alert, intelligent, and personable, literally changed into a killer right before his eyes. He went from laid-back and friendly to agitated, nervous, and high-strung as he gave more and more details about the murder. Jones became wild-eyed and was shaking, the detective said. It was as though he was reliving the crime and the excitement he had experienced while murdering Katherine, according to Asaro.

Jones told the officers that he had gone to New Orleans for Mardi Gras and had been on a methamphetamine bender for nearly a week, leaving him disoriented and strung out. He and Katherine Collins had hooked up in the French Quarter, he claimed, and then went to an abandoned "drug house" to have sex. Jones said Katherine took her clothes off, but then he backed out on their deal and they began to argue. When Katherine ran, naked, out of the house, Jones said he chased her, stabbing her as he ran her to ground.

When the officers asked him why he had killed Katherine Collins, Jones gave a chilling answer.

"The bitch deserved it," he growled.

Days later, on January 20, 2005, after checking out and confirming several of the details of Jones's confession, formal action was taken against him for the murder of Katherine Collins. The investigators had compared Jones's account of the injuries Katherine received during his assault to those that the coroner had listed at the autopsy of her remains, and they matched exactly. Additionally, Jones had passed six polygraph tests in which he confirmed that he had killed Collins. An arrest warrant for first-degree murder was issued for Jones by the New Orleans authorities, the third death with which he would be officially charged.

Burch admired Asaro and Walls for their tenacity after what the two men called "an old-fashioned police hunch" proved to be fruitful.

"Their persistence and good detective work paid off," Burch told reporters.

Katherine Collins's brother, Randy Heckaman, was astounded to learn the details surrounding the man who had been charged by authorities with the murder of his sister. He grew angry as he began to realize the full extent of the carnage that had allegedly occurred after the IAFIS failure to

identify Jeremy Jones. Heckaman said there were "a lot of innocent girls that lost their lives" because the FBI didn't do
their job correctly.

"What's their excuse?" he wanted to know.

Chapter 13

During his many hours of nonstop confessions, Jeremy Jones had also claimed to be the person who was responsible for the abduction and murder of Patrice Tamber Endres, the Georgia hairdresser who vanished from her beauty salon on April 15, 2004. He gave the authorities plenty of details about where he claimed her body had been dumped, saying that he had left her in a North Georgia creek that fed into the Chattahoochee River. A massive search of all the waterways in the area that he had indicated was immediately started. At first, the authorities did not confirm that Jones himself had named the location where he said that Patrice Endres could be found. Instead, they told the media, they were acting on an "anonymous tip" they had received pertaining to the site where her body had been left. The search continued for a couple of months but yielded no results in the exact locations Jones gave. He claimed that he had been so high on methamphetamine at the time that he had abducted Patrice Endres that he hardly knew where he was.

He had been driving around aimlessly on April 15, 2004. Lost, Jones said. He claimed that he drove through the town of Canton, Georgia, then said that he got "turned around" and couldn't find his way back toward Douglasville. When he saw Patrice's beauty shop, Tamber's Trim-n-Tan, located on the side of Georgia Highway 369 in North Forsyth County, in a little community called Matt, he stopped to get directions.

When Jones saw that Patrice Endres was there alone, about to have lunch before her next customer arrived at noon, he noticed that she was just his type, with her long, dark hair and striking good looks. On the spur of the moment, he said, he deicided to kidnap her.

Jones told Forsyth County sheriff Ted Paxton's investigators that he forced Patrice to leave with him, threatening her with an unspecified type of weapon. He said that he then raped and killed her, and dumped her body off the Riverside Parkway Bridge, which spanned Sweetwater Creek, near the Chattahoochee River.

Later, Jones denied to the media that he had ever claimed responsibility for Patrice's disappearance, and adamantly said that he had never killed anyone, not Lisa Nichols or anyone else, despite his ongoing series of confessions, which continued to take place during his sessions with the investigators. Jones told an Atlanta television reporter that he was only in jail because he was in the wrong place at the wrong time. At the time of Patrice's disappearance, Jones claimed, he had been at work, on the job at the Lafarge Rock Quarry in Douglasville. He said that he had the time cards and witnesses to prove it. That, he said, was why no charges had thus far been brought against him in the case.

As time passed and the weather changed, the search for Patrice's remains, undertaken earlier but yielding no results, had been halted temporarily due to rising waters in Sweetwater Creek. After the water levels in the creek began to drop back to normal once again, the search for Patrice was resumed, with Sheriff Paxton requesting assistance from the state's forensic anthropologist. Searchers went through the thick undergrowth along the sides of the creek, looking at every square inch of the creek bank and collecting soil samples, and cadaver dogs were brought in to aid in the search. The dogs were some of the most reliable means available for locating the site of a clandestine grave or of finding the place where a body might have, at one time, been dumped. The highly trained dogs seldom make mistakes, and sometimes they can even locate a body underwater. On two separate occasions, the dogs indicated that a body might have once been left in a location along the creek bank, but no trace of Patrice Endres's remains were found. The authorities said that no evidence had been found at the salon, either, with Paxton expressing his frustration that hair samples and fingerprints were all but impossible to obtain from a hair salon. He told the media that in a hair salon, there was hair everywhere, and "fingerprints on top of fingerprints." He said that out of all the aspects of the crime scene investigation, the setting itself was one of the biggest obstacles his detectives faced.

Aerial searches of bridges in the area were planned, divers were brought in, and countless other bridges and their surroundings were checked out, all to no avail. And Paxton couldn't bring charges against Jeremy Jones without some good, solid evidence.

"There has to be corroboration," Paxton told the press when he announced that Jones was a suspect and admitted to them that the search had been under way for some time, since Jones's initial confession months earlier. "Sometimes people confess for the notoriety, or just to play games."

It was beginning to look like Jones might have done just that, in regard to some of the murders for which he so freely claimed credit.

Evidently, Jeremy Jones had not been alone in his desire for attention from law enforcement and the media. Sheriff Paxton also announced that the "eyewitness" who had come forward immediately after Patrice disappeared, Michelle Lee Grant, thirty-two, of Jasper, Georgia, had been charged with giving false information about seeing a white van parked outside the salon at the time of Patrice's disappearance. Grant had even given Paxton's investigators a detailed description of the man she claimed she saw standing beside the van. Composite drawings were made up and distributed far and wide in a search that resulted in the loss of countless man-hours looking for an imaginary suspect and following up worthless courses of investigation.

Captain Frank Huggins, of the Forsyth County Sheriff's Office, told the press that Grant had confessed to lying about what she said she had supposedly witnessed. Huggins said that Grant's false claims had caused the drawings of the suspect and descriptions of the vehicle to be distributed all over the country and featured on several Web sites and national television programs.

"It has caused us to spend valuable time running down nonexistent leads," Huggins said.

According to Huggins, his department had received a tip that Grant might not have actually seen anyone outside Patrice Endres's salon on the day of her disappearance. When Grant was questioned once again, she finally broke down and admitted that she had made up her story.

Sheriff Paxton, and all the many other law enforcement personnel, volunteers, and friends and family members who were sidetracked in their search for Patrice Endres by Grant's made-up eyewitness account, were understandably furious. Paxton said Patrice's family had suffered a great disappointment because of Michelle Lee Grant's false statements, and the investigation might have been more successful had it not been sidetracked for months into a wrong direction.

"Why someone would want to pull a stunt like this is beyond comprehension," he said.

Paxton might not be able to charge Jones until there was positive corroboration of his confession, but the sheriff would, and did, charge Michelle Lee Grant with giving false information to the authorities, a charge that could bring the false witness up to five years in prison.

Chapter 14

Continuing with the hundreds of hours of interviews he had been giving to the Mobile County investigators, Jones confessed to two additional cases of rape and abduction, which brought Craig County, Oklahoma, authorities rushing to Mobile to question him about the December 30, 1999, disappearances of missing Welch, Oklahoma, teenagers Ashley Freeman and Lauria Bible. Jones also said he'd committed the murders of Ashley's parents, Danny and Kathy Freeman, claiming he killed the Freemans over a debt that he said they supposedly owed to a friend of his.

Craig County, Oklahoma, authorities Sheriff Jimmie Sooter and District Attorney (DA) Gene Haynes, along with Oklahoma Bureau of Investigation (OBI) agent Steve Nutter, traveled to Mobile in January and talked to Jeremy Jones for a total of almost eighteen hours. During that time, several details emerged from the interviews that convinced the investigators that Jones was indeed responsible for the Oklahoma murders, and his knowledge of those details left the Craig County sheriff feeling that Jones was a very credible suspect.

In the years since the Freemans were murdered and the two girls had disappeared, Sheriff Sooter had received tips from sources that ranged from truck drivers to psychics, all of which amounted to wild-goose chases. He had initially been somewhat skeptical about making a trip all the way to Mobile to interview Jeremy Jones. Sooter previously had made a similar trip to Texas to question serial killer and death row prisoner Tommy Lee Sells, after Sells claimed responsibility for the deaths of the Freemans and the disappearance of Ashley and Lauria.

Sells, who had sent a letter to the *Joplin Globe* saying that he had been in Welch during the night when the girls disappeared, told the newspaper that he had been returning from a trip he had made to St. Louis. Sells claimed that his memory of the incident was unclear because of his drug usage at the time. He said that he was "trying to remember a fire" and the location of the site where he had buried Ashley and Lauria. Sells told Sooter that he could lead searchers to the location of the two girls' bodies, and the prisoner was taken out of his cell on death row and away from the prison to a field in Marshall, Texas, to point out the site he had named in his confession. The search, however, was fruitless.

Later, authorities said that the field where Sells had claimed to have buried the bodies looked nothing at all like the location he had described earlier when he first "confessed." Since Sells had already claimed to have killed more than seventy people, with many of those claims totally unsubstantiated, his admission of guilt was discounted as yet another of his many bids for attention. Sheriff Sooter conducted an intensive check of Sells's whereabouts at the time of the Freeman/Bible abductions, and he had found that there were no indications that Sells could have been responsible for killing the Freemans and taking the two girls.

Sells was also unable to give any convincing details of the crime at the Freeman trailer and the abduction of Ashley and

Lauria, such as the layout of the trailer or what the girls were wearing, claiming that he was omitting information "out of respect for some other things," which he coyly declined to name.

Jeremy Jones, on the other hand, seemed to know far more credible details about the crime. He seemed initially to make a connection with the Oklahoma sheriff, who had coached and taught school before going into law enforcement, then was elected as sheriff by a landslide vote. Sooter, incidentally, had been a teacher at the schools Ashley and Lauria had attended, and had known the two girls, who had been enrolled in some of his classes. Because of Sooter's kindly demeanor and his personal interest in the case, he was able, over the long hours of questioning, to lead Jones into gradually letting down his guard and discussing the murders and abduction.

Jones told Sooter and the other investigators what he claimed was the true story of what happened on the night the Freemans were murdered and the two girls were abducted, saying that he hadn't expected the girls to be at the trailer, and he had been surprised when they came running out.

Jones told Sooter that he barely knew Danny and Kathy Freeman. Once, he said, Danny Freeman had stopped by a garage in Commerce, Oklahoma, where Jones and some of his friends were hanging out. Kathy Freeman had been sitting in Danny's truck while Danny went inside, Jones said. That was the only time he had seen Kathy, and about the second time he'd met Danny, before he went to their trailer to kill them. They owed one of his friends some money, he said, first claiming the amount the Freemans owed was $20,000, then the next day changing his story and saying it was $5,000. Sooter said Jones told him that he killed the Freemans because he believed that people should pay their debts. The friend who was owed the money hadn't asked him to kill the

Freemans, Jones said; he did it on his own, as a favor to his friend. He didn't specify that the debt was over a drug deal, but the friend he had named, like most of Jones's other acquaintances at that time, was widely known by law enforcement in that area to have been an active drug dealer prior to his death.

Jones told Sooter that he had been high on methamphetamine when he went looking for the Freemans' home, and he claimed that it took him several hours to find it. Then, he said, he located the trailer sometime after midnight, and got a twelve-gauge shotgun out of his truck. He said that he had entered the unlocked trailer, shot the Freemans in their bedroom while they were sleeping, scattered some clothing on the floor and doused it with accelerant, then torched the room and went back outside to his truck. Then, according to Sheriff Sooter, Jones said he was surprised when the two girls came running out of the burning trailer toward Jones's truck, believing that he had been passing by, had seen the fire, and had just arrived to see if there was anything he could do. He got the girls to get into his truck, telling them they'd go to get help. Then, Jones said, he drove them to a remote area of Kansas, in the Galena area, where he shot the two girls and threw their bodies into an abandoned mine pit, a hole formed by the collapse of an underground mine shaft. He claimed that he had sexually assaulted one of the girls, and also told Sooter that one of the girls had tried to escape, but said that he shot her as she ran away.

Jones showed Sooter four possible locations of the mine pit on a map of around four square miles, but he said that he couldn't remember exactly which of them might be the one where the bodies of the missing girls could be found. As he would claim in so many other instances, Jones said he was so high on drugs at the time that he couldn't recall some of the details about that night's events. Also, he said, locations on the map didn't look like they did from the ground, and he just couldn't be completely sure.

"He knew some things about the crime scene that people shouldn't have known," Sooter told reporters. "We just have to go look and see if he's telling us the truth. He's very smart, and he knows the right things to say. If we find bodies, we'll know he's telling the truth."

Sooter told reporters that Jones had been quite accurate in his descriptions of the interior of the Freemans' trailer and how the fire had been set. Jones told Sooter that the guns he had used that night were long gone; he bought and sold guns "all the time," he said, and didn't know what had happened to them.

Jones soon recanted his confession to the press, saying that he had never taken a human life and hadn't told the investigators anything that would have indicated that he had. He told reporters that the searchers wouldn't find anything when they went to look for the girls' bodies; they were wasting their time, he said. Plans were made, however, to search the Kansas locations that Jones had indicated in his confession as soon as weather conditions in the area made such a search possible, with several of the law enforcement agencies in Oklahoma and Kansas scheduled to take part, along with the Kansas Bureau of Investigation (KBI), the OBI, and an agent of the FBI. The KBI also hired a Colorado organization called NecroSearch International, a nonprofit agency specializing in using high-tech methods and equipment to aid law enforcement agencies in their searches for cadavers.

NecroSearch, based out of the Douglas County, Colorado, Sheriff's Office, had developed innovative techniques specializing in the location of clandestine grave sites and evidence. Their research facility was located at the Highlands

Ranch Law Enforcement Training Facility in Douglas County, and was utilized by NecroSearch personnel, as well as students from the University of Colorado, Colorado State University, and the Colorado School of Mines. There they studied magnetic, electromagnetic, and ground-penetrating radar applications, as well as aerial photography that could indicate changes in characteristics of the ground and the surrounding plant life in areas where bodies might have been buried.

NecroSearch studied the changes a buried corpse might cause in the entomology, plant ecology, and animal-scavenging activity of a crime scene. Cadaver dogs were also employed to help locate bodies. Forensic anthropologists examined excavated remains, and thermal imaging was employed using infrared cameras to generate images of the radiation being emitted by a possible buried corpse. NecroSearch also provided training and information to law enforcement on all levels, and had helped in more than two hundred cases in half the states in the nation, as well as helping with cases in a number of other countries.

In order to assist in a case, NecroSearch International was required to receive a formal request from the law enforcement agency involved. Such a request had been made in the search for the bodies of Ashley Freeman and Lauria Bible, and NecroSearch was ready to go to the search area and prepared to use all its available resources and high-tech expertise. The search, authorities said, was going to be a large-scale effort that would be conducted like an archaeological dig, slowly and carefully. Even though it would be costly and time-consuming, all the agencies involved felt that the time and expense would be very much worthwhile if the search turned up any evidence that would help to solve the mystery of what had really happened to Ashley and Lauria.

Initially the search was stalled due to poor weather conditions, but a few months later, when the weather began to improve and conditions permitted, the search for the bodies of the two girls began as planned along Schermerhorn Road in Galena, Kansas. Permission was obtained from both private landowners and from the local authorities for the search personnel to enter the property. However, the search team was initially met with a disappointment. NecroSearch was unable to use their ground-penetrating radar because the search areas had been used for many years as trash dumps, and countless numbers of cans and other metal objects abounded in the many mine pits that dotted the bleak landscape. Instead, another approach was tried. NecroSearch's cameras were lowered into the dangerous abandoned mine shafts that were filled with water, but that effort, too, was to no avail. Next, cadaver dogs from Southeast Oklahoma Action Dogs, a Wagoner, Oklahoma, volunteer organization, were brought in to search for any indication of the bodies of the two girls being present in the mines. The dogs were expected to aid greatly in the search, and were normally able to detect the presence of bodies at depths of almost twenty-five feet, but there were just so many problems with the search location. The areas that Jones had indicated on the maps that Sooter had provided to him were pocked with countless numbers of abandoned mines, and the trash-filled pits provided many distractions for the dogs. They and their handlers spent hours going over the search site in several different sessions, but it was looking as though the search was going to prove to be very difficult. The dogs ranged back and forth over the search areas, again and again, finding many things among the trash heaps that caught their interest. Unfortunately, none of those things turned out to be related to the search for Ashley and Lauria.

Sheriff Sooter still felt that Jeremy Jones's confession was, in part, very credible because of his knowledge of the interior layout of the Freemans' trailer and several other details of the crime scene, and also because of his continuing insistence to the investigators that he was responsible for the murders. The sheriff felt that the information Jones had given him was right in line with the evidence, and said he remained "cautiously optimistic." One of the problems with Jones's admissions, however, was the time frame of the initial setting of the fire and the fact that Jones had been arrested around four o'clock that same morning in Miami, Oklahoma, about eighteen miles from the Freeman home. The last person to see Danny and Kathy Freeman and the two girls alive had been Ashley Freeman's boyfriend, who had been visiting Ashley and left the Freeman trailer to go home sometime between 9:30 P.M. and midnight. Sooter said he believed that after that time, Jones would have had sufficient time to shoot the Freemans, set fire to the trailer, take the girls to the area where he said he dumped their bodies and kill them, then return to Miami in time to get arrested at 4:00 A.M. for public intoxication and possession of drug paraphernalia.

Jones had been arrested on that occasion by an Ottawa County, Oklahoma, deputy, who said that Jones had come running up to his patrol car yelling for help and saying that he was being chased by someone who was trying to kill him. Jones told the officer that the police had raided his supposed chaser's meth lab earlier that night and the man was in hot pursuit of Jones because he believed that Jones was an informer who had turned him in and was therefore responsible for the bust. A search failed to locate anyone who had been chasing Jones, however, and officers later learned that there had been no meth lab raids anywhere in the area that night. Jones was placed under arrest because he had been drinking and also had a used hypodermic needle in his possession. The arresting officer reported that he observed a "strong odor of an alcoholic beverage" on Jones's breath, and said in the report that the subject's eyes were bloodshot and his speech was slurred. That was enough to earn him a bed in the Ottawa County Jail for the next several hours, where he slept off his drinking and drugs while firemen battled the flames at the Freemans' trailer, eighteen miles away. Jones was released the following day at 10:23 A.M., according to the records at the Ottawa County Sheriff's Office.

Lorene Bible, Lauria Bible's mother, said that if Jeremy Jones had given truthful information and Ashley and Lauria's bodies were found, it would at least put an end to the long years of torment from not knowing what had happened to her daughter. She believed, she said, that if Lauria had been alive, she would have somehow been able to get to a phone at some time during the previous five years since her disappearance, and she would have called to let her mother know where she was. It had been a terrible five years, she said, dealing with the rumors that the girls might have been sold into prostitution or worse. But, she said, perhaps other people might now be encouraged to come forward with new information about the girls because of Jones's claims.

"We're aware of Jones's lack of credibility," KBI agent Kyle Smith told reporters when asked about Jones's denial of his earlier confessions, adding that the KBI's plans were to conduct a "complete and thorough search" of the areas Jones had indicated, on the possibility of finding anything, however remote that possibility might be.

"If there's any chance of recovering those girls, we're going to do it," Smith said.

Lorene Bible said that she hoped with all her might that the search would bring results, but she also said that she was afraid that the searchers would find nothing and they would then be left not knowing where to look next.

Dwayne Vancil, Danny Freeman's brother, said he would wait and see what the search results proved before he ventured any opinions about Jones's truthfulness.

"I'll wait and see what they come up with," Dwayne Vancil told reporters. "I'm not too optimistic," he said, that Jones was telling the truth. More proof was needed about his possible involvement, he said.

At the time that Craig County, Oklahoma, district attorney Gene Haynes and Sheriff Jimmie Sooter announced Jeremy Jones's confessions in the Freeman/Bible case, Haynes also confirmed that Jones was being looked at as a possible suspect in the deaths of Delaware County, Oklahoma, residents Danny Oakley, forty-eight, and Doris Harris, fifty-one, who were shot to death in Oakley's trailer on February 21, 1996. Like the Freeman murders, the trailer was set on fire after Oakley and Harris were killed. Family members of the victims in both cases had gotten together and compared notes years earlier because of the marked similarities in the manner of the deaths in the two cases, and the fact that the trailers were both set on fire. Both families, however, remained skeptical that Jeremy Jones could have been the only person who was involved in both sets of the murders. In the Oakley/Harris case, neighbors had reported seeing a man come out of the trailer carrying a shotgun or rifle, put it into the trunk of Danny Oakley's car, and ride away in the car shortly before smoke began to come from the trailer. The next day, a man was arrested in a nearby town after he was found, passed out, in Oakley's car. The man was never charged in the murders.

"If [Jones] is involved at all, or has any information, I hope the authorities will continue to pursue this," said Doris Harris's younger sister, Paula Barnett. She told the *Joplin Globe* that she didn't want to be left without any closure in her sister's murder.

"I want to know if he's involved."

Danny Oakley's father, Carl, told a *Joplin Globe* reporter that, as far as he knew, Jones's name had not come up previously in connection with his son's murder.

"I saw Danny almost every day, and I never saw this Jones down there," Carl Oakley said, "but I hope he keeps talking."

In addition to the admission of Oklahoma authorities that Jones had confessed to the four murders in Welch and was a suspect in the Oakley/Harris murders, Ottawa County sheriff Dennis King announced that Jeremy Jones was also a person of interest in the 1997 murders of Harmon Fenton, thirty-three, and Sarah Palmer, nineteen, of Commerce, Oklahoma. Their bodies had been found in the bed of a pickup truck near Melrose, a town in Cherokee County, Kansas. The truck was parked inside a shed, and Fenton and Palmer had both been shot. When word began leaking out that Jeremy Jones was possibly involved in their deaths, the authorities grudgingly admitted that Jones had, at one time, been used by the Ottawa County Drug Task Force as an undercover informant, and that he had made a "buy" from Harmon Fenton during an investigation in 1996. Needless to say, this news raised more than a few eyebrows in several Oklahoma counties, and created an immediate buzz in Internet chat rooms where Jones was being discussed.

By his hundreds of hours spent dangling tidbits of information to investigators who were coming from all over the country to talk to him, Jeremy Bryan Jones had received a lot of favors, which included extra phone privileges and special foods, such as crab claws, pizza, and hamburgers. Those perks got him out of his cell to be fed like a king, and he liked it a lot. He was also getting a tremendous amount of attention from the media, which he enjoyed perhaps even more than the tasty treats and the almost unlimited phone calls. As the body count with which he credited himself continued to rise, followed closely by his denials of having confessed at all, more and more families were left to wonder whether or not Jeremy Jones could really be the person responsible for the deaths or disappearance of their missing loved ones.

Chapter 15

For months, Detectives Paul Burch and Mitch McRae had fielded great numbers of phone calls from law enforcement agencies around the country regarding Jeremy Jones. Countless cold cases in many states were being checked out to fit his profile, and in many of them, Jones could be placed near the area at the time that the crimes had occurred. In several of the cases, he was eventually ruled out as a viable suspect. But many of the investigators around the country who had been interested in Jones were now considering the possibility that Jones might be responsible for some of the frustrating, unsolved cases that they had been working on without success for several years.

One such case was the unsolved disappearance of a young woman in Atmore, Alabama. Melinda Wall McGhee was a licensed practical nurse who was about to graduate from nursing school. While taking classes in the daytime, she worked on the night shift at a nursing home in nearby Bay Minette. Melinda also worked occasionally in Atmore, the location of Holman Correctional Facility, as a prison nurse. She was the mother of two little boys, and she and her husband, Troy, and their children lived on Kent Road, a dead-end dirt road in a remote rural area lying on the fringes of the Poarch Creek Indian Reservation. They had close ties to the Poarch Creeks, Alabama's only federally recognized Indian tribe. Melinda herself did not claim Creek ancestry, although she had dark hair and eyes and certainly looked as though she was part Native American. Her husband's family, however, were Poarch Creek tribe members.

When the Escambia County, Alabama, investigators learned some of the details about Jeremy Jones and examined the patterns of the murders that he was confessing to, they traveled to Mobile to check into the possibility that he might be connected to Melinda Wall McGhee's disappearance. Melinda was, after all, a dark-haired, dark-eyed beauty who appeared to be part Native American, as were the majority of the other women in the cases to which Jones had confessed.

On the morning of March 24, 2003, Melinda came home around eight o'clock, after working all night at the nursing home. Troy had already left on his way to work at Masland Carpets. The couple's two sons, a five-year-old and a one-year-old, were with their babysitter, and Troy's fourteen-year-old son had been taken by his grandmother to a dental appointment. Before she went to sleep, Melinda called her mother and her husband to check in with them at around 8:30 A.M.

When her husband got home from work that day, at around 4:00 P.M., he walked into their house and into a nightmare. There was evidence inside the house that a violent struggle had taken place, and some media reports claimed that a great deal of blood was also found at the scene, but Melinda was not there. Like so many of the others in the cases that Jeremy Jones had claimed responsibility for, she had vanished without a trace.

Following the discovery of Melinda's disappearance, Escambia County sheriff Grover Smith told the media that his investigators were following every possible lead in the case. Smith said that state forensic personnel and Alabama Bureau of Investigation (ABI) officers were working the case as well.

"There are signs of a struggle inside the house," Smith told the press, adding that a great deal of forensic evidence had been gathered from the scene.

"We are afraid foul play was involved. We'll be searching for Melinda, or anything that might relate to her disappearance: clothing, personal items, disturbed soil, burned areas—anything unusual or out of place."

More than two hundred volunteers turned out to search the acres of dense forests that surrounded the McGhee home, located in a remote area with only two other homes that sat at the end of a dead-end dirt road over a mile long. Nothing was found, despite the intensive searching. No leads, no clues, no suspects, and no motives had been found—not until the similarities in the Jones cases and Melinda's disappearance caught the attention of the Escambia County authorities.

"I would be overjoyed to solve this case," Sheriff Smith told the press, adding that he was hopeful that some link would be found connecting the case with Jeremy Jones. Earlier, Smith had compared notes with Louisiana authorities whose serial-killings task force in Baton Rouge had looked at suspects around the nation. Derrick Todd Lee, the man who had been charged with the deaths of six women in the Baton Rouge area, was a suspect in a number of other murders, rapes, and abductions in Baton Rouge. For a time, Lee had been thought to be a possible suspect in Melinda's disappearance. However, he was later ruled out of serious consider-ation because of the distance between Baton Rouge and Atmore, 250 miles to the east. Smith hoped against hope that Jeremy Jones might prove to be the key to finding out what had happened to Melinda.

It came as a great disappointment to Smith and his investigators when they had to announce that Jeremy Jones had been officially ruled out as a suspect in Melinda McGhee's disappearance. Melinda had been reported missing on a day when there was positive proof that Jeremy Jones was at work. His time card and the testimony of his coworkers confirmed that he had been present on the job in Douglasville, Georgia, that day.

Jeremy Jones was also being closely scrutinized by investigators in four other states who were searching for a man who had come to be known as the "Truck Stop Killer," a man believed to be responsible for a long string of murders of prostitutes. The killer was thought to be picking up the women at truck stops, then leaving their bodies—raped, strangled, and beaten to death—by the side of interstate highways. The possible connection to Jeremy Jones? Like Katherine Collins, whose murder in New Orleans he had already been charged with, several of the prostitutes who were believed to have been murdered by the Truck Stop Killer had been beaten to death with a tire iron. But the most compelling similarity between the cases was the ethnic background that was shared by Collins, several of the other women Jones had claimed that he had killed, and most of the Truck Stop Killer's victims.

Nearly all of the women were of Native American descent, or looked as though they might be.

Those Native American and part–Native American victims included Vicki Anderson, forty-six, of Oklahoma City, whose body was found off I-40 in Texas, after being last seen at a Flying J Travel Plaza in Oklahoma.

Casey Jo Pipestem, a member of the Seminole tribe, was from a traditional Native American family that continued to observe some of the older customs of their people. Casey Jo had been a shell shaker, a special dancer, at tribal gatherings when she was younger. The girls and women who serve as shell shakers at the all-night "stomp dances" are given a great deal of respect among the people of their tribes. But as she grew older, Casey Jo's life began to go downhill. She had developed a drug habit and eventually ended up as a prostitute. Her nude body was found by the roadside after she was dropped from an overpass bridge onto the highway below.

Witnesses saw Taddemika McHenry getting into a truck parked at a rest stop, and she had not been seen since then. No body had been found, but her disappearance was looked at as possibly involving foul play.

Buffie Rae Brawley, a prostitute who frequented truck stops in Indiana, was found brutally murdered at an abandoned truck stop after she disappeared from a highway fuel station near Indianapolis. Another victim, Vesta B. Meadows, was found along the Pennsylvania Turnpike. She had last been seen at a Knoxville, Tennessee, truck stop.

Margaret Gardner, who was also seen alive for the last time at a truck stop, was found, killed by blunt-force trauma to the head, on an on-ramp of Interstate 40 in Arkansas. Sandra Richardson died from similar injuries, and her nude body was dumped at a highway intersection east of Oklahoma City. And another Oklahoma prostitute, Sandra Beard, was found, nude and dead from asphyxiation, dumped at an I-40 exit.

The nude body of Jennifer Hyman, also from Oklahoma, was thrown off the Tallahatchie Bridge in Mississippi after she had been strangled. Jennifer was a prostitute who was last seen at a truck stop in Oklahoma City.

Patsy Laverne Leonard, a prostitute who frequented truck stops, was seen for the last time in Texas. She was found, nude and strangled, in a creek in Oklahoma.

All of these homicides, and several other very similar cases around the country, were believed to be the work of the Truck Stop Killer. The murders included as many as ten likely victims, and the Truck Stop Killer was believed to almost certainly be a truck driver. Some of the background information on Jeremy Jones described him as a "former truck driver." His investigation as a suspect in the Katherine Collins murder in New Orleans immediately caught the attention of authorities who had been working to identify the Truck Stop Killer. Those investigators noted that Collins, like the majority of the victims in the Truck Stop cases, was a part–Native American prostitute whose body had been found near the truckers' entrance to the Port of New Orleans. It fit the pattern of the Truck Stop Killer's crimes, as well as those that Jeremy Jones had been confessing to with such abandon. Investigators of the Truck Stop Killer cases began to check out Jones's whereabouts at the time the other murders that had been attributed to the Truck Stop Killer had taken place, hoping that they would be able to place Jones in any of the areas where some of the crimes had taken place.

Despite the many similarities to the crimes Jones had confessed to, however, in a short time he was eliminated as a suspect in the Truck Stop Killer case when another person of interest emerged. A truck driver from Nebraska, Carl Lawson, had been arrested for rape, kidnapping, and assault and battery with intent to kill, when he assaulted a woman in Oklahoma who had detailed his truck at a truck stop. When she got into his truck to collect her pay for the detailing work, she told police, he locked her in and began assaulting her. She was unconscious for several hours before she woke up on the side of the interstate near the Nebraska-Kansas border with her clothes scattered near her, where they had been thrown from her assailant's truck and left along the shoulder of the highway.

The woman, who considered herself lucky to be alive, was able to give the authorities a great deal of information about

Lawson and claimed that he told her that he didn't mind her frantic efforts to bite him and scratch him. He told her, she said, that it "bothered him" when the first three or four women he killed had scratched and bitten him as they fought for their lives, "but I kinda like it now."

Lawson, obviously, became the immediate focus of interest in the Truck Stop Killer cases, and investigators scrambled to compare DNA evidence and trace his whereabouts during the time periods of the long list of murders.

Investigators of yet another case, this one in the St. Louis area, announced shortly after Jeremy Jones's arrest in Mobile that he was being looked at as a potential suspect in the murder of an unidentified woman in their jurisdiction. The torso of the victim, a Caucasian estimated to be in her twenties, had been found at an interstate rest stop, and there was no clue as to her identity. Autopsy reports indicated that the woman had scars from a cesarean section, and that she'd had an appendectomy at some point in her life. Other than those facts, nothing else was known about her.

Warren County sheriff Michael Baker announced his department had "a man we're very interested in," referring to Jeremy Jones, following a funeral service for the unidentified woman. She was buried after a small service that was attended by the sheriff, the county coroner, and some of their staff members. The efforts to identify her and locate her family continued, and learning the woman's identity was a priority for the sheriff's staff.

Baker's investigators and officers from the St. Louis Major Case Squad considered Jones a likely enough suspect that they, like so many others before them, made the trip down to Mobile to question him.

"We understand he's been somewhat cooperative in some

other investigations," Baker told reporters, but went on to say that Jones had made no confessions to his officers.

Jones was looked at so closely in that particular case because a white van he had owned was similar to one that had been seen in the Ann Parden Road area at the time Lisa Nichols was murdered. A white van had also allegedly been spotted outside Patrice Endres's hair salon in Forsyth County, Georgia. And other witnesses said they had seen a white van at the rest stop on I-70 where the unidentified woman's torso was found. But, as in the case of Melinda McGhee's disappearance and in many of the other cases in which Jones was, at one time or another, considered to be a possible suspect, he was soon ruled out. The moniker of Truck Stop Killer would not be assigned to him.

Chapter 16

While Jeremy Jones spent his time in jail freely talking to the countless law enforcement agencies from around the country that came to interview him, detailing and then denying the murders that he claimed to have been responsible for, his court-appointed attorney, Habib Yazdi, just wished that his client would shut up.

Yazdi did everything within his power to convince Jones not to speak to anyone at all without an attorney present, but Jones just kept right on talking, agreeing to interview after interview with both the authorities and with countless members of the media, who spoke with him both by phone and in person. Jones alternated between the confessions of guilt, which he made to the law enforcement officers, and denials of his responsibility for any of the crimes, when he was speaking to the media. Needless to say, this pattern of behavior was creating even more confusion for the investigators, while Jones continued to brag about all the special foods and the almost unlimited phone calls that he was getting in return for agreeing to the many interviews.

Yazdi did what he could in the way of damage control, but his client was so out of control that little could be done to stop the flow of inadvisable talk. Jeremy Jones was the center of everyone's attention, and he liked it that way. It was getting him exactly what he wanted, and he wasn't about to change his tactics just because some lawyer suggested that he pipe down.

In the meantime, Yazdi gave several interviews of his own, flip-flopping back and forth, trying to convince anyone who would listen that Jones was either a very smart individual, or that he was mentally incompetent and any "confessing" that he did could not be relied on to be factual in any way. Shortly after being appointed by the court to represent Jones, Yazdi told the press that his new client was an intelligent man who could have been a success at almost anything that he chose to do.

"He is a supersmart man," Yazdi said, adding that if Jones had chosen another path in life, he could have been a successful doctor, businessman, or even an attorney. But a short time later, Yazdi had completely changed his tune about his client's mental competency.

"From the conversation we have," Yazdi told CNN's Sara Dorsey, "I realize he's not in the right mind to talk to law enforcement agencies without the presence of a lawyer."

Yazdi and Jones went before a Mobile County judge in early October, with a motion attempting to stop the numbers of investigators traveling to Mobile from other states to question the talkative Jones about unsolved cases in their jurisdictions. Yazdi wanted to be present whenever Jones was questioned, but no ruling was made on that motion. The questioning was going to continue whenever Jeremy Jones wished, without Yazdi's presence.

Chapter 17

On Thursday, October 27, 2005, Jones was brought before Mobile County District Court judge George Hardesty, who heard a great deal of testimony, which ran the gamut from the ludicrous to the horrific, during a preliminary hearing in the murder case of Lisa Nichols. Hardesty was to decide whether the four counts with which Jones was charged—capital murder, burglary, kidnapping, and rape—would be sent on to a Mobile County grand jury.

The lengthy hearing quickly turned into a defense attorney's nightmare. Jones often seemed as though he was far more interested in turning around in his seat and looking outside the courtroom at the large crowd of news media gathered for the hearing, instead of paying attention to the proceedings that were going on in court while crucial testimony was being given against him.

Detective Paul Burch took the stand and told the judge about the events of September 18, when Lisa Marie Nichols's children found their mother's body in her dark, smoke-filled trailer. She had been shot three times in the head; then an attempt had been made to burn her body, with her assailant mutilating her face and genitals with fire. When he first entered the murder scene, Burch said, he found Lisa's body lying in the bathroom of the trailer. An attempt had been made to bind her hands with an electric cord. The bathroom was all but destroyed, with clothing scattered, fixtures broken, and the tub filled with bloody water. Jones, Burch told the judge, had been staying at that time with his former employer in a residence less than a hundred yards away from Lisa Nichols's trailer. Burch said that it was not long before he and his team had more than enough incriminating evidence about the man, who was known at that time as Oklahoma, to arrest him for Lisa's brutal murder.

When Burch initially questioned Jones, the suspect claimed that Lisa Nichols had asked him to buy some drugs for her, then willingly had sex with him three times in various locations, both inside and outside the trailer. Later, he said, she had overdosed on the drugs and subsequently died. Jones then launched into a series of elaborate excuses for his alleged behavior. He told Burch that he was fearful that he would be blamed for Lisa's death due to the drugs he said that he had gotten for her, on which he had claimed she had overdosed. He shot her three times in the head "to make it look like something else," he said, then claimed that he had set fire to the trailer in the hopes of further covering up the crime. When he was asked why he tried to set fire to his victim's face and genitals, Burch said that Jones had no explanation to offer.

While Jones busied himself in the courtroom by sneaking glances at the press and smiling for their cameras, Habib Yazdi came up with some far-fetched excuses for his client's admissions of guilt during his initial series of interviews with Detective Paul Burch. Those explanations did little to impress either the judge or the spectators in the courtroom, who had listened in shocked silence as Burch related what Jones had told him about the murder. Mobile County's district attorney pointed out that Lisa Nichols neither used drugs nor invited strange men into her home, and certainly would not have had consensual sex with Jones, as he had claimed. A jury would have the opportunity to hear from Lisa's friends and family later on during a trial, he said, about what kind of person she was.

Yazdi tried to explain away several details of the slaying, saying the electric cord found tied around Lisa's wrist had been part of a bondage scenario. Then he asked the court to explain how his client could be guilty of capital murder if Lisa had already been dead of an overdose before Jones shot her. Then Yazdi made a statement almost as horrifying as it was insensitive.

"It's not that much of a crime to shoot a dead person," he said. "It's now a thing."

That statement created an immediate, outraged stir in the courtroom. Upon hearing Lisa referred to in such a callous manner, some of her family members jumped up out of their seats and fled from the courtroom in shock and anger. The earlier testimony, filled with the awful details of Lisa's murder, had been almost unbearably painful for her friends and family to sit there and listen to, but Yazdi's incredibly tasteless remark was more than they could bear.

At the conclusion of the lengthy hearing, Judge Hardesty's ruling came immediately; he showed no hesitation whatsoever in sending Jeremy Jones's capital murder case on to a Mobile County grand jury.

Chapter 18

In the coming months, Habib Yazdi began to see that he was going to have his hands full controlling the damage done by Jones's fascination with the attention he was getting from the press and law enforcement agencies around the country.

In addition to his attempts to convince the media that his client was mentally incompetent, Yazdi also tried to blame Jones's apparent confessions on claims that his client had been given the wrong antipsychotic medication by the Mobile County jailers, "and would say anything because of that. We don't agree with those confessions."

Yazdi told the media that Jones was given the medication Risperdal for a couple of months, from around the time of his September arrest until sometime in November. Yazdi planned to argue at one of the upcoming court hearings that anything that Jeremy Jones said to anyone during that time, when Yazdi claimed that his client had been under the influence of the Risperdal, should be suppressed. Jones, Yazdi said, was unable to make the decision to waive his rights and to voluntarily make statements to the investigators without his attorney being present, because his judgment had been compromised by the effects of the medication.

The Mobile County authorities, however, said that Jones had confessed to the murder of Lisa Nichols on several different occasions, with at least one of those confessions taking place prior to the time that he had allegedly begun receiving the Risperdal. And Jones, by that time, was beginning to deny to the media that he had ever made any of the confessions to the investigators in the first place and certainly had not killed anyone, not ever. Perhaps Habib Yazdi's advice to shut up was finally beginning to sink in.

"We are not going to let them dump all the unsolved murders on my client," Yazdi told the press, adding that Jones had told the investigators anything he thought that they wanted to hear in exchange for getting special foods and telephone privileges. As an explanation for his client's confession to the Freeman/Bible murders, Yazdi claimed that Jones had only told the authorities what he had heard from drug dealers while he was in jail in Oklahoma, and Yazdi claimed that Jones, himself, had nothing whatsoever to do with the crime.

In April, Yazdi and Jones were back in court once again, this time to answer federal charges brought against Jones for being a felon in possession of a firearm. The weapons charge was filed against him in order to block any attempt to transfer Jones out of Alabama to face charges in Georgia or New Orleans before he was first tried in Mobile County for the murder of Lisa Nichols. Alabama prosecutors told the press that the weapons charge was filed to serve as insurance against authorities in other states who might be planning to file similar federal charges in order to move Jones out of Alabama to face charges in their jurisdictions. But the Alabama authorities were determined that Jeremy Jones was going nowhere until Lisa first received the justice she and her family were due. Once he was tried for Lisa's murder, they said, then the other states that wanted him in their courts could stand in line to see who was going to get him next.

Jones was indicted by a grand jury for the rape and shooting death of Lisa Marie Nichols, in early May 2005, and was arraigned on May 10 before Mobile County Circuit Court judge Charles Graddick, who heard Jones's not guilty plea. But following the entry of his plea, Jones dealt his beleaguered attorney yet another unexpected and quite unpleasant surprise. When Habib Yazdi and his newly appointed cocounsel, Greg Hughes, requested that Judge Graddick order that Jones should undergo a psychiatric evaluation at Taylor Hardin Secure Medical Facility in Tuscaloosa, Alabama, the judge had no hesitation in issuing the order. But Jeremy Jones apparently had some other ideas of his own.

"I ain't crazy!" Jones reared back in his seat and bleated out to the judge, much to the amusement of the spectators in the courtroom. A dismayed Yazdi quickly reached over and tried to clap his hand over his client's mouth to stifle any further damaging comments, but it was too late—the damage had already been done. Yazdi and Hughes had intended to keep the possibility of an insanity plea on the table, just in case the psychiatric evaluation gave them any hopes of being able to use such a plea. Jones, however, didn't want to go that route, and let the judge know in no uncertain terms that he didn't feel that he had any mental problems that would justify what would likely be a fairly unpleasant stint with the evaluators at Taylor Hardin.

Yazdi later told the reporters who were waiting outside the courtroom that he'd had to physically try to stop his client from blurting out something that might further hurt his chances in court.

"He is so unpredictable," said Yazdi. "He's excited. He's afraid. He's scared." Yazdi said the heavy charges Jones was facing would cause anyone else to react in a similar manner.

"We tried to stop him from talking further," Yazdi said of the hand-over-the-mouth incident, "because he may damage his case."

Judge Graddick had allowed Yazdi and Hughes to take Jones out of the courtroom for a quick conference following his shouts of "I ain't crazy!" When the trio returned several minutes later, the two attorneys had apparently done some straight talking with their contrary client, because Jones was noticeably more calm. Judge Graddick warned Jones that any statements he made concerning his sanity could later be used as evidence against him. Then the judge ordered that Jones's murder trial would start on August 15, 2005.

On the following day, Jones told a Mobile *Press-Register* reporter that he felt Yazdi had done the right thing by putting his hand over his mouth to silence him. He said that he had been unnerved by the prospect of going to Taylor Hardin, but he claimed that he was planning to cooperate with the psychiatrists there because he wanted to know if he had mental problems. The doctors would tell him, he said, if "maybe I do got something wrong with me."

While he waited to be sent for his mental evaluation, Jones busied himself by building up a large stash of the drug Thorazine, along with some other medications, which the jailers said he had obtained from some of the other inmates. When the cache of drugs was discovered, Jones was placed on a two-week suicide watch. He was removed from the cell that he had been sharing with two other inmates and was put in a one-person cell. Jones immediately gave another of his interviews to the media claiming that the drugs weren't his, and he said that the jail's authorities were trying to break him down mentally.

"I wouldn't try to kill myself," he said, "I love life."

"So did his victims," one of their family members pointed out.

Chapter 19

As reports of Jones's continuing string of confessions kept on appearing in the media around the country, Habib Yazdi found himself doing everything he could to discount the credibility of his client's claims, saying Jones would "tell them anything they want to hear" as long as he was allowed to call his mother and Vicki Freeman and get special foods and time out of his jail cell. Even though Jones had begun to deny ever having killed anyone or having ever confessed to doing so, Yazdi was still having to work constantly to contradict the growing number of news reports that outlined Jones's previous admissions of guilt to so many unsolved slayings. There had been no official announcements concerning Jones's many confessions at that point in time, but nonetheless, for several months, word had been leaking out about his statements, and it was becoming common knowledge that he had claimed to be responsible for a score of murders around the country.

"He has confessed to all sorts of things," Yazdi told the Mobile *Press-Register,* adding that Jones had hoped to be able to use his supposedly bogus confessions during his trial for the murder of Lisa Nichols.

"He has so many confessions and comes up with phony

facts," Yazdi said. According to Yazdi, Jones hoped this would confuse the jury when they were faced with all of the confessions that he had made about the murder he was going to be on trial for; confessions that he now denied having ever made at all, despite the fact that each and every one was on videotape. Yazdi said he and Jones "didn't agree with those confessions," adding that the truth was going to come to light whenever Jones took the stand at his trial and testified in court.

Jones was not the first contrary court-appointed client Yazdi had dealt with; another one of his previous clients had been on trial for raping a seventy-eight-year-old woman, who bit off part of his tongue while he was assaulting her. As his explanation for his client's injury, Yazdi claimed that the man was having consensual sex with the seventy-eight-year-old woman, who got jealous over another woman, enticed his client to "give her some sugar" during sex, then bit off part of the man's tongue in a fit of jealous rage.

Another disgruntled client, William John Zeigler, asked the judge in his capital murder trial to remove Yazdi, his court-appointed attorney, from his case because Yazdi had told him he was "stupid" for refusing to talk with the Mobile County district attorney about a plea bargain in his case. The judge refused to relieve Zeigler of his unwanted attorney, and the trial proceeded, with Zeigler facing the death penalty and being represented by a lawyer he no longer trusted or liked.

"He told me I was stupid not to take it," Zeigler claimed Yazdi told him regarding the plea bargain offer.

"I'm scared, I don't know what to do," Zeigler said. "I would like to know what to do about getting my counsel changed."

In yet another death penalty case, Habib Yazdi argued unsuccessfully that his client, Eric Buras, should not be extradited to Louisiana to be charged with first-degree murder in the death of nineteen-year-old Katie Wilkerson, whose body was found floating in the shallow waters of Louisiana's Pearl River. Yazdi called for the prosecution to show probable cause and produce evidence that his client committed the crime, but his calls fell on deaf ears. Alabama governor Bob Riley agreed to Buras's transfer to Louisiana and sent a warrant to that effect to the Mobile County Sheriff's Office ordering the extradition to proceed, despite the objections of Buras and Yazdi.

Habib Yazdi was clearly an attorney who was accustomed to dealing with difficult cases, and his court-appointed defense of Jeremy Bryan Jones was looking as though it was going to be one of the most challenging murder trials of his career.

Chapter 20

The Jeremy Jones cases had been the focus of a nationwide media frenzy since shortly after his arrest in Mobile, with the surprising disclosure of the FBI's admitted bungling of his fingerprint identification during his Georgia arrests. Jones had granted interviews, in person and by telephone, with countless news media outlets, and none of those interviews had been with the permission or the presence of Habib Yazdi, his court-appointed attorney. In return, Jones was given something that he seemed to enjoy even more than the phone privileges and special foods he was being treated to while he was interviewed by law enforcement. The clamoring national media gave Jones a constant flood of attention, which he craved far more than food or contact with his loved ones.

America's Most Wanted had featured Jeremy Jones at the time of his arrest for Lisa Nichols's murder. The show detailed the Nichols case and added that Jones was also being looked at as the most likely suspect in the murders of Amanda Greenwell and Katherine Collins. The program's Web site, which had covered the Patrice Endres disappearance at length for quite a while, had shown the composite of the alleged suspect in that case. After Jones's confession, it had told its viewers that according to the authorities, Jones was being compared to that likeness. Taken side by side, Jones's mug shots from his Georgia arrests bore an eerie resemblance to the composite, with the exception of the longer hair shown in the drawing. That resemblance, of course, turned out to be merely coincidental, since the supposed eyewitness who gave the information that was used to prepare the composite later admitted that she had actually made up the entire story.

In October 2005, *A Current Affair* featured the story of the relationship between Jones and Vicki Freeman, who was still steadfastly supporting her fiancé and insisting to everyone who would listen that he simply could not be guilty of all the terrible crimes that he had confessed to. Producers of the syndicated television news program were interested in the case because Freeman had continued to insist that she planned to marry Jones, and thus far had remained a loyal and faithful girlfriend "in the face of mounting evidence that [Jones] is allegedly a serial killer."

Producer Bob Higgins said his show wanted to get to the story before any of the larger national programs, such as *48 Hours* or *Dateline,* got wind of it; so he and his crew came to Mobile in May to interview some of the people who had been involved with the Jeremy Jones cases, including law enforcement officers, reporters, and family members of some of the victims. Higgins said the Jones/Freeman jailhouse romance would be one of the main elements of the story, but the fact that Jones had been named a suspected serial killer by the FBI was one of the first things that caught the producer's attention.

When the program aired in October 2005, Vicki Freeman was quoted as saying that Jones was everything she'd always been looking for in a man, "the love you only find once in a lifetime," and swore that she was going to stay in the relationship for keeps.

"You'll meet the woman standing by her man . . . only on today's *Current Affair,*" the promo for the episode said.

When CNN/Court TV's Nancy Grace featured the story of the FBI's failure to identify John Paul Chapman as Jeremy Jones, Lisa Nichols's daughters, Jennifer and Amber, appeared on the program and talked with Grace about what had happened to their mother and how their lives had been impacted by her murder.

Grace began the segment, aired a few days before Mother's Day, by asking her viewers if a clerical error on the part of the FBI had allowed a suspected serial killer to walk free and add four additional victims to his list. Grace then went to CNN correspondent Sara Dorsey for details.

Dorsey told the viewers that the FBI had basically admitted that their national database had failed and was not able to match the prints of John Paul Chapman to Oklahoma fugitive Jeremy Jones. Dorsey added that Jones had been arrested three times in Georgia without a match being made.

"The significance of this," she said, "is that he was wanted in Oklahoma on a sexual assault charge."

Jones was allowed out of jail after the Georgia arrests because of the fingerprint matches never being made, Dorsey said, and since that time he had been charged with three murders and was being looked at for possible involvement in several others.

Grace then introduced Jennifer and Amber, who had brought along several pictures of their mother. The camera zoomed in on the photos of Lisa Nichols, giving the viewers a good look at Lisa's beautiful smile. Some of the photos were taken in the brilliant sunshine on the beach at Jennifer's wedding, and Lisa's joy at the occasion was very apparent. In one of the photos, she smiled into the camera, her hair wet with salt spray from the ocean, and another shot, one of her daughters' favorites, was of a vibrant Lisa in a bright red sequined dress, looking forward to a special occasion. Other photos had been taken during a water balloon fight Lisa was having with her grandchildren. In all the photos, Lisa Nichols looked as though she was the same age as her daughters, youthful and happy.

While the photos were being shown on-screen, Grace talked with Jennifer and Amber, asking the two girls if they felt that but for Jones's release, due to a clerical error, their mother might still be with them.

"Absolutely," Jennifer answered. She said that she and her sister had questioned how something like the print mix-up could have happened, when the FBI was supposed to have the best technology available, and a budget to match.

"What went wrong?" Jennifer asked. "And what are they going to do in the future to prevent things like this from happening again?"

Grace told her audience she had obtained a copy of the criminal complaint in the murder case, and said that Jones had, in a sworn affidavit, confessed to killing Lisa with a pistol stolen from a neighbor. She asked Jennifer what she and Amber had found when they got to their mother's home.

"We didn't know at the time that it was, indeed, a homicide," Jennifer said. "They were looking more toward an accident, because there was a fire."

The girls had been given the shocking news on the following day, she said, that their mother's death had been a homicide.

Grace asked Jennifer and Amber how they would spend the upcoming Mother's Day, without Lisa.

"I haven't even thought about it," Amber said. "I don't know if it's something that I want to think about, because to me, the whole thing is still not real."

Jennifer told Grace that normally, the girls would have gone to Lisa's house and spent the day with their mother.

"And now that's not going to happen," she said, "so I think it's going to be different; it's just going to be a very emotional day."

Chapter 21

Jury selection for the case of capital murder against Jeremy Bryan Jones was set to begin on October 17, 2005, but on Thursday, August 25, the prosecution lost an important witness due to a freak accident. The death of Scooter Coleman, the man who rode out Hurricane Ivan with Jones in the trailer home of Mark and Kim Bentley, came as quite a surprise to the Alabama Attorney General's Office, which had taken over prosecution of the case from the Mobile County district attorney at the request of Lisa Nichols's family. The communications director for the attorney general's office, Chris Bence, would not confirm whether or not Coleman would have been a witness in the trial, and would not comment on how Coleman's death would affect the prosecution. Other law enforcement officials involved in the case, however, suggested that Coleman would have not only testified at the trial, but would have been one of the key witnesses.

Fortunately, with the abundance of other evidence, testimony from other people, and Jones's own confessions, Coleman's accidental death did nothing to lessen the likelihood that Jones would be convicted.

The Mobile County Sheriff's Office issued a news release

on Friday, the day following Coleman's death, stating that his body had been found by one of his relatives at a Roberts Road residence in Chunchula, Alabama, on the previous afternoon. There was no indication that Coleman had met with any sort of foul play, the release said, and his exact cause of death was in the process of being determined by sheriff's investigators and the Alabama Department of Forensic Sciences. Later, some media reports stated that Coleman had been accidentally electrocuted while trying to restore power to his mother's home following a storm.

When Scooter Coleman had been interviewed by Detective Paul Burch on January 14, 2005, he told what he said had happened when he and Jones, whom Coleman knew at that time as Oklahoma, were the only two people who rode out the storm in the Ann Parden Road neighborhood, where Lisa Nichols and the Bentleys lived. Jones, Coleman said, had tried to steal a gun from one of the neighborhood homes, but Coleman claimed that he objected to the theft and said that he had told Jones to put the .25-caliber pistol "right back where he got it."

Coleman also told Burch that when Lisa Nichols returned home from waiting out the rough weather with her daughter Amber and Amber's boyfriend, Todd McKerchie, she found that her home had been burglarized while she was gone and a pistol was missing.

During the interview, Coleman also told Burch that Jones had been seen "messing around" with some gasoline cans in the hours before Lisa's body was found—shot, mutilated, doused with gasoline, and set on fire.

Coleman told the investigators about hearing Lisa's family screaming for help when they arrived to check on her and found her body in the sooty, smoke-filled trailer. Coleman said that people from all over the neighborhood came running to try to help, and were horrified to learn what had happened. Coleman said he ran from the trailer, knelt outside in the yard, and prayed for Lisa, asking someone else to come and pray with him. When Burch asked about the behavior of Oklahoma during all the commotion, Coleman said he stayed inside, watching television, and never showed any interest whatsoever in coming outside to see what was going on next door.

Coleman's testimony to the investigators lasted around a half hour, and would have played a major role in Jones's prosecution. His death was a loss to the case against his onetime friend, although there was still plenty of evidence to secure a conviction. Jones would later begin hinting to interviewers that Coleman's death might have been a suicide, telling them it was undoubtedly due to the overwhelming guilt Coleman felt at having incriminated his good buddy Oklahoma in the murder of Lisa Nichols. Jones even seized what he saw as a good opportunity, and attempted to convince the authorities that Coleman himself had been the actual murderer, but that effort was too transparent to ever be taken seriously.

Chapter 22

The constant flood of media attention surrounding Jeremy Jones and all the interviews he had granted so freely had been referred to frequently as a "circus," but as Jones's trial date neared, it soon became evident that the real circus was just beginning, and the clowns were about to be sent in. Even from the point of the initial court appearances for jury selection, it was obvious that the capital murder trial of Jeremy Bryan Jones was going to be the biggest show in town, and no one wanted to miss it.

Hordes of reporters and photographers flocked to the enormous sixth-floor ceremonial courtroom at Mobile's Government Plaza, hoping to size up the pool of one hundred prospective jurors that turned up on Monday, October 17, 2005, for the proceedings. The members of the press also hoped to get another look at the notorious Jeremy Bryan Jones, who seemed so greatly to enjoy being the object of their attention.

At all his previous court appearances, Jones had worn the orange coveralls that had been issued to him by the jail, and he had been in handcuffs. But when jury selection began, his hands were free of restraints and he was dressed in a dark, quite respectable business suit, with a white shirt and a tie. Under the suit, however, was a security restraint designed to be worn beneath the clothing and intended to prevent inmates from making a break from the courtroom during trial appearances. The leg restraint was made to snap into a rigid position if the wearer tried to run, quickly and easily preventing any escape attempts.

Jones and his attorneys, Habib Yazdi and Greg Hughes, had tried unsuccessfully to get the trial moved from Mobile because of the extreme amount of media attention that the case had received in the months following Lisa Nichols's murder. There was no way, the attorneys claimed to the judge, that their client could face a completely impartial jury because of all the press coverage of the case. But the prosecution pointed out that since the vast majority of that publicity had been generated gleefully by Jones himself, with his many voluntary interviews and statements, the trial should not be relocated.

Jones and his attorneys sat at a table in the courtroom as Mobile County Circuit Court judge Charles Graddick began asking questions of the members of the jury pool, beginning the selection process by narrowing down the field. Graddick asked the pool of prospective jurors if anyone had heard of the case in the media; then due to the great numbers of them who indicated that they had indeed heard of the case, Graddick asked, instead, who among them had not heard about it.

By the date that the jury selection had started, reports had already been widely circulated that, in addition to being charged with the murder of Lisa Nichols, Jones had also been charged with the deaths of Amanda Greenwell and Katherine Collins, and was a suspect in many other such crimes in several states. There still had been no formal statement issued by the Mobile authorities confirming the rumors or indicating just how many cases Jones had confessed to, but word had still managed to leak out about most of the confessions. Television and print media reported widely on developments in the many states and cities where Jones had claimed responsibility for cold cases that stretched back for years. Formal statements about his confessions might not have been made yet, but the news was definitely out, all the same, and reporters were on full alert for any new information.

Graddick determined that sixty-nine out of the one hundred prospective jurors had heard of some aspect of the Jones case, and he told the group that they would be questioned individually about the media coverage they had heard, their views on the death penalty, and other issues that might affect their performance on the jury if chosen to serve. Prosecutors had announced they would seek the death penalty in the case, so the prospective jurors' opinions on capital punishment would matter a great deal in the case, both to the defense and to the prosecution.

Twelve jurors and two alternates would be selected, Graddick told the jury pool, and the trial would, more than likely, last around two weeks. The selected jury members, he said at that time, were going to be sequestered in a Mobile hotel during the course of the trial.

While the questioning of prospective jurors took place, a large group of people listened from the prosecution's side of the courtroom. At the table with Alabama assistant attorney generals (AAGs) Will Dill, Don Valeska, and Corey Maze were Paul Burch and Mitch McRae, the Mobile County investigators who had worked so diligently on the case, as well as Lisa Nichols's family members. Jennifer Murphy had earlier asked the attorney general's office in April to take over the prosecution of her mother's killer, when she and other family members grew impatient at the continuing delay in Jones's prosecution. They had been told it might be many months before Jones would be brought to trial, and they felt matters had already been delayed long enough. They requested that the case be taken over by the attorney general's office.

Attorney General (AG) Troy King personally granted Jennifer's request, and his staff immediately took the reins and began to speed matters along considerably. King was going to be opposed in the upcoming election by Mobile County's district attorney John Tyson Jr., but King told the media that his office's takeover of the prosecution from Tyson had nothing whatsoever to do with his reelection bid and was not a political matter.

"There was no campaign going on," King said at the time that Jennifer came to him with her plea for help.

While the jury selection was under way, everyone seated at the prosecution table listened carefully and paid close attention to the questioning of the jury pool. They were determined not to miss a word that was said by any one of the prospective jurors; the outcome of the case was too important to overlook any details in the process of jury selection.

After Graddick adjourned the court for the day and sent the jury pool home to return the next morning, AAG Don Valeska spoke to the press. He told them that his office planned to do everything possible to see that the jury had all the evidence they needed to convict Jeremy Jones of capital murder. Then, Valeska said, Jones would no longer pose a threat to other innocent women, like Lisa Nichols, that he might come into contact with.

The following morning, at eight-thirty, the individual questioning of the potential jurors began, with Graddick, the prosecution, and the defense all asking jurors some very straightforward questions about their feelings on the death penalty, specifically whether or not they would be able to recommend death for Jeremy Jones in the event that he was to be convicted of capital murder. Some members of the jury pool were quite adamant about their feelings and told the court outright that they could not, and would not, vote in favor of the death penalty under any circumstances. Others cited their religious beliefs as their reason for not supporting the death penalty, and still more said they just couldn't condemn a fellow human being to death and would not want such a thing to be weighing on their conscience.

On the other side of the coin, prospective jurors were also let go if they said that they had already formed an opinion that Jones was guilty. Graddick announced at the end of the day that his goal was to winnow down the one hundred potential jurors to a group of sixteen, twelve jurors and four alternates, as opposed to the original two alternates. The selection process was taking a great deal longer than the court had hoped, and Graddick gave instructions to the remaining group to return again the following morning to continue with the questioning.

Chapter 23

On the evening of the third day of jury selection, Judge Charles Graddick finally struck a jury and was prepared to begin Jeremy Jones's murder trial. But Jones, always ready and eager to talk to the press and smile for their cameras, had a surprise in store. The media, which previously had been his favorite audience, had requested to the court that they be allowed to bring their cameras into the courtroom. Much to their chagrin, Jones opposed the request and asked to have cameras banned from the courtroom during his trial. Jones's attorneys, Habib Yazdi and Greg Hughes, also tried again for a change of venue after the jury pool had been polled concerning the media coverage of the case, hoping that they could convince Judge Graddick that Jones couldn't receive a fair trial in the Mobile area because of all the pretrial publicity.

To the chagrin of the many photographers and cameramen, Graddick allowed the motion to exclude cameras in the courtroom, but denied the request for change of venue because, once again, Graddick pointed out that Jones himself had voluntarily generated the lion's share of the media attention he had received, gleefully granting interviews to one and all.

Graddick had ruled previously that several of the videotaped statements that Jones had made to Detectives Paul Burch, Mitch McRae, and their team could be admitted as evidence, despite the fact that the interviews were conducted without Jones's attorneys being present. Since Jones had willingly agreed to those interviews, and countless others, without his attorney's knowledge or approval, the videotapes would be allowed to be shown to the jury in court.

The following morning, Thursday, October 20, the trial started, with the team of prosecutors from the Alabama Attorney General's Office primed and ready to go to work. The press had been told by AAG Don Valeska that, in addition to Jones's own confessions, there was also a great deal of very solid forensic evidence in the case, and Valeska and his fellow prosecutors Will Dill and Corey Maze were ready to present that evidence, and much more, to the jury.

In their opening arguments, the charges against Jeremy Jones were explained for the jury, along with a detailed account of Jones's activities from the time he first arrived at the Bentleys' home on Wednesday, September 15, until he left there on Sunday, September 19, slipping away unnoticed, without any explanation, while Mark Bentley was sleeping.

The charges against Jeremy Bryan Jones, as told to the jury, were as follows:

Capital murder–rape—Lisa Marie Nichols was shot with a firearm by Jeremy Jones while he was engaging or attempting to engage in sexual intercourse with her by force.

Capital murder–kidnapping—Jeremy Jones shot Lisa Marie Nichols during his abduction of, or attempt to abduct, her with the intent to inflict physical injury upon her or to violate her sexually.

Capital murder–burglary—Jeremy Jones caused Lisa Marie Nichols's death while he entered, or remained unlawfully, within a dwelling with the intent to commit a crime therein, rape or sexual abuse. While entering the dwelling, or while inside or while in flight from the dwelling, Jones caused physical injury to Lisa Marie Nichols.

Capital murder–sexual assault—Jeremy Jones intentionally caused the death of Lisa Marie Nichols by shooting her during the time that he subjected, or attempted to subject, Lisa Marie Nichols to sexual contact by force.

The prosecution also presented the jury with a detailed time line account of everything that had taken place from September 15, when Jones turned up on Mark Bentley's doorstep unannounced, through the events following the hurricane, the discovery of Lisa Nichols's body, to Jones's disappearance from Bentley's home and his subsequent arrest by Mobile County authorities on September 21 at 8:30 A.M.

In his opening statement, Assistant Attorney General Will Dill, the lead prosecutor of the case, told the jury that as dangerous as Hurricane Ivan had been as it approached Mobile in the days before Lisa Nichols was murdered, there had been an even more dangerous threat—what he referred to as a "malevolent force"—approaching from the north: Jeremy Bryan Jones. Dill said that Hurricane Ivan came with plenty of advance warning, but no one had been given any warning that Jeremy Jones was preparing to stalk Lisa, rape and sexually abuse her, shoot her in the head three times, then try to set her body on fire to cover up his murderous actions and destroy as much of the evidence of his crime as possible.

The jury learned for the first time, that morning, about some of the horrifying testimony they could expect to hear in the coming days of the trial. Dill described to them the awful experiences of Lisa's family, who would be testifying themselves about what happened when they went to check on their mother and discovered her body, and Dill said that DNA evidence would positively link Jeremy Jones to the crime. Other witnesses, Dill said, would tell the jury about Jones's strange behavior, both before and after Lisa's body was discovered, and his later, unannounced disappearance from the Bentleys' home.

The jury heard Dill describe how Lisa's family and her neighbors were hysterical, crying for help and rushing to the scene, while Jones sat next door in the Bentley home casually watching television.

"He knew it was his handiwork," Dill said of Jones.

Opening for the defense, attorney Greg Hughes claimed that the police had arrested the wrong man, a man who was addicted to methamphetamine, who would tell them anything that he thought they wanted to hear. Hughes admitted that Jones had given statements to the detectives working the case, and ultimately those statements had been the cause of his indictment for the murder. His client had given those statements, Hughes said, in order to get to spend time out of the "miserable living conditions" he had been suffering in the cell, where he was being kept under suicide watch.

The prosecution began calling witnesses later that day, beginning with Amber and Todd McKerchie. Amber and Todd, who had gotten married since Lisa's death, told of the horrors they faced when they and Amber's sister, Jennifer Murphy, went to Lisa's home to find out why they had been unable to get in touch with her by phone for an entire day. They knew the electricity was still out in most of Lisa's neighborhood, so they carried flashlights. As they walked up the driveway toward the mobile home that evening, they noticed there were further signs that there had been an additional break-in and other indications that caused them to suspect something was very wrong.

When they entered the house, their flashlights showed a room full of smoke. They began to frantically call Lisa's name, walking farther into the trailer to look for her. Todd McKerchie told the jury what he saw when he looked into the bathroom and found Lisa lying on the floor.

"She was just about unrecognizable," he said. He blocked Jennifer and Amber's view into the room, pushing them back and telling them to call 911. But despite his efforts to shield the girls from the terrible sight of their mother's burned and mutilated body, they saw what had happened and became hysterical. Amber stumbled out of the trailer and fell off the porch, and Jennifer ran down the driveway, screaming for help, toward the neighboring houses.

Ironically, Mark Bentley was the person who first heard their cries for help. He made the initial call to 911; then he went with Todd back into the trailer to see if there was any possibility that Lisa could be helped. Others in the neighborhood hurried to the trailer to find out what had happened, and to help if they could, but only one person didn't react to the commotion outside, Todd said. Jeremy Jones—the man Mark Bentley and Scooter Coleman called Oklahoma—sat calmly on the Bentleys' sofa, watching television while everyone else in the neighborhood was outside, trying to determine what had happened to Lisa and attempting to console her hysterical daughters.

During Todd McKerchie's cross-examination, defense attorney Habib Yazdi, employing tactics that courtroom observers deemed extremely tasteless and inconsiderate, tried to imply that Jones had an "affair" with Lisa Nichols. He even went so far as to suggest that Lisa might have also been intimate with Mark Bentley. Yazdi said that he had been told that Bentley spent a couple of days following the murder, crying, "perhaps for the loss of Lisa." But McKerchie promptly told him that it was no wonder that Mark had been upset and devastated after seeing Lisa's burned, mutilated body lying in her bathroom.

McKerchie had successfully undermined Yazdi's attempts

to malign Lisa and discredit Mark Bentley, who was scheduled to testify the following morning. Yazdi dreaded Mark taking the witness stand; he knew that Mark Bentley's testimony was going to be highly incriminating for his client, and there was nothing he could do to prevent it.

Chapter 24

When the prosecution resumed calling witnesses to give their testimony on Friday morning, beginning with Mark Bentley on the witness stand, the jury heard his account of the events surrounding Lisa Nichols's death. They also heard one of the key pieces of evidence in the trial, a long recording of a phone call Jeremy Jones had made to his former employer from the Metro Jail after his arrest.

Mark Bentley explained to the jury that he had let Jones and Scooter Coleman stay in his home while Hurricane Ivan approached. Mark and his wife, Kim, had made plans to go north of Mobile to a town farther inland and spend the night there, leaving Jones and Coleman to wait out the storm in the Bentley home, next door to Lisa Nichols. Jones had gotten a look at Lisa when she had returned to her home for the first time after the storm to survey the damage, then left again to spend another night with Amber and Todd. The trim, attractive forty-four-year-old could easily have passed for a woman half her age, and Jones took notice, claiming later to one of his friends, "I need a woman." Scooter Coleman let him know right away, in no uncertain terms, that Lisa was way out of his league, but the damage was already done. Jones had sighted and targeted his victim, and he would not be discouraged, not by Scooter or anyone else. Jones knew exactly what he wanted, and he was determined to get it.

Mark Bentley told the jury about what it was like for him, going with Todd McKerchie into the smoky trailer and seeing Lisa's body. He said he was "freaked out. She was burned up. It just about killed me."

Mark confirmed Todd McKerchie's account of Jones's behavior after the murder was discovered. He said that Jones didn't come outside at the time Lisa's body was first discovered, but asked Mark later on, "What did it look like over there?"

During the course of the trial, the jury would hear many long taped conversations and interrogations, and they would see many videotaped statements. That day, they heard one of the most compelling of those tapes. As they sat, listening intently, the recorded phone call Jeremy Jones placed to Mark Bentley on December 10 was played for them. It included the first of a multitude of confessions they would hear Jones make, on recordings and on videotapes, freely admitting to the murder of Lisa Nichols.

Mark Bentley answered the phone that day with no idea who it was that was calling him, saying, "Yeah."

"Hey, buddy," Jones said, "what's up, Mark?"

"Who is this?" Bentley asked.

"Oklahoma," Jones answered.

"What you doing calling me, dude?" a surprised and angry Mark Bentley asked, hardly able to believe that Jones had the nerve to be on the phone, calling him.

"I just said 'emergency' and asked if I could call you," Jones told him.

"Well, why would you do that?"

"'Cause I just want you to pray for me."

"Pray for you," Mark said. "Huh. Do you think it will do any good?"

"Yeah," Jones said, "it can't hurt, can it?"

Mark was totally disgusted with his former friend.

"I don't know, man," he told Jones, "I tell you, you just . . . I don't know what even to say to you, dude, I mean—"

"I know you don't," Jones said.

"You ain't the man I thought I knew, anyway," Mark told him. "I don't know what to say to somebody like you, man. You deceived me and everybody else around you. I mean, you killed my neighbor, man, and then let me go in there and see it. I won't ever get over that. You hurt me more than anything else, because I trusted you."

"Yeah," Jones said, apparently unable to come up with any better reply.

"I mean, I always liked you and believed in you, but that right there, it just done something to me, you know. . . . You can ask forgiveness, but a man ain't gon' forgive you, I can tell you that. You know that."

Jones stuck with his one-word reply. "Yeah," he said.

Mark was warming to his subject now, and he had a lot he wanted to say to this man he had befriended.

"And whatever happens to you, I hope you get forgiveness for what you done. I don't hate you, but I just don't know you. I thought I knew you, but I don't."

"You knew me," Jones told him, "You just didn't know me on drugs."

"Well, I mean, I ain't never seen no drugs that would cause somebody to kill somebody, John. You didn't have to go that far, you know. You didn't have to take the woman's life. You didn't have to take her life, man. You could have let her live. I mean, what's worse, dying in the electric chair, going to prison for life, or, you know, raping somebody and getting seven or eight years? You didn't have to kill her, and you didn't have to let me go over there and see what I saw and then go back there and us pray together. I mean, that right there was sorry."

"I needed it," Jones told Mark.

"Huh," Mark said. "Oh, you needed it. I know it. We all need it. It messed me up; it messed up my life; it messed up my way of thinking; it tore my family up. You messed with a lot of people's lives that won't ever be the same."

Jones reverted to his one-word answer. "Yeah," he said.

"You know, like I said, I don't know what to tell you, bro. I really don't. Up until the end, I vouched for you and told them ain't no way you could have done that, ain't no way, but that wasn't the man I knew. I just didn't know you. Hell, man, I let you stay at my house, *at my house,* and I took care of you!"

"I know," Jones said.

"I mean, if you was going to do something like that, man, why would you do it to my neighbor? It's questions I have to ask, and I won't never know the answers."

"I don't even know myself," Jones said.

Mark Bentley, growing flustered, fumbled to find the words he wanted to use.

"You know, I mean that's . . . it's just . . . I mean, I don't . . . I'll be honest with you. I don't see how one man, one human being, can do that to another human being and walk around with a straight face like you did. I can't see that, you know. I can't; it's hard for me, it's hard for me to just . . . it's like it's not a reality to me."

"It ain't reality for me, either, you know," Jones said, "not until after I came down and realized what I did. I mean, I was that fucking high, excuse my language, but I was higher than I had ever been in my whole life. I don't care about shooting drugs or whatever; that was the highest I had ever been in my whole life and it wasn't even a high, it was like a nightmare. I was in a movie. When you can't stop what you're doing and you're thinking, 'God, I'm out of control,' you know, and then you just teeter-totter and then you just feel like coming down and you're thinking, 'Was that just a dream, or was I hallucinating?' you know. For two days, I thought that didn't really happen. I really did, Mark."

"I don't believe that," Mark stated flatly. "You knew what happened."

"I was in denial then," Jones claimed.

"Well, you knew what happened and you didn't want to face it; now, I can believe that," Mark told him.

"Okay," Jones said.

"You know, I wouldn't want to face it, either," Mark said. "Who would, once you know you done it, once you've gone so far, you know you're going to have to face it sooner or later. And you think about it; anybody that can do something like that, hell, you sat here and ate hamburgers, we worked together, and we was laughing, you know? I was talking about how I shot my rifle over that way and I was thinking a stray bullet might have went over there, and this and that and the other, until I found out what happened. Anyway, I know you've talked about it so much now, you probably don't want to talk about it no more."

"That's all right," Jones told him.

"I just wish you wouldn't have done it, man," Mark said.

"Me, too," answered Jones.

"I ain't lying," Mark told him.

Jones then admitted to Mark Bentley that he and Mark's cousin Scooter Coleman had done drugs in the Bentleys' home after Mark and his wife had left. Mark was irate to hear what had taken place without his knowledge.

"See, and I saved his life," Mark said about Scooter Coleman. "I literally saved his life, and took him in my house and fed him when he couldn't even get up off the couch; I let him stay at my house and he swore on his life and his children that he wasn't fooling with no drugs, because you know, and he knew, how I felt about them and how I feel, right now, about it. I looked at you (when you came to my house) and I asked you in your face [if you were doing drugs]."

"I wasn't doing nothing," Jones claimed, "I wasn't when I came down, I wasn't."

"Well, that was a day or so after you had been here, and y'all had went to [the home of someone known to do drugs]. Yeah, you was doing it, you just lied to me. I guess I'm a little bit gullible because I try to help people."

"Yeah," said a chastened Jones.

"Like I said, I always, always liked you up until you got on that shit because I don't think, when you was working for me that year and a half before, I don't believe you were on it."

"I wasn't," Jones said.

"[Police] are wanting me to tell them something about you, but I can't tell them nothing. I don't know where you've been and what you've done," Mark told Jones.

"Yeah," Jones said, "Everybody swore up and down everybody down here knew who I was, that's what the police thought."

"No," Mark said, "ain't nobody down here knew who you was."

"No, they thought they knew my name and everything," Jones told him.

"You're a damn good liar, I can tell you that," an angry Mark Bentley answered. "You fooled me, now I can tell you that."

"I just really, I just had to change my life, you know what I'm saying, and I didn't want to get in no trouble and I thought I'd change my ways and I did, you know what I'm saying?" Jones scrambled to explain away his behavior. "When I first met you and worked for you, I was one hundred percent who I was, except for my name."

"Well, I know, and I told them . . . Hell, I ain't never had anything but good to say about you up until that point where I told you I was going to send your ass back to your mother in a box (for doing drugs), you remember that?"

"Yeah," Jones said, "I remember that."

"Up until that time, hey, me and you was good buddies," Mark said.

"Yeah, oh yeah," Jones whined, "my life's fucked."

"You don't have a life anymore," Mark told him flatly.

"It's gone," Jones said, "but they told me I could use the phone and wanted to know who I wanted to call and I told them I wanted to call you."

Jones had evidently forgotten about telling Mark Bentley earlier that he had gotten to use the phone because he claimed to have an "emergency," and Mark remained skeptical about Jones's statements of regret.

"Well," Mark told him, "I mean, hey, I don't know—"

"I'm sorry for anything I ever caused," Jones said.

"Well, you know, it's like anything, man," Mark told him, "once you do it, it's too late to be sorry, because you can't take it back."

"Yeah, I can't," Jones agreed. "We had some good times fishing, we had some good times hunting, shooting gators, whatever, you know; you showed me fun and I appreciate it, okay?"

"All right, man," Mark Bentley said, hanging up the phone, thankful that the uncomfortable conversation with his former employee was over.

Chapter 25

Also present in the courtroom and hearing Jeremy Jones's taped phone call to Mark Bentley that day was Vicki Freeman, Jones's long-suffering girlfriend, and his mother, fifty-year-old Jeanne Beard, who had come from Miami, Oklahoma, for the trial of her oldest son. She and a group of other relatives sat in the courtroom and listened to Jones freely admitting on tape to Mark Bentley that he was guilty of all the heinous acts for which he was being tried. Even though she heard for herself as her son confessed in his own words to Lisa Nichols's murder, Jeanne Beard still believed that Jones wasn't guilty.

"He's a good boy," she told reporters.

Jones was seen mouthing the words "I love you" to his mother and Vicki Freeman during the proceedings, and courtroom observers reported that he seemed to be much more concerned with what the two women were thinking of him than what was being said about him on the witness stand.

Jeanne Beard almost didn't get to make the trip to Mobile for her son's trial; early in October, she and her younger son, Jeremy Jones's half brother, were arrested at their Oklahoma home for a number of gun and drug charges after a raid on her house turned up methamphetamine, a multitude of different items of drug paraphernalia, a stash of currency totaling more than $1,000, and around twenty guns, including a loaded derringer.

Detective Danny Green, of the Miami, Oklahoma, Police Department, said that the raid was the result of three weeks of surveillance and investigation after the Miami Police had been informed by the authorities from another neighboring town that Jeanne Beard had been observed delivering what was described as a "white, powdery substance" to someone who was being watched there by the police for suspected drug activity.

Jeanne Beard had prepared herself and her home for the possibility that she might, at some point, be paid a surprise visit by narcotics agents, and she had carefully set up several surveillance cameras covering all angles of the outside of her house. Anyone approaching the house from any direction could be watched by Beard from a monitor in her bedroom. However, as luck would have it, she happened to be in the shower on the day when officers from the Miami, Ohio, police, the Oklahoma Bureau of Narcotics and Dangerous Drugs Control, and the Thirteenth District Drug Task Force came calling with a search warrant in hand.

Beard was wearing a towel when the officers arrived on her doorstep at midmorning, and after they entered the house, she hurriedly got dressed. Green reported that Beard came out to the living room, sat down on the couch, and held on to her purse protectively. When the purse was pried from her grip and was searched, the top part of a set of scales, of the type commonly used for measuring out drugs, was found, along with a substance that the officers had reason to believe was methamphetamine residue.

Beard became quite belligerent and uncooperative after her purse was searched, Green said, and she had to be arrested and taken to jail in order to keep her from interfering with the continuing search of her house. After Beard was removed and the search was resumed, the officers found the surveillance equipment, which had been set up in her bedroom, and seized it. Then they found plastic bags and the bottom part of the scales, the stash of currency, and weapons that were hidden under Beard's bed. The loaded .25-caliber derringer and the other guns were also seized and removed from the house. The officers also found a large number of letters written by Jeremy Jones to his mother and brother from the Mobile County Jail.

The search of Beard's seventeen-year-old son's room turned up more scales, pipes for smoking marijuana or hashish, and a few pieces of that old high-school favorite, marijuana brownies. The boy, who would be turning eighteen years old in only two days after the bust, came home from Miami High School while the search was in progress and was promptly taken into custody. He was released into his father's custody with orders to show up for a court date a few days later. Because of his upcoming birthday, Green said, the boy could possibly be charged as an adult with possession of marijuana with intent to distribute.

Likely charges against Beard included possession of drug paraphernalia, possession of a loaded weapon in the process of committing a felony, and possession of methamphetamine within a thousand feet of a school.

The arrests of Beard and her younger son received a great deal of publicity in the Oklahoma, Kansas, and Missouri areas, where the media had been covering the Jeremy Jones cases with just as much fervor as in the Southeast. Dozens of comments on the coverage were posted on one newspaper's Web site. A few people expressed their sympathy for Jones and his family, but the overwhelming majority felt different.

One post said that it was "about time [Jeanne Beard] got in trouble for something," and another called Jones "a convict, murderer and complete skank," saying he had ruined many people's lives, and both he and his family "deserve to rot."

Another post accused the newspaper and its reporters of "participating in a media campaign to slander and libel Jeremy Jones." That one brought a flurry of furious responses from Internet readers across the country, and even some posts from family members of Jones's alleged victims.

One relative of young Amanda Greenwell expressed a wish that people would quit "whining about Jones," and asked how anyone of sound mind could or would defend him.

One of those defenders asked why Jones had to be constantly brought up in the press, considering that he hadn't yet been convicted, and saying there was no proof he had killed anyone, "so why keep printing it?" The writer added that the charges against Jeremy Jones shouldn't be "spread all over the news," and said that Jones, if innocent, wouldn't stand a chance at a fair trial.

"He had nothing to do with his mother's or half-brother's [*sic*] deal," the writer said.

During the early days of the trial, Jeanne Beard was present in court in support of her son, but she would soon have court appearances of her own to worry about back in Oklahoma.

Chapter 26

On Saturday, the prosecution played another tape for the jurors. It had been made on September 21, following Jeremy Jones's arrest, and recorded the initial questioning sessions with Jones, conducted by lead investigator Paul Burch and other Mobile County detectives. On the tape, Jones alternated between tearful confessions and adamant denials, admitting that he shot Lisa Nichols and attempted to set fire to her body. However, he doggedly stuck to his story that her death was due to a drug overdose and that the sexual activity that took place prior to her death was consensual, not a case of rape. Lisa was already dead when he shot her, he continued to claim, dead from a heart attack caused by an overdose of speed. He then shot her and set fire to her body, he said, because he didn't want Mark Bentley to know that he had been doing drugs.

The jurors heard investigators telling Jones that he might as well admit what actually happened, since they had more than enough forensic evidence to prove that he had shot Lisa in the head three times with a .25-caliber pistol while she was still alive. Paul Burch told Jones that he wanted to know exactly what happened to Lisa.

"We have a right to know that, and the family has a right to know that," he told Jones. Since Jones had already admitted to killing Lisa, he told him, he'd gotten over the hard part of his statement.

"Raping her doesn't much matter after you've killed her," he told Jones. "I don't understand why you're having such a hard time with that. We're going to be able to prove it."

"'Cause myself, I don't picture me raping nobody, I mean that's just something I wouldn't do," Jones protested.

Burch and his colleagues told Jones that they had a pretty good idea of what had happened, and why; they believed he was high on drugs, annoyed after an over-the-phone disagreement with Vicki Freeman, and tried to make advances toward Lisa Nichols after seeing her earlier that day when she returned home. Jones, who had a very high opinion of his attractiveness to women, was not used to being turned down.

"I could charm the pants off a nun," he had claimed on several occasions, bragging about his sexual prowess. But when Lisa would have nothing to do with him, he attacked her, then raped and killed her, setting fire to her body in an attempt to cover up his crime and destroy evidence. When the investigators let Jones know that they didn't believe the stories he was telling them, they also let him know that Lisa Nichols was too much of a lady to ever behave as he had described. The hardworking, responsible grandmother would have never sullied herself or her home in such a manner, they knew.

Jones also claimed that Lisa had given him $20 to buy the drugs that he said they used on the night she died, but the investigators already knew that was a lie. Because of Hurricane Ivan's visit, Lisa hadn't been able to pick up her paycheck at the usual time and had borrowed $10 from a friend at work that evening before she left for home. The $10 bill was the only money she had.

During the questioning session, Jones appeared very ill at ease, with his voice growing loud, then dropping almost to a whisper. He alternated between cocky confidence and nervous whimpering, and seemed to be most worried about what Mark Bentley would think of him when he realized that Jones, whom he knew as John Paul Chapman, was addicted to methamphetamine.

Later that day, the jury heard testimony from deputy state fire marshal Gary Cartee, who analyzed the fire that was set in Lisa Nichols's trailer. Cartee said that a large amount of gasoline had been poured onto Lisa's body and set afire, but the fire didn't burn long because of the lack of oxygen in the closed-up trailer.

"The only thing that sustained significant fire damage was Ms. Nichols's body," he told the jury, saying that in his professional opinion, her body had intentionally been set on fire.

Chapter 27

Since the next day, October 23, was Sunday, Judge Graddick resumed the trial at 12:30 P.M. and planned to remain in session until 4:00 P.M. The jury had spent another sequestered night in their motel rooms, and they returned to the courtroom to listen to more taped interviews. Then they viewed a video of Jones that had been made during a questioning session the previous November.

In the video, Paul Burch and his team began gradually bringing Jones nearer to the truth than in their previous sessions. He began to change his story, and finally appeared to have realized just how close he was to the possibility of receiving the death penalty. Jones cried aloud as he admitted that he had lied when he claimed that Lisa had done drugs with him. He told the investigators that he had made up the whole story about a drug overdose because he was trying to save his life.

"I don't want to die," he bawled, shedding crocodile tears with all his might. "I don't know why I did what I did to her, I don't; and I'm sorry for her family, I am."

Jones also admitted that they didn't have consensual sex, downgrading his previous story to saying that there had only been one single attempted kiss that Lisa had promptly pulled away from, then turned her back on him.

"I put my arm around her neck like that, and come up like that," he said, showing the investigators the moves he had made after Lisa rejected his advances. "She was like, 'What are you doing?' and I told her, 'I don't know, I don't know what I'm doing.'"

Jones also told the investigators that he had ordered Lisa to take her clothes off "right now," and said that she was "scared." And despite his claims that he was not the sort of person who could ever rape a woman, he finally admitted that he had, indeed, raped Lisa.

It had taken some time, and several interview sessions, before Paul Burch and his team had worked Jeremy Jones around to telling them what had actually happened on the night Lisa Nichols was murdered. The men had patiently talked for hours about many of the things Jones liked—like fishing and hunting—in order to work their way to the truth, but their careful questioning had finally begun to pay off.

"I can't believe I'm sitting here telling y'all this," Jones told them, "but it's the truth."

Chapter 28

Jeremy Jones took the stand in his own defense the following day, steadfastly claiming that the many taped confessions the jury had watched and listened to during the previous days had all been a lie.

"Whenever I wanted something," he bragged, "I made the magic phone call," getting word to the detectives that he was ready to talk to them some more about Lisa Nichols's murder or about some of the many other crimes to which he had begun confessing. He confessed, he claimed, because when he got questioned by the investigators, he always got whatever special foods he requested, was allowed to make calls to Vicki Freeman and to his family back in Oklahoma, and was given other privileges that he otherwise would not have had.

"They treated me like a king," Jones said of the detectives, claiming later that he had only admitted to the murders because they wanted him to do so, and because of the many "perks" he got whenever he was making his confessions.

But once on the witness stand, he insisted that all his admissions of guilt had been nothing but lies, and he began trying to shift the blame for Lisa Nichols's murder to the late Scooter Coleman, who had been slated to be a prosecution witness.

Coleman, Jones claimed, had gone with him into Lisa's trailer and was the person who had actually committed the crime. Coleman had threatened him, Jones said, and had forced him to take the blame for Lisa's death by saying he would kill Jones's family if he didn't say he was the guilty party. Jones even fell back on one of the oldest clichés around, going so far as to claim that he had stumbled on to the scene after Lisa had been killed and had seen Scooter Coleman standing over the body and literally holding "a smoking gun."

"Yeah," one of the prosecutors muttered, "blame the dead guy."

From the start of the trial, the media had eagerly awaited a confrontation between the attorney general's prosecutors and Jeremy Jones himself. On Tuesday, October 25, the time for the much-anticipated showdown had finally arrived. Jones took the witness stand to spend well over an hour being grilled by AAG Don Valeska, who had been waiting for his opportunity to put Jones in the hot seat. Valeska had several points he looked forward to making, most having to do with testimony the jury had heard during the previous days, testimony that Jones now tried his best to contradict. His efforts, however, were unsuccessful.

Jones frequently gave answers to Valeska's questions that left the courtroom spectators choking back snorts of laughter. It wasn't as much what he said, one of the observers claimed, but how he said it. His Oklahoma accent came across with a distinct "redneck twang," and the listeners sometimes just couldn't muffle their snickering. And occasionally his answers left the courtroom laughing out loud at his outright conceit.

When Valeska asked Jones what had made him think that a woman of Lisa Nichols's caliber would ever be interested in a loser like him, Jones had an immediate answer.

"I think I'm very good-looking," he pronounced confidently, a statement that was met with hoots of laughter from the courtroom gallery.

Jeremy Jones was enjoying the attention he was getting from the spectators, the media, and even the prosecutors. He and Valeska argued back and forth during his time on the stand, with Valeska losing his temper on several occasions despite his best efforts to keep a cool head. Jones was so flippant that his answers infuriated the veteran prosecutor.

When Jones told Valeska that he was lying when he had confessed to Lisa Nichols's murder several times on tape, Valeska heatedly replied, "You're always lying!"

"Except under oath" was Jones's glib answer, which brought another round of muffled chuckles from the gallery.

Following the lengthy and heated Jones/Valeska dustup, both the defense and the prosecution rested, and Judge Graddick announced to the court that the trial would reconvene Wednesday at 8:30 A.M., when both sides were slated to begin presenting their closing arguments.

Chapter 29

Assistant Attorney General William Dill stood before the jury on the morning of Wednesday, October 26, and started the prosecution's closing arguments by calling Jeremy Jones "a coward" and a vicious murderer who hated women. Dill also brought up the late Scooter Coleman once again, reminding the jury of how they had heard Jones repeatedly confess to Lisa Nichols's murder on tape during the trial, and how Jones had subsequently changed his story and blamed the murder on Scooter Coleman, once Coleman was dead and gone, unable to refute anything Jones had to say about him.

"Blame the dead guy," Dill told the jurors. "He can't come in here and defend himself. It's one more vicious lie."

Dill then recapped the events leading up to Lisa Nichols's murder, and described Jones's behavior following her death, telling the jury that Jones had casually gone back next door to Mark Bentley's home, took a shower, then watched hunting videos for a while before going to bed, as if nothing out of the ordinary had happened.

When the defense took the floor to present their own closing arguments, Greg Hughes claimed that his client had been frightened and had tried to cover up the killing, which the defense continued attempting to attribute to Scooter Coleman. What he alleged that Jones had done, Hughes told the jury, could not be classified as capital murder. And the many taped confessions, Hughes said, were not valid. The investigators were "slicking" his client, who had been manipulated into making untrue statements while he was high on drugs and had not actually intended to confess to anything.

"He felt he could improve his living situation" by confessing, Hughes claimed. The confessions got him out of his cell, provided him with good food, and allowed him to make phone calls, Hughes said, and Jones kept on telling the authorities whatever he thought they wanted to hear.

When Don Valeska took over his portion of the prosecution's closing arguments, he reminded the jurors that, in addition to Jones's confessions, there was also a great deal of forensic evidence that pointed directly to Jones as the murderer. Lisa Nichols's blood had been found on Jones's clothes, he told them again.

In answer to the many claims by the defense that Jones had been coerced and bribed into admitting guilt for things he had not done, Valeska read part of the transcript of Jones's phone call from jail to Mark Bentley. Once again, the jurors heard Jones's own words to his former employer as he freely admitted to killing Lisa Marie Nichols.

"'It was like a nightmare,'" Valeska read. "'I was in a movie. I was higher than I had ever been in my whole life.'"

That confession, Valeska said, was not made to the investigators, but directly from Jones, by his own choice, to his former friend. There was no way, Valeska claimed, that Jones had been coerced or manipulated into saying the things that he had told Mark Bentley in that phone call he made from the jail.

Valeska closed by telling the jurors that there was no reasonable doubt in the case, and they should have no hesitation in pronouncing Jeremy Jones guilty.

"If you want to see evil, look at him," he told them, categorizing Jones as an immoral, cowardly drug user who had stalked and brutally murdered an innocent woman for no reason other than his own gratification.

The jury left the courtroom to deliberate, and within only two hours, they filed back in to return their verdict. Jeremy Jones was found guilty on all the counts against him.

During the final day of the trial, Jones had looked frequently at his mother, Jeanne Beard, who once again sat in the courtroom beside Vicki Freeman. He seemed to be worried about what the women would believe, considering the testimony they were hearing, much of it his own taped confessions. But when the verdict was read, Jones didn't look around the courtroom. He sat at the table, facing forward, between his two defense attorneys, showing no emotion at all and remaining still and quiet.

Judge Graddick announced to the courtroom that on the following day, the jury would give him their recommendation for Jeremy Jones's sentence: either the death penalty, or life in prison without parole.

Chapter 30

There were tears of relief from the family of Lisa Nichols when the guilty verdict, which convicted Jeremy Bryan Jones of Lisa's murder, was read. The trial had been an ordeal for them, with graphic photos and descriptions of the crime scene, and they had sat through some very hurtful testimony, which continually reminded them of the horrors inflicted on Lisa before her death. But Jennifer Murphy spoke to the media after court was adjourned, and expressed her gratitude to the Mobile County Sheriff's Office and the Alabama Attorney General's Office.

"I'll always have a place in my heart for them," she said.

Lead investigator Paul Burch told reporters that he had believed all along that Jones would be found guilty when a jury heard the abundance of hard evidence against him, his own confessions in particular.

"We've got justice for Lisa Nichols today," he said.

The following morning, Attorney General Troy King released a statement giving the highest praise to Sheriff Tillman and his investigators for their work on the case.

"I commend Jack Tillman and the Mobile County Sheriff's

After his arrest for the murder of Lisa Marie Nichols, Jeremy Bryan Jones confessed to so many other murders that investigators called him "the redneck Ted Bundy." *(Photo courtesy of the Dawson County, Georgia Sheriff's Office)*

Lisa Marie Nichols, the Alabama woman whose murder brought an end to Jeremy Jones' alleged killing spree. *(Photo by Jennifer Murphy)*

Following his arrest in Mobile County, Alabama, Jeremy Jones claimed the sores on his face were the result of hepatitis C.
(Photo courtesy of Mobile County Sheriff)

This gun was used by Jeffrey Jones in the murder of Lisa Marie Nichols.
(Photo courtesy of Alabama Attorney General's Office)

Sergeant Jeffrey Walls and Investigator Armando Asaro with the photos they used to identify murder victim Katherine Collins. *(Photo courtesy of New Orleans Police Department)*

The reconstruction made by Louisiana State University's Faces Laboratory from the skull of Katherine Collins shows a remarkable resemblance to the photo of Collins. *(Photo courtesy of New Orleans Police Department)*

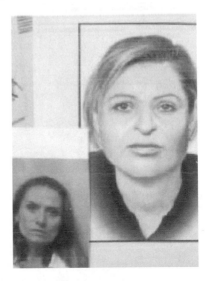

This driver's license photo of Patrice Endres was circulated nationwide by the Forsyth County, Georgia Sheriff's Office following her disappearance. *(Photo courtesy of the Forsyth County Sheriff's Office)*

Forsyth County, Georgia Sheriff Ted Paxton and his officers followed up hundreds of leads on the Endres case after it was featured on "America's Most Wanted" and other television news programs. *(Photo courtesy of the Forsyth County Sheriff's Office)*

This composite drawing was made after an alleged eyewitness described a suspect she claimed to have seen outside Patrice Endres' hair salon at the time of her disappearance. *(Photo courtesy of the Forsyth County Sheriff's Office)*

A van like this one was reportedly seen by an eyewitness, parked outside the hair salon when Patrice Endres vanished, but the eyewitness later admitted she lied. *(Photo courtesy of the Forsyth County Sheriff's Department)*

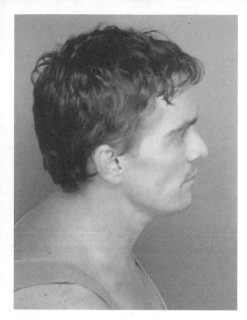

This mug shot was taken of Jeremy Jones by the Dawson County, Georgia authorities, who believed at that time that he was named John Paul Chapman. *(Photo courtesy of the Dawson County Sheriff's Office)*

When photos of these eight women were found in Jeremy Jones' storage shed, authorities feared they might have been among his victims. The women were later identified, and had not been harmed.
(Photo courtesy of the Forsyth County Sheriff's Department)

Lorene Bible and her brother Lonnie Leforce, left, wait for reports on the renewed search for the bodies of Lauria Bible and Ashley Freeman after Jeremy Jones confessed to their murders.
(Claremore Progress photo by Linda Martin)

Lorene Bible keeps a memorial for her daughter Lauria and Lauria's best friend, Ashley Freeman, on the gate to the Freeman home where Ashley's parents were killed and the two girls disappeared. (Claremore Progress photo by Linda Martin)

Alabama Attorney General Troy King and his staff took over the capital murder prosecution of Jeremy Jones at the request of Lisa Marie Nichols' family. *(Luverne Journal photo by Kevin Pearcey)*

These photos of Jeremy Jones, assembled from case files, show the many different faces of the man who confessed to over 21 murders in several states. *(Photo courtesy of the Alabama Attorney General's Office)*

Jeremy Bryan Jones
April 12, 1973

Alabama Assistant Attorney Generals Will Dill, left, and Don Valeska were the prosecuting attorneys at Jones' trial for the murder of Lisa Marie Nichols. (Luverne Journal photo by Kevin Pearcey)

Less than a week after Jeremy Jones was moved to Death Row to await execution, the body of Patrice Endres was found far from the location where Jones claimed to have left it. (Photo courtesy of the Forsyth County Sheriff's Office)

Elbert Clark, left, with Dawson County Sheriff Billy Carlisle, church member Larry Jones, and Elbert's son Andy Clark. Elbert and Andy Clark discovered the skeletal remains of Patrice Endres. (Dawson Community News photo by George Herrera)

A crowd of area law enforcement from several counties and organizations gathered at the edge of the woods where Patrice Endres was found. (Dawson Community News photo by George Herrera)

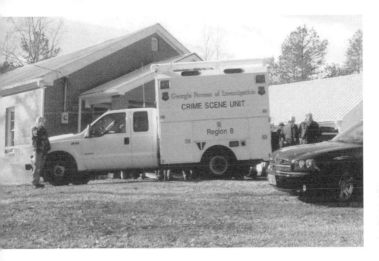

The Georgia Bureau of Investigation's Region 8 Crime Scene Unit came to the Endres recovery site in Dawson County to aid in the investigation.
(Dawson Community News photo by George Herrera)

After receiving instructions, the search and recovery team started down into the heavily wooded ravine where Patrice Endres' remains were discovered.   *(Dawson News and Advertiser photo by George Herrera)*

Georgia Bureau of Investigation Medical Examiner Dr. Rick Snow, who identified Patrice Endres' skeletal remains, talking with an investigator at the recovery site. *(Dawson Community News photo by George Herrera)*

Satellite trucks from Fox News and Atlanta's NBC affiliate, 11 Alive News, along with several other network and local news crews, came to a press conference at the Lebanon Baptist Church parking lot. *(Dawson Community News photo by George Herrera)*

Authorities announced at the press conference, held the day following the discovery of skeletal remains, that they had been positively identified as those of missing hairdresser Patrice Endres. (Dawson Community News *photo by George Herrera*)

GBI Special Agent in Charge John Cagle, left, along with Dawson County Sheriff Billy Carlisle and Forsyth County Sheriff Ted Paxton, answered questions from the media on the day after Patrice Endres' body was discovered. (Dawson News and Advertiser *photo by Brian Blackley*)

When he and his son walked into the woods behind their church, Elbert Clark noticed a skull and other bones lying beside a log at the bottom of this ravine. (Dawson Community News *photo by George Herrera*)

A bouquet of flowers was left as a memorial at the site where Patrice Endres' skeletal remains were found, over an hour's drive from the Chattahoochee River location Jeremy Jones had earlier described for the authorities. (Dawson Community News *photo by George Herrera*)

Amber McKerchie, with husband Todd and daughter Katelyn, worked tirelessly with her sister, Jennifer Murphy, to insure that their mother, Lisa Marie Nichols, received justice. *(Photo courtesy of Jennifer Murphy)*

Lisa Marie Nichols, shown here while playing with her grandchildren, was loved and respected by everyone who knew her. *(Photo courtesy of Jennifer Murphy)*

This photo of Lisa, in a favorite dress, was shown on Nancy Grace's television program when Jennifer Murphy and Amber McKerchie appeared to talk about their mother's case. *(Photo courtesy of Jennifer Murphy)*

The memory of Lisa Marie Nichols' beautiful smile, the smile her daughters said could "light up the world," will remain with all her family and friends forever. *(Photo courtesy of Jennifer Murphy)*

Office for their professionalism and resolve," King said, "a resolve that never wavered and without which this verdict would not have been possible. Mobile County is fortunate to be served by a man as committed to justice as is Sheriff Tillman. Yesterday's verdict begins the process of holding Jeremy Jones to account for his deceit and his murderous cold-bloodedness."

Later that morning, the seven women and five men on the jury heard from Lisa's family members, who took the stand to tell the jury how important Lisa Nichols had been in their lives and how much suffering her loss had caused. Lisa's sister, Lori Hardesty, told the jurors that she lived in New Mexico and had received the news of Lisa's murder by phone. She described her grief and anguish when she learned that her sister was dead, and said that she fell to her knees in shock when she heard that Lisa was gone.

Jurors also heard pleas for mercy from Jeremy Jones's mother and stepfather, who begged the jurors to spare his life. Attorney Greg Hughes told the jury that regardless of what they chose to recommend, Jones's life was essentially over. He would likely die in prison, Hughes said, angling for a life sentence, which he claimed would "neither excuse nor forgive him." Jones, he said, would have to "grind his life away" in prison every day until he died.

The jury heard the appeals on Jones's behalf, but when they filed out of the courtroom, they deliberated for only forty-five minutes before they voted 10 to 2 to recommend the death penalty for Jeremy Jones. During their time out of the courtroom, they voted four times and the vote remained 10 to 2 throughout the deliberations. Their options had been to either recommend life in prison or execution by lethal injection, and there seemed to have been little doubt by the majority of the jurors about what their recommendation should be.

Sentencing by Circuit Judge Charles Graddick was set for December 1. In the state of Alabama, judges have the power to overturn jury decisions in capital murder cases, either setting greater or lesser punishment than recommended by the jury. Although Judge Graddick was not bound by the jury's decision, it was widely believed that their recommendation of the death penalty would stand.

This time, the family of Lisa Nichols left the courtroom with smiles on their faces. Jennifer Murphy told reporters that the jury's recommendation of the death penalty had been her family's goal.

"We have accomplished that goal," Jennifer said. "This is not a time for tears." She told reporters, "It's what we wanted. We weren't going to settle for anything less for the man who did this to our mama."

Jeremy Jones, however, appeared stunned when he heard the jury's verdict. He wiped his eyes when the decision was read, saying, "I love you" to his girlfriend, Vicki Freeman, putting his hand over his heart, then reaching out to her as he was led from the sixth-floor courtroom back to his jail cell. Vicki Freeman, obviously shaken to the core by what she had seen and heard during the trial, stood outside the courtroom in tears, saying, "I'm sorry. . . . I'm so sorry" to several members of the Nichols family as they filed past her without making eye contact. Following Jones's arrest for murder, Vicki Freeman had told reporters and TV news magazine programs that she intended to marry Jones while he was in the Mobile County Jail, but that event had not come to pass as she had planned. Now it seemed highly unlikely that it ever would, unless the easily manipulated Freeman continued to stand blindly by her man.

Paul Burch talked to reporters about the "path of destruction" Jones left when he left Oklahoma and headed south, and seconded his previous statement that Lisa Nichols had received justice. Mark Bentley, who had been one of the primary witnesses for the prosecution, told the press that he felt the verdict and the subsequent recommendation for the death penalty proved that the members of the jury "saw right through" Jones's attempt to switch the blame for the murder to Bentley's cousin, the deceased Scooter Coleman.

When the jurors left the courtroom, one of them, Diana Grant, stopped to answer a few questions from a reporter with a local television station. When the reporter asked her how she felt the deliberations had gone, she said, "We looked at the evidence with open minds, and we prayed before and after we made our decisions."

Later that day, Alabama attorney general Troy King's office released a statement saying, "The members of the Mobile County jury today performed a duty no citizen would want to perform, a duty which justice and the facts demanded. They recommended that Jeremy Jones pay with his own life for the callous and brutal murder he committed. I hope that Judge Graddick will follow this recommendation and ensure that Jeremy Jones pays for these crimes with his own life."

King also told the media that the jury in Jeremy Jones's murder trial had sent a very clear message to other would-be killers that in Alabama courtrooms, they could expect to be given a punishment that was "commensurate to the evilness of their deeds."

Jeremy Jones was the first man recommended by a Mobile

jury to die for his crimes since the case of William Zeigler, who had been sentenced in 2001 to the death penalty for the murder of a Mobile County teenager. Ironically, Zeigler was also represented by the same court-appointed attorneys, Greg Hughes and Habib Yazdi, who had attempted without success to exonerate Jones. The judge in William Zeigler's case had accepted the jury's recommendation, and Zeigler was sent to death row. It was likely that he would soon have some company there, someone with whom he might have several things in common.

Chapter 31

During Jeremy Jones's trial, there were a couple of observers in the courtroom gallery who were there not only to give their support to the family of Lisa Nichols but also to get a close look at the man who had confessed to, and later denied, the murders of their own loved ones.

Rob Endres, the husband of Patrice Endres, the Georgia hairdresser who disappeared from her salon on April 15, 2004, attended the last days of the trial. While Jeremy Jones was being interviewed about other crimes he had claimed that he'd committed, during the months preceding his trial, he had told the investigators that he was the person who had abducted and murdered Patrice Endres, giving them some very accurate details of the incident and telling them where he claimed to have dumped her body. Jones immediately became the prime suspect in the case because of his seemingly viable confession, and several Georgia law enforcement agencies named him as the person who might have been responsible for Patrice's disappearance. Later, Jones told the investigators that he was lying when he'd claimed to have killed Patrice, but he still remained a suspect while Georgia authorities searched diligently for any clues that might place him at the scene of the crime.

"I don't know why they haven't charged him," Rob Endres said.

Patrice's father, Richard Tamber, told the press that Jones's confession meant nothing unless some hard evidence was found that proved his guilt and was sufficient for an arrest warrant.

"He's a suspect, but he hasn't been charged," Richard Tamber said. "Did he, or didn't he? Nobody knows."

Patrice's sister, Kyleen Kramer, agreed with her father, saying that the confession meant little to her unless there was enough physical evidence found to enable the Forsyth County investigators to bring charges against Jones. All the authorities had was Jones's word, she said, "but what good is his word?"

Brian Tamber, one of Patrice's brothers, told reporters that Patrice hadn't just vanished off the face of the earth.

"If Jeremy Jones didn't do it," he said, "I don't know. It could be anyone."

But there was a reason that Jones hadn't been officially named as the person responsible for Patrice's disappearance, even though he already had been charged with the murders of Katherine Collins in New Orleans and Amanda Greenwell in Douglasville, Georgia.

So far, not one single trace of physical evidence had been found near Sweetwater Creek in Douglas County, Georgia, where Jones had told the authorities that he had thrown Patrice's body, and countless searches by cadaver dogs had turned up no indication that Patrice's body had ever been there. The dogs had given some signs that, at one time, a body might possibly have been at that location, but heavy rains and the passage of time had weakened or eliminated any more positive indications. And without a body, or any other clues or evidence that linked Jeremy Jones to the crime in any way—other than his own claims of guilt, which he later denied—there was no way for the Georgia authorities to bring charges against him.

Rob Endres told reporters at the trial that he came to Mobile because he wanted to see his wife's self-confessed killer face-to-face, as well as to offer his support to the Nichols family. When he heard the guilty verdict, he said, he knew that at least Jones would not have the opportunity to ever hurt any other women.

"He never made eye contact with me," Rob Endres said. "I think he knows who I am."

Rob said that he was repulsed by the thought that Jones might have laid hands on his wife, and said that he hoped that the Mobile conviction would send a strong message to other sexual predators across the nation, letting them know that the public would not tolerate their crimes or allow them to go unpunished.

Rob Endres also told the media that he hoped Jones would provide more information about Patrice as well as about any other women he might have assaulted, since he was now convicted of capital murder and no longer had anything to lose. Although Patrice's disappearance might never be solved and her body might never be found, he said, he was glad to see that justice had been done for Lisa Nichols.

Amanda Greenwell's father, Rick Greenwell, also came to Mobile to sit in on part of the trial. Unlike Rob Endres, Rick Greenwell knew that charges had been brought officially against Jones for Amanda's murder. Rick told the press that Jones had taken the only thing from him that he'd ever had, the beautiful daughter who meant everything to him. Whether or not Jeremy Jones would ever leave death row in Alabama and be taken to Georgia to actually stand trial for Amanda's murder remained to be seen. But Rick Greenwell and Amanda's other relatives, like the families of so many of the other possible victims of Jeremy Jones, at least had the satisfaction of knowing that Jones would be punished. There might never be full closure for their families, but for Lisa, Amanda, Katherine, and all the other victims he might have killed, Jeremy Jones would pay the ultimate price.

Chapter 32

Although there had never been any official confirmation of Jeremy Jones's multiple confessions to murders in several states, it had been widely reported, within months after his Mobile arrest, that he had been classified as a "serial killer" by the FBI's standards. In several instances, word had quickly spread in other states about Jones's confessions to murders there, and the investigations were resumed in those unsolved cases based on what Jones had told the many investigators who had traveled to Mobile and questioned him at the Metro Jail prior to his trial. But after his conviction, Mobile authorities and the Alabama Attorney General's Office felt there was no longer any need to withhold their official announcement about the large number of murders for which Jeremy Jones had claimed responsibility.

A standing-room-only news conference was held at the Mobile County Metro Jail, with Attorney General Troy King, Mobile County sheriff Jack Tillman, and his detectives Paul Burch and Mitch McRae giving statements and fielding questions from the press. Also in attendance were the two daughters of Lisa Marie Nichols—Jennifer Murphy and Amber

McKerchie—who listened from the sidelines while the long list of Jones's alleged victims was read to the assembled reporters.

This was the occasion that the media had been waiting for, and the press conference was even more well-attended by reporters and photographers than the trial had been. Camera crews from several states were present to film the official confirmation of the off-the-record rumors they had constantly been hearing during the previous several months. Prior to the trial, the Alabama authorities had refused to comment officially about the confessions so as not to risk jeopardizing their case against Jones for the murder of Lisa Nichols. Now that they had a conviction, though, they were free to tell the press about all the other killings that Jones had told them he'd committed.

While the cameras rolled, AG King stated that Jeremy Jones had confessed to more than thirteen murders in several states, in addition to the two in Louisiana and Georgia that he had already been charged with. King said that Sheriff Tillman had told him that Jones had been able to give details during his confessions that only a person who had been intimately involved with the actual murders would have known.

"The killing spree that Jeremy Jones engaged in stretches across this land," King said, adding that because of his history of violent criminal acts, Jones might have also committed even more murders that had not yet come to light.

"This is something we've wanted to do for some time," Paul Burch said about the press conference, telling the reporters that Jones had not shown any trace of regret while reciting the details of the murders he described.

"He was just matter-of-fact," Burch said. "He enjoyed raping and killing."

When asked how Jones said that he had chosen his victims, Burch said Jones had contacted them in several different ways: meeting them in the clubs and bars he frequented, targeting someone that he was already acquainted with, or even attempting to snatch his victims out of parking lots or off the street. Jones told the detectives that his methamphetamine use was the cause of his murderous impulses, and he blamed all his troubles on his drug of choice.

"He said that brought the urges out in him," Burch said.

King described for reporters how Jones was believed to have been able to successfully maintain the identity of John Paul Chapman for so long.

"He moved in and out of personalities without any effort at all," King said. "It made him a more effective killer."

A composite photo had been made up of several mug shots, driver's license photos, other ID photos, and candid shots of Jones. It clearly showed that he was able to change his appearance very easily to match all those different personalities that King had attributed to him.

Among those murders that Jones claimed to have committed was the killing of Jennifer Judd, the beautiful newlywed who was slain in her Baxter Springs, Kansas, apartment on May 11, 1989. Earlier, when rumors of his confession had first reached the press, a spokesman for the Kansas Bureau of Investigation had said that there was no evidence linking Jeremy Jones to the case in any way. He was no longer considered to be a person of interest in Jennifer's death, the spokesman said.

Jones also claimed to have killed Danny Oakley and Doris Harris, who died on February 21, 1996, when they were shot to death and their trailer in Delaware County, Oklahoma, was burned.

Justin Hutchings, of Picher, Oklahoma, died on September 11, 1999, after being injected with a "hot shot," a combination

of methamphetamine and other drugs. Jones said that he was
the person who had administered the lethal drugs to Justin.

On December 30, 1999, Kathy and Danny Freeman were
shot to death inside their trailer in Welch, Oklahoma. The
trailer was set on fire, and their daughter, Ashley Freeman,
and her friend who was spending the night, Lauria Bible, disappeared from the scene. When Oklahoma authorities traveled to Mobile and interviewed him about the incident, Jones
claimed that he had killed the Freemans and started the fire,
then abducted the two sixteen-year-old girls when they came
running from the burning trailer. He took them to a remote
location, he said, shot them, then dumped their bodies into an
abandoned mine pit in Kansas. Sheriff Jimmie Sooter, of
Craig County, Oklahoma, told reporters that searches of the
area had been conducted after Jones's initial confession. So
far, the efforts to search in the area filled with abandoned
mines and mine pits had been unsuccessful, he said, and he
intended to interview Jones further in the hope of narrowing
down the location of the bodies of the two missing girls.

Sooter called the information Jones had provided "very
convincing," and told the press that he still believed that Jones
had been somehow involved with the disappearance of
Ashley Freeman and Lauria Bible. He hoped that the families
might finally be able to have some closure if the bodies of the
girls could be found.

"They still could be somewhere over there," Sooter said of
the search area near Galena, Kansas, adding that word of
Jones's confession had resulted in some new leads in the case.
Another mining location, this one north of Picher, Oklahoma,
was being investigated, Sooter said, and cadaver dogs had
shown some interest in an abandoned mine's water-filled air
shaft. It was too dangerous, however, for divers to explore,

and other means of searching the air shaft would have to be developed before the mine could safely be checked out.

Jones told the Mobile investigators that he had killed four or five prostitutes with whom he had come into contact when he was in the Atlanta area. He did not know their names, he said. He additionally claimed to have murdered three prostitutes whom he picked up in the Prichard, Alabama, area during his first period of residence in Mobile, and said that after he killed them, he had dumped their bodies in a swamp near Chickasaw, Alabama. Sheriff Tillman told the media that the swamp had been partially drained and cadaver dogs had been brought in to search for bodies, but up to that point, nothing had yet been found.

King described Jones as "a monster who would kill without remorse. I think the description is appropriate, that he is a monster."

Because Jones had told the press that all of his confessions—even his several taped admissions of guilt in the murder of Lisa Nichols—had been untrue, reporters asked Tillman if there was a possibility that Jones had lied about committing the murders.

"I think if someone tells you the victims' names, where they lived, how he killed them, and where he dumped their bodies," Tillman said, "don't you think that would be a good profile to follow through?"

Paul Burch added that Jones had maintained all along to investigators that what he was telling them was the truth.

"He stands by all the information that he has provided to us in the past," Burch said, even though Jones had proclaimed long and loud to the media that his confessions were lies. When his mother and girlfriend were present, Burch said, Jones claimed to be innocent. But during interviews with the investigators, he had given names, details, and other information that only a person directly involved with the killings could have known.

During the press conference, King told reporters that one of his plans, which he said had been suggested by the Lisa Nichols murder case, was to draw up and propose an item of legislation that he said would "close the loopholes" in current Alabama law. Even though the jury had convicted Jeremy Jones without any knowledge of his prior criminal deeds in other states, King wanted to change current state law and enable prosecutors to inform juries of a defendant's prior cases in which pleas of nolo contendere, or no contest, had been entered. Jones had entered such a plea to his charges from Ottawa County, Oklahoma, for sexual battery. This March 1997 plea was not allowed by law to be mentioned during his Mobile murder trial. Alabama, King said, was one of a few remaining states in the nation with laws on the books that did not permit such pleas to be used as evidence in trials, and King wanted to change that situation. He planned to go to work on the legislation immediately, and he would be aided by Jennifer Murphy, who felt such a change in Alabama law would serve as a lasting tribute to her mother's memory.

King and Tillman told the press that they would be assisting in every way possible the local authorities in the several other states that were in the process of investigating the possible series of Jones's killings. Those authorities had been provided all of the information Jones had given about the murders as soon as Jones had confessed to each of them, Tillman said, and it now remained up to the states in question to pursue their investigations. The Alabama authorities would assist any other law enforcement agencies that wanted to charge and try Jones in their states, King said. The requests for extradition would be considered on a case-by-case basis, with Georgia and Louisiana first in line. Jones had already been charged in those two states with the murders of Amanda Greenwell and Katherine Collins, and there was a strong probability that additional charges would be filed in other cases. Jeremy Jones might still have a long route to travel through the legal system in several states around the nation.

"He's a sociopath," Tillman told the press, adding that Jones reminded him a great deal of the infamous serial killer Ted Bundy, who was known for his personable manner and good looks. When talking to Jones, Tillman said, he came across as being "as nice of a fellow as you'd ever want to meet, someone you'd never suspect" of being a killer.

"We will never know how many people he killed."

Chapter 33

Jeremy Jones would not learn Judge Graddick's decision as to his fate until December 1, 2005, but as soon as his trial was over, with the jury recommending the death penalty, he immediately set out on another of his trademark public relations campaigns. Taking advantage of the kind, sympathetic nature of a local newspaper reporter with whom he had established a fairly friendly relationship, Jones publicized a claim that he allegedly had an advanced case of hepatitis C. He would not live long enough for the state to execute him, if he was to receive the death sentence, he told the reporter, and he just might not be healthy enough to help law enforcement in solving the many other crimes he had confessed to, as the authorities had hoped that he would. He was locked in a tiny cell on suicide watch, he said, and his clothes had been taken away; only a synthetic blanket was left, one that he could not use to hang himself.

Jones claimed that he didn't know exactly when he had contracted hepatitis C, but said that doctors had told him that he had the disease when he had been seen for medical treatment while he was working in Douglasville, Georgia, a few years earlier. He wouldn't live more than a few years, he said the doctors had told him, if he continued on with his habits of drinking and drug use and if he didn't get proper treatment for the condition. He also claimed that he had told the authorities at the Mobile County Metro Jail that he was ill with the disease, and had asked the jailers repeatedly to take him to see a doctor, but he said that the jail had not allowed him to be treated.

A spokeswoman for the Mobile County Sheriff's Office, when contacted about Jones's allegations, said that the jail would never have refused medical treatment to any prisoner, and said that she could not comment further on any inmate's health issues, which were, by law, confidential information.

Jones told the reporter that the authorities wanted the governor to sign his death warrant, but said that he could die in a couple of years if his hepatitis C went untreated.

"That's fucked up," he said, calling his allegedly neglected case of the disease "just suicide two years down the road."

When asked about the situation, Habib Yazdi took what was, for him, an uncharacteristic conservative approach. His client had just recently told him that he was ill with the disease, he said, but Yazdi didn't want to comment on whether or not he knew if Jones had been refused treatment at the jail. Apparently, Yazdi had gotten a bit leery of making too many controversial comments in the press prior to the upcoming sentencing date. He more than likely wished that his overly talkative, contrary client would do the same.

Jeanne Beard, Jones's mother, stood by her boy as usual, claiming that she had known all along that her son had been diagnosed with the disease. He had been sick while working at the refinery in Douglasville, she said, and he had found out then that he had hepatitis C. She railed at the unfairness of jail officials who had allegedly refused to allow him to be taken for treatment.

"If it's not treated," she said, "his liver will get worse."

Jones's claims of hepatitis C infection were inadvertently bolstered by a story that ran in the New Orleans *Times-Picayune* concerning his interviews with the New Orleans detectives who came to Mobile to question him about the murder of Katherine Collins. The story mentioned that while Jones was being questioned by the officers, he "began furiously picking at sores on his face and neck, symptoms of his advanced case of hepatitis C." Although health professionals agreed that sores of that sort were not known to be caused by the disease, the officers might have been told during the interview that the sores on Jones's face, clearly visible in his Metro Jail mug shots, were the result of hepatitis C. In fact, they were far more likely to have been the result of his rampant methamphetamine addiction. One of the most recognized signs of the meth user is ulceration or sores of the skin, particularly on the face and hands, caused by an uncontrollable feeling of the skin crawling or itching. The addicts then pick and scratch at their skin, causing the sores to appear and worsen.

The prosecutors in the attorney general's office said that they had no knowledge of Jones being ill with hepatitis C. They were understandably skeptical, since Jones had made so many confessions, then recanted them and said he was lying. If not presented with official medical proof of his alleged disease, they were not going to be buying his story.

As time drew near for Judge Graddick to pronounce sentence on Jones, Alabama attorney general Troy King told the press that he would personally go to Mobile to present the prosecution's case for the death penalty. He told reporters that Jones had lied without remorse and killed without remorse, saying that the only remorse he had ever seen Jones exhibit for anyone was for himself.

"He was a monster," King said.

Mobile County sheriff Jack Tillman stated that Jones had confessed to many murders, but said that there were even more that fit Jones's modus operandi, "not just here, but everywhere he roamed around." It had already been established that Jones could be placed either in or near the area of each one of the many murders that he had confessed to, and he knew details in most of the cases that only a person who had actually been at the scene when the crime was committed could possibly have known. Jones later spent a great deal of time denying all of his confessions and making excuses, claiming that he had learned the details of the crimes when he heard them being talked about by some of the other inmates in the jails that he had been in.

Like so many of his other stories, however, those claims of overheard jailhouse gossip weren't plausible, and the investigators and prosecutors weren't buying them any more than they had bought Jones's tales of hepatitis C.

Chapter 34

When the official announcement of Jeremy Jones's many confessions had finally been made public, the press immediately began contacting the family members of some of his alleged victims. Most of them had already been told of his admissions of guilt, shortly after those admissions were made to the investigators, but like the authorities in their states, the relatives had, for the most part, remained silent until the Mobile trial was over and a conviction had been secured. Then they felt free to speak their minds, something that many of them had wanted to do for quite a long time.

Richard Tamber, a restaurant owner in Birmingham, Alabama, and the father of Patrice Endres, told the media that he and the rest of his family still held on to the hope that maybe Jeremy Jones had been lying. Even though Jones had claimed that he'd killed Patrice and then dumped her body into Georgia's Sweetwater Creek, Richard Tamber hoped with all his heart that his beautiful daughter might still be alive.

"It's the only thing that keeps me going from one day to the next," he told the media.

Lorene Bible, mother of the missing Oklahoma sixteen-year-old Lauria Bible, had known for some time that Jones had actually confessed to killing her daughter, along with her friend Ashley Freeman and Ashley's parents, Danny and Kathy Freeman. Sheriff Jimmie Sooter had told her that Jones had given him information, almost a year earlier, about a specific location in Kansas where the girls might be found, and the search had begun immediately. The media had spotted the search activity and soon learned of the confession, but like Richard Tamber, Lorene Bible had continued to hold out hope that maybe there was still a chance her daughter might somehow be alive. Jones might be using his alleged confessions, she had suspected, as a way to get a reduced sentence in Lisa Nichols's murder. Lorene told the press that she thought Jones knew something about the disappearance of the two girls.

"How much for sure, I don't know," she said. "At this point, he seems to be the only one having enough information" about the incident to have been responsible. Lorene Bible still had some doubts, however, that Jones was telling the truth, and if he was being truthful, she felt he might not be telling the entire story.

"If Jeremy Jones is found to have done something," she told reporters, "he's not the only one." Jones didn't go into the Freemans' home by himself, she believed.

"I can guarantee you that," she said.

Before Jones made his confession to Sheriff Sooter, Lorene said, she had never heard his name mentioned in connection with her daughter's disappearance. She said she doubted that he would have acted alone, or that he would be willing to take all the blame by himself if anyone else had been involved.

"Why would he not implicate other people?" she asked. "There is somebody out there that will come forward" with further information about what had happened to the missing girls.

"We've been there before," Lorene said of the thus-far-unsuccessful searches for Ashley and Lauria.

Danny Freeman's younger brother, Dwayne Vancil, also told reporters that he personally doubted Jones's confession.

"I think they're trying to pin it on somebody as far away from Craig County as possible," Dwayne said. He told the reporters that he, too, had never heard Jeremy Jones being mentioned previously in connection with the crimes, and said that he believed someone else had killed his brother and sister-in-law. Another man, he said, had admitted to a couple of different people in the area that he'd had something to do with the murders. That man, Dwayne said, might possibly have known Jones.

Dwayne Vancil also discounted Jones's claims that the murders had been drug-related, saying that his brother occasionally smoked some marijuana, but was not a cocaine user and did not use or deal in drugs like crystal meth.

Despite his skepticism, Dwayne Vancil told reporters that he would like to view the tapes of Jones's confessions to the murders of his brother, sister-in-law, and the two girls, saying that Jones was "no dummy," but was definitely a pathological liar. Dwayne said his family had developed some information, with the assistance of a private investigator, that had indicated to them that other people might have been involved in the Freeman/Bible case. Jones might have played a role in the crime, Dwayne said, but like Lorene Bible, he was still convinced that, if so, Jones had not acted alone.

Tina Mayberry's stepfather, Kenneth Timms, told the media that he and his wife and Tina's other relatives had been waiting for such a long time, hoping for any new developments in Tina's murder case. The delay, he said, had been costly.

"It's really devastated us," he said. He and the family hadn't been able to find any closure in the years since Tina's death, Kenneth Timms said, and were unable to move on with their lives because of the lack of answers as to what had really happened to Tina. Now, with Jeremy Jones's confession, the family once again had a gleam of hope that they might eventually be getting justice for Tina. But once again, unless positive physical evidence could be found to link Jones to the murder, that closure for Tina Mayberry's loved ones might still be very far away. There was also the matter of a Web site that had been placed on the Internet after Tina's death, containing a bold statement that named another individual, claiming outright that the person was Tina's killer.

"I should know, I saw him right before it happened!!!" the maker of the Web site proclaimed, alleging that the person had been seen wiping fingerprints off the gas pumps and off his car after he had been pumping gas at a local station on Halloween, 2002, the night when Tina was killed.

The Web site stated that either the authorities "does not see two inches in front of their nose, or is there some funny bizz [*sic*] going on?"

The author of the Web site extended deepest regards to Judy and Kenneth Timms, and told them, "I tried to get the truth known," and wished that they would receive the justice and closure they deserved, with peace and serenity as their reward.

"But most of all," the posting ended, "may Tina's soul finally be rested."

The murder of Tina Mayberry would, for the time being, remain an open investigation, with searches continuing for conclusive physical evidence that would finally prove the real identity of her killer.

The news that Jones had confessed to the murder of Jennifer Judd, who supposedly had been his first victim, came as a shock to Jennifer's parents, Dale and Debbie Bryan. Debbie, a teacher at an Oklahoma school, said that she wanted Jones to stand trial, but only if he really was the person who had murdered Jennifer thirteen years earlier.

"If it's him, that's what we want," she said, adding that if

Jones was not guilty, then the family most certainly did not want him to be charged, while allowing the real killer to continue walking free and unpunished.

"I want who did it, not a substitute," she said.

Jeremy Jones's revelations also came as a surprise to Jennifer's sister, Amanda Davis. She said she hoped that if the confession was, indeed, truthful, then Jones would be held accountable for Jennifer's death. If Jones was lying, however, as her mother had said, Amanda felt that the false confession might then allow the real murderer to walk. There were too many contradictions to Jones's confession, she told reporters, because there was no indication that Jones had been in Baxter Springs, Kansas, where Jennifer's murder occurred.

Jones had told investigators that he had killed Jennifer because they had been having a "secret love affair" and he was angry because she had thrown him over and married Justin Judd. Neither the family nor anyone else had any reason whatsoever to believe that tale, or to think that Jones had been acquainted at all with Jennifer, Amanda Davis said, but if he had any knowledge of the murder, she continued, "we want to know." But a few of the facts surrounding Jennifer's death coincided, to a certain extent, with some of the things that Jones had said.

A short time before Jennifer's murder, her family had claimed that Jennifer had seemed uncomfortable when she had to stay alone at night in the convenience store where she worked, and she told a friend that she believed that she was being stalked by someone. And Jones had told the investigators in Mobile, while claiming that he had murdered Jennifer, that he had stalked her for several days beforehand. Jennifer had also told one of her girlfriends that someone had tried to break into her home a few days before her murder, pounding on the front door and trying to force his way inside. Jennifer told the friend that she had hidden behind the sofa until whoever was at the door had finally given up and left.

Jennifer's family considered the possibility that Jeremy Jones could indeed have been the would-be burglar and the "stalker" she had seemed to be worried about, even though they had never heard the name of Jeremy Jones before his confession. Paul Burch said that in his opinion Jones's account of Jennifer's murder had rung true. He called the information Jones had given during questioning by the KBI "overwhelmingly convincing," saying that, like in the other cases that he had confessed to, Jones had once again given "details no one else could have known." But, like in most of those other cases, there was not yet enough corroborating physical evidence to bring charges against him.

Jennifer Judd's family was left to wonder if they would ever know with certainty who had killed the beautiful young bride just days after her wedding. They were determined the search for Jennifer's murderer would continue, whether it would turn out to be Jeremy Jones or if someone else was guilty.

"I owe it to her to seek justice," Jennifer's father told the press. "I don't want people to forget about this." Dale Bryan went on to say that he would do everything in his power to see that the case would be eventually solved, "and I really believe it will be."

The families of Danny Oakley and Doris Harris told reporters that they had not been contacted by the authorities about any of the alleged confessions Jones had made concerning the murders of Oakley and Harris. Harris's sister, Paula Barnett, said that both of the families wanted to know just exactly what it was that had made the confessions believable, and she said that it was high time for law enforcement to make some use of that information. She believed there might be a link between the case and that of the Freeman murders, and said that she had also spoken, years earlier, to Lorene Bible about a possible connection. Her family was disappointed, she said, that they had not been told whatever it was that Jones had said in his confession concerning the murders, for they might have then been able to take what they already knew and "connect the dots" with whatever Jones had claimed.

Danny Oakley's father, Carl, also denied being given any information from the authorities concerning Jones's confession to the murder of his son. Oakley denied ever having seen Jones or heard him mentioned in connection with the crime, but like the family members of some of the other victims, he believed that if Jones was responsible, others were surely involved also.

A neighbor of Danny Oakley's had reported the fire at Oakley's trailer, and had also reported at the time that a man was seen leaving the residence shortly before smoke began to come from the trailer. He said the man came out of the trailer carrying a gun, put it into Oakley's car, got in the car himself, and drove away. Later that day, a man was found, passed out in Oakley's car in a nearby town, but he was never charged in relation to the murders. Carl Oakley told reporters that he had always felt that if the man didn't commit the murders himself, he very likely knew who did. But Jones's professed involvement, he said, was something that remained to be proven.

"I hope he keeps talking," Carl Oakley said of Jones, adding that he hoped Jones "drags them all into it."

Carla Chappell, the sister of Danny Oakley, believed that if Jeremy Jones knew any of the facts about her brother's murder, then he must have either been at the scene himself or had close contact with the person or persons who were guilty.

"If Jeremy Jones is the answer," she said, "I say, thank God, it's about time."

When asked about his department's reaction to the press conference announcing Jeremy Jones's confessions, Delaware

County sheriff Jay Blackfox told reporters that he intended to schedule a meeting with the Oklahoma State Bureau of Investigation to plan the next steps to be taken in the Oakley/Harris investigation.

The family of young Justin Hutchings had always believed Justin's death was not an accident or an overdose, but was instead a homicide. They had spent six frustrated years hoping to find some proof of that belief and praying for justice in the case, and with Jeremy Jones's confession to killing Justin with a "hot shot," a mixture of drugs, their hope was revived.

"I want the killer to be caught," said Justin's mother, Donna Lyons. "If Jones is the one, then he should face justice for Justin's murder." She felt that, with Jones's confession, Justin's case should surely get the proper investigation that it had always deserved.

"I plan to push this until Justin gets justice," Donna Lyons said. "His blood cries out."

Will York, Justin's uncle, had also believed for six years that his nephew had been murdered.

"Everything points out to [Jeremy Jones], and his story is credible in every detail," Will York said. "Nothing was ever mentioned about it in any papers, and why would Jones pull Justin's name out of thin air, unless he did it?"

Will York and his sister had conducted their own investigation of Justin's death, and they had learned that there was a female driver in the car at the time, Jones said, that he had given Justin the fatal injection. Jones knew the name of the woman and, according to Will York, knew about the vehicle that was involved. According to Paul Burch, Jones claimed that when Justin realized what was happening to him, he jumped out of the car and started to run for help before he was overcome by the drugs and collapsed on the street.

The family, Will said, was extremely frustrated with the

authorities who, they said, did not want to reopen Justin's case, and Will said he planned to continue the fight for justice for Justin.

The loss of his nephew had a deep and lasting effect on Will York, causing him to change careers and begin to work for a sheriff's department while pursuing a law degree. Will said he believed that, out of something bad, always comes good. Out of Justin's death and the homicide of another family member, he said, had come his career change and "an opportunity to change some things along the way." Will York firmly believed that Jeremy Jones was Justin Hutchings's murderer, and he made a plea to law enforcement to change their decision and investigate the case further.

"Do not again let Justin's death ring a solemn bell for yet another unsolved crime," he said. "Jones is the man who murdered Justin."

Craig County, Oklahoma, district attorney Gene Haynes, who had accompanied Sheriff Jimmie Sooter to Mobile for his interview with Jones about Ashley Freeman and Lauria Bible, said he hoped that he would eventually be able to bring the man that he called "our best suspect" and "the best chance of finding the girls" back to Oklahoma. He felt that if Jones was taken to the site where he had claimed to have dumped Ashley and Lauria's bodies, he might be able to pinpoint the location better in person than he had by looking at maps of the area.

Haynes admitted, however, that since no official charges had been filed, either in his own jurisdiction or in Kansas, it would be extremely difficult to justify his attempting to extradite Jones with so many other agencies already in line hoping to prosecute him. If Jeremy Jones was to ever be taken back to Oklahoma, it would probably be a long time coming.

Chapter 35

One group of Jeremy Jones's alleged victims had, for the most part, no friends or family members waiting to speak for them. As a result, they were largely overlooked by the authorities and the media alike. Jones had said that he had murdered four Atlanta prostitutes, and he had passed a polygraph test about those murders. He told Paul Burch that he had picked up the women on the streets of Atlanta, then killed them, getting rid of their bodies by throwing them off bridges into rivers or leaving them in the woods. But Atlanta area authorities discounted Jones's accounts, telling the press there was nothing there to substantiate his claims.

"The connection could not be made to Atlanta," said Atlanta police spokeswoman Sylvia Abernathy.

Fulton County, Georgia, officials also said there were no unsolved homicides in their county that had any apparent connection to Jones.

Atlanta investigators had intended to question Jones about his confessed prostitute murders in Mobile, on March 11, 2005, Burch said, but their trip was suddenly canceled because of the shootings that took place that day in Atlanta's Fulton County Courthouse. A defendant set for a court appearance,

Brian Nichols, had escaped custody while in the courthouse, took an officer's gun, and fatally shot a judge, a court reporter, and a deputy. He later also shot a U.S. Customs agent while fleeing his pursuers. That incident made national headlines and got the undivided attention of every officer in all the law enforcement agencies in the Atlanta area and beyond. The canceled interview with Jones was rescheduled, but once again, it was not to be. Unfortunately, on that second try, it was set to take place around the time when Hurricanes Katrina and Rita paid their destructive visits to the Gulf Coast. Once again, the Atlanta authorities had to postpone their trip to Mobile.

There would be an indefinite delay in the questioning of Jeremy Jones about his alleged murders of the group of unidentified Atlanta prostitutes. Burch told reporters that the courthouse shootings and the hurricanes might have gotten things off track, temporarily disrupting the plans of the Atlanta authorities, but they would still have the opportunity to talk to Jones whenever they liked, at any time in the future.

"He's not going anywhere," Burch said.

In Mobile, where Jones had claimed he'd murdered several prostitutes earlier, during his first period of residence in the city, his confession was given somewhat more priority than in Atlanta. However, no proof of his claims in that city were found, either; the swamp where he said he had dumped the women's bodies had been partially drained, and the cadaver dogs, brought in to check for bodies, found nothing.

A Mobile prostitute told a reporter that she thought it was unlikely anything would ever be followed up concerning Jones's claim of murdering the prostitutes in Atlanta and Mobile. No one really cared what happened to hookers, she said, and the women always knew they were taking their lives into their own hands whenever they made contact with potential customers on the streets. There was nothing new, she said, about prostitutes disappearing without any investigation; it happened every day and was just a part of life on the stroll.

The possibility existed that Jeremy Jones had never murdered any prostitutes in either locale, since he had claimed that his other confessions had all been lies. He had never killed another human being, he continued to insist to the media, all the while giving investigators more and more information about the murders for which he had already claimed responsibility. And there was the polygraph test concerning the murdered prostitute story to take into consideration. He had, after all, passed it; was he a skilled enough liar to fool the polygraph? It had happened before.

Another of Jones's confessions had also been discounted by the authorities in Oklahoma. Jones told Paul Burch that he had shot Commerce, Oklahoma, residents Harmon Fenton and Sarah Palmer in March 1997, but Commerce police chief Bob Baine later claimed that much of what Jones had described about his alleged murders in Commerce didn't coincide with the facts in the case. Baine said he had no plans to travel to Mobile to question Jones.

"What he is saying doesn't fit the crime," Baine told reporters after he was informed by the Mobile investigators of Jones's confession, adding that he didn't feel at that time that Jones was the person who was responsible for the murders.

Chapter 36

The official confirmation of Jeremy Jones's long chain of confessions to murders in several states immediately set off a flurry of comments in Internet chat rooms, message boards, and Web sites devoted to following the stories of serial killers. The opinions expressed by the writers ranged from condemnation of Jones and hope that he would pay the ultimate penalty, to doubts that he had committed any of the murders for which he had claimed responsibility.

One writer suggested that Jones's admitting to the murders didn't necessarily mean that he did them. He could claim to be the king of England, the writer said, but that wouldn't necessarily make it true. The authorities would have to back up Jones's claims with hard evidence; otherwise, they would only prove to be due to his "psychotic, ego-driven need for attention."

If there was no proof, he said, then the person who actually committed the crimes might walk away free.

Another person posted the opinion that Jones was causing the victims' families renewed grief by the statements he was making, and the investigators should keep his confessions confidential until bodies were actually found and physical evidence was developed in the cases.

One very astute writer brought up the Henry Lee Lucas/ Ottis Toole syndrome, which he described as being the confession to a crime in order to get attention, or what might be perceived as media adulation—when, in fact, the confessor might not be guilty at all. Lucas and Toole, between the two of them, had confessed to over six hundred murders all around the nation, and even in foreign countries (which, it was later proven, they had never even visited). Lucas was interviewed by investigators from forty states and was questioned about over three thousand homicide cases.

Henry Lee Lucas, like Jeremy Jones, later denied his confessions and told reporters that he made up all the hair-raising accounts he had related during his countless questioning sessions because, once again like Jones, he was being given good food during his interviews. He said he "wanted to make the police look stupid," which, unfortunately, he did. The authorities who questioned Lucas about crimes he confessed to, but could not possibly have committed, were soundly criticized for "coercing" confessions from him.

The writer made a comparison between the endless wild-goose chases that Henry Lee Lucas and his sidekick, Ottis Toole, had led law enforcement on, and the motives behind the confessions and subsequent denials that were being made by Jeremy Jones. He described Jones as "a twisted con with absolutely nothing to lose" by confessing to every unsolved crime in the northeastern Oklahoma area in order to get attention from the public and curry favors from the authorities.

One woman, the widow of an Oklahoma detective-turned-private-investigator who had been shot and killed by an unknown assailant, had been using the Internet since her husband's death to research further into some of the unsolved murders to which Jones had later confessed. She said that the news of Jones's possible guilt in those crimes would likely

have come as no surprise to her husband. He had been looking into the death of Jennifer Judd and the disappearance of
Ashley Freeman and Lauria Bible, she said, and by coincidence, he had arrested the young Jeremy Jones at some time
in the 1990s when her late husband had worked with the sheriff's department.

The woman said that her husband had talked about Jones
at times in later years, during his time as an investigator. After
he was shot and killed under suspicious circumstances, she
wrote to Jones in the Mobile Metro Jail, asking him if he had
any information about her husband's death. She wasn't accus-
ing him, she told Jones, but she hoped that perhaps he might
have heard something. She said that she had received no re-
sponse from Jones.

The woman said she would continue to hope for information on her husband's death, and in the meantime, would continue searching the Internet for possible leads. She also spent
time contacting the families of other crime victims to offer
her condolence and support, leaving a very touching letter of
sympathy on young Amanda Greenwell's memorial Web site.

Another person posted an opinion that might have per-
tained to the dead husband of the previous writer. The person
said, in his or her opinion, that quite a few murders in the area
where Jones had lived were Mafia-related. "They also shut up
the private investigator," the writer said, when the man had
been shot two years earlier. The private investigator had some
volatile information that he was getting ready to disclose, according to the writer, information that would have had some
far-reaching consequences for more than a few highly placed
figures in area politics and law enforcement.

One of the other comments posted on the Internet was a
rather sarcastic account referring to Jeremy Jones's multitude
of confessions. With tongue in cheek, the writer claimed that

a recent news flash had revealed that Jones had just confessed to setting fire to the City of London in 1666, starting the Chicago Fire early last century, the kidnapping and killing of the Lindbergh baby, the assassination of JFK, the crimes that had previously been attributed to the Manson Family, and the Bonnie and Clyde bank robberies. With Jones off the streets, the writer said, the four-state area should remain forever crime-free. There would probably be even more "confessions" from Jones, according to the writer, because with his likely death sentence, he'd have plenty of time to think of them.

One very large message board was devoted to the disappearance of Ashley Freeman and Lauria Bible, and it contained a multitude of postings, from all over the United States to as far away as Australia and England. Relatives, friends, complete strangers, and even psychics left messages offering support to the girls' families and encouraging law enforcement to never give up their search for answers.

Many other Web sites were constructed as memorials to some of Jones's alleged victims and to those whose murders he had already been charged with formally. Memorial sites for Lisa Nichols, Patrice Endres, and Amanda Greenwell drew a large number of visits and many touching messages of condolence. One such message was left for Rick Greenwell, Amanda's father, from a family that the Greenwells had known years earlier when they lived in Key Largo, Florida.

"Word travels slow sometimes," they said; they had just found out about Amanda's murder, which had happened months earlier.

"We are so upset for you and your family," they wrote, adding that they could still remember an adorable, young Amanda attending one of their daughter's birthday parties when Amanda was only about seven years old.

"Who could have imagined this would happen? We will never forget her."

Perhaps the most poignant posting to be found on any of the Web sites, however, was left by Jennifer Murphy, who reached out to the other victims' families to offer her help and understanding:

"Please do not give up on your loved ones, and fight for them, for we are the only ones who can. Demand justice from your local law enforcement office. Please, if I can in any way, help, contact me, for you are forever in my thoughts and prayers."

Chapter 37

On Thursday, December 1, 2005, a crowd gathered once again in the courtroom of Circuit Judge Charles Graddick to hear for themselves, firsthand, the judge's sentencing of Jeremy Bryan Jones. And like so many other occasions during the trial, a circuslike atmosphere prevailed both in and outside the courtroom, with television cameras allowed inside to film the proceedings. There were camera crews and on-air reporters on hand representing a number of television stations from Mobile to Atlanta and beyond. There were so many, in fact, that Judge Graddick had made a rare exception to his usual rule and had allowed them to set up inside the courtroom itself, instead of in their usual designated location, outside in the exile of the hallway, some distance away from the action.

Deputies brought Jeremy Jones into the courtroom in leg irons and handcuffs, and seated him at the defense table between his two attorneys, Habib Yazdi and Greg Hughes. When the deputies had come to take him from his cell to the courtroom that morning, they had to make Jones remove something he had fastened to his clothing before he was allowed to leave the cell. They found the audacious, unrepentant prisoner wearing a handmade sign that read: "I am the victim." That accessory, the deputies determined, would definitely not be making its way into the courtroom and in front of the battery of cameras. The sign came off, a disgruntled Jones came out of his cell, and the deputies shepherded him into court to hear his fate.

The judge would hear arguments that morning of December 1 in favor of the death penalty from Alabama attorney general Troy King, and would allow pleas for mercy from Yazdi and Hughes. Jones, himself, would be given an opportunity to speak on his own behalf before Judge Graddick announced his decision.

AG King told the judge that Jones had never shown "an ounce of regret" for what he had done, and showed no feelings for anyone or anything but himself. King called Jones's crime "blood-chilling" and told the judge that Jones "targeted his prey like any predator."

Attorneys Greg Hughes and Habib Yazdi were aware that time was fast running out for them to generate any trace of sympathy for their client, and they made their best effort. Obviously grasping at straws, they made the outlandish statement that Jones's crime was not particularly heinous, and they claimed that his problems stemmed directly from his stepfather, who had physically abused him when he was a child, they said.

Hughes told the judge that his client had a long history of drug use, which had eventually compounded his mental problems, claiming that there were "factors at work" in Jones's mind over which he had no control. One of the defense attorneys even went so far as to make the crude statement that Jones "got it in the butt and it came out in his head." And since Jeanne Beard and her husband were not present in the courtroom that day, Habib Yazdi took advantage of their absence and tried his utmost to lay the blame for Jones's murderous actions on his family.

Standing behind Jones and grasping his shoulders like a kindly uncle, Yazdi said that his client had been an "innocent boy," born to "savage people." Yazdi described them as petty criminals, drug addicts, and alcoholics. Their many social and sexual perversions, he claimed, had eventually caused the young Jones to escape into a life full of episodes of violence. He did this, Yazdi said, in order to mask the pain that he felt because of his unwholesome family situation.

Yazdi even told Judge Graddick that he'd had the occasion to attempt to meet with Jones's family when they had come to Mobile earlier, during the trial. When he went to their motel room, hoping to talk to them about Jones's defense, he said, he found them too drunk even to discuss the case with him.

After thoroughly reviling the family of Jeremy Jones, Yazdi then turned his attention to Lisa Nichols's family, saying that if Jones received the death penalty, he would sit in prison for as long as ten to twenty years during the appeals process. Every time Lisa's relatives heard Jones mentioned in the media during that time, Yazdi said, it would reopen their wounds and cause them to relive the "hell" of their mother's death, time after time.

AG Troy King took immediate issue with that statement, and told Judge Graddick that Lisa's family would never be free of the pain of her loss, no matter what happened to her murderer.

"[The family] is not going to come out of the hell, even when Jones is no more on the earth," King said in no uncertain terms.

Judge Graddick then gave Jeremy Jones the opportunity to speak on his own behalf. This was what everyone in the courtroom had been waiting for, but Jones's statements weren't what the people were expecting him to make. The entire courtroom was taken by surprise, shocked at what Jones had to say.

Jones began by telling Graddick that the judge had given him a fair trial, but to everyone's amazement, he then announced that if anybody was expecting to hear him begging for mercy or forgiveness, they were mistaken. He didn't know how to do that, he said defiantly.

He went on to call himself a "scapegoat" who had been used by the attorney general to promote his upcoming election battle against the man from whom he took over Jones's prosecution, Mobile County district attorney John Tyson Jr.

The attorney general's office shouldn't have taken over his prosecution, he said.

Jones then told the judge that as far as his many confessions were concerned, he had made all of them up and said he would have "said anything" to get access to the extra food and phone calls his claims of guilt had earned him.

Jones next waxed biblical, with veiled threats to Judge Graddick that if he was put to death, Graddick would "reap" God's anger and would, himself, be punished.

"You shall surely be put to death," Jones told the judge, adding that, instead of asking the court for mercy, he was feeling joy.

"My soul is right," the convicted murderer and rapist announced.

After hearing these brazen and unrepentant statements, Judge Graddick began the summation of his decision. With Jones standing before him, the judge began by saying that Jones had intentionally put Lisa Nichols in a situation from which she could not free herself.

"The circumstances were that you had to have your own way," Graddick said, "and nothing was going to stop you until you got your way."

Graddick told Jones that when he raped and murdered Lisa and set her body on fire, he had forfeited his own right to live.

"She was an innocent, hardworking mother and grand-mother," Graddick said of Jones's victim.

Graddick next reviewed the evidence that had convinced the jury to recommend the death penalty, evidence that clearly showed that Jones had arrived at Lisa Nichols's home, had burst in on her, restrained her, and then forced himself on her. Then, Graddick said, Jones had fired three bullets into her head and doused her body with gas in an effort to "burn away the evidence" of his guilt.

Some of the strongest evidence against Jones, the judge said, was provided by Jones himself in the series of recorded and videotaped confessions, along with the taped phone call that Jones had made to Mark Bentley. In all of these, Graddick said, Jones had freely admitted his responsibility for Lisa's death.

The judge then reminded Jones that when he'd had the opportunity to speak for himself, he seemed only to be interested in defiantly announcing to the court that he was not going to ask for mercy.

"No mercy will be given," Graddick told him, calling Jones "a danger to civilized society," and announcing that his sentencing decision was to uphold the jury's recommendation that Jeremy Jones should be condemned to death by lethal injection for the murder of Lisa Marie Nichols.

Chapter 38

Finally, after the long and painful ordeal of the trial and the sentencing, the family of Lisa Marie Nichols believed she had received the justice that she was due. Her family was emotionally exhausted from the experience, but they were relieved their time in court was over and that they had gotten the outcome they had hoped to get.

"It was what we wanted," Jennifer Murphy told the media representatives who were waiting outside the courtroom to get her comments on the judge's sentencing. She went on to say that the execution of her mother's killer, however, could never equal what had been done to her mama.

Jennifer said that one of the reasons she and her family wanted Jeremy Jones to spend the rest of his life, prior to execution, on death row was so that he would be locked up in solitary confinement. He would be allowed only an hour a day outside his tiny, cramped cell, and conditions in the prison would not be comfortable. Jennifer said that perhaps his being in that situation would force Jones to think about what he had done.

She was astonished, however, by the flippant, unrepentant statements that Jones had made to the judge.

"He said that he was not going to beg for mercy," she told a reporter for the *Joplin Globe*. "He said that the people who wanted him dead should be the ones begging for mercy. It's just the kind of person he is," she said, adding that Jones apparently didn't care about anyone or anything but himself and his own family. He had never shown any trace of remorse for the suffering of Lisa Nichols's family, Jennifer said, or any of the other families whose lives he had torn apart.

When Judge Graddick announced that he was upholding the jury's recommendation for the death penalty, Jeremy Jones had shown no emotion at all, which caused prosecutor Don Valeska to tell the press, "He realized it was a foregone conclusion."

AAG Will Dill, lead prosecutor in the case, described Jones as a "classic sociopath," and said that the facts in the case were so "awful," and Jones was so unsympathetic, that the death sentence was inevitable under the circumstances.

While Jennifer, her family, and members of the prosecutorial team spoke with the media outside the courtroom, Jeremy Bryan Jones was being whisked out of the courtroom by deputies and was taken back to his cell in the Metro Jail. Acting quickly, the authorities immediately made preparations to transfer Jones to Atmore, Alabama, where a cell on death row at Holman Correctional Facility was ready and waiting for him.

Chapter 39

When Jeremy Jones arrived at Holman Correctional Facility in Atmore, Alabama, a maximum-security state prison, he immediately began being processed into the system. One of the first things he got upon his arrival was a haircut and a new set of prison clothing—this time, a set of white pants and shirt instead of the orange coveralls he had worn at Mobile Metro Jail. He was put in segregation, where he would remain for three months prior to being moved to a cell on Alabama's death row, where, like the more than 190 other inmates already there awaiting execution, he would spend twenty-three hours a day in a cell measuring six feet by eight feet.

Even though Jones would not have a great deal of contact with them, there were up to 998 other prisoners at Holman, housed in the 630 general population beds, 200 single cells, and 168 death row cells. Quite a few of Jones's fellow inmates were serving life without parole, and some others were considered to be medium-custody prisoners. All of the state's death row prisoners were housed at Holman, where the state's death chamber was located and where all executions were conducted.

Jones would only be allowed a very small television and

only a few personal items in his tiny cell, and he was required
to make a list of visitors that would be strictly limited to eight
people. Six of those people could be relatives; the other two
could be a male friend and a female friend. Weekly visits would
be allowed, but both the length of the visit and the amount of
personal contact permitted between the prisoner and his visitors were strictly limited—only a brief hug was allowed, once
upon the visitor's arrival, and once on the departure.

The rules that inmates' visitors were expected to abide by
at Holman Correctional Facility were lengthy, and had been
designed to prevent any possibility of money or any form of
contraband being passed to prisoners during visits. Visitors
could only enter the visitation area with $20 in change; no
paper money was allowed. Money could not be left for prisoners; they could only receive money by mail, in the form of
authorized money orders. The $20 or less in visitors' change
had to be carried in a clear plastic bag, along with car keys.
Other than those items, nothing else except for baby items
would be allowed, and the baby items were also strictly limited. Only four disposable diapers could be brought into the
prison by fathers or mothers of young babies, and one of
those would have to be changed in front of the prison guards
during their initial search of the visitors and their belongings.
One blanket and two plastic bottles were the only other things
that would be allowed in the visiting area for the baby.

If Jeanne Beard had had problems following the visitation
rules at Mobile Metro Jail, she would likely find Holman's re-
quirements all but impossible to understand or to follow.
There were also a lot of very strict regulations concerning the
clothing and accessories that could and could not be worn by
visitors, and the list of prohibited items included hats, caps,
scarves, headbands, sunglasses, wigs, jewelry, and medications. Neither male nor female visitors were allowed to wear

any white clothing, or even light-colored clothing that might appear to look white. Women's dresses and skirts would have to be knee-length or longer, with no splits higher than knee-length. No button-up, wraparound or sheer, see-through dresses or skirts; no sundresses; no see-through or sleeveless blouses or tops; no tank tops, halter tops, or low-cut tops; no shorts, stretch pants, sheer pants, or spandex; no jogging or athletic-type clothing. The rules also bluntly stated that female visitors "must wear a complete set of undergarments. Panty hose do not take the place of panties."

To make sure the rules were followed, all visitors were also informed that they would be subject to being searched, and all those who were over sixteen years old would be required to produce a valid photo ID. And if visitors failed to follow the rules, there would be no visit and they would be told to leave the prison facilities.

One of the people on Jeremy Jones's visitors list, his girlfriend, Vicki Freeman, was once again telling the press that she and Jones still planned to be married during his time at Holman, but given the on-again, off-again nature of their tempestuous relationship, the reporters speculated that particular event would probably never be taking place.

Jones told the Mobile reporter who had befriended him that he was being treated better at the prison than he had been in Mobile Metro Jail. He hadn't known what to expect when he got to Holman, he said, but he was more satisfied there than he had been in Mobile. He had his own bed, toilet, and sink, and said that he was much more comfortable with the prison-issue clothing than he had been with the tacky orange jumpsuits he'd had to wear for the previous several months.

After Jones and the eight people on his list of family and friends had time to learn about all the strict regulations governing prisoners and their visitors at Holman Correctional

Facility, however, the Mobile Metro Jail might have begun to look somewhat better in comparison. There would be no conning the prison staff to get extra food or phone calls; Jones was in a whole different world now, and he would probably not be liking it very much.

Jeremy Jones could spend fifteen years or more on Holman's death row in his five-by-eight cell, wearing his white prison togs and watching his little television, while his case slowly inched its way through Alabama's lengthy appeals system. If his attempts to overturn either his conviction or the judge's death sentence failed, then once the time for all of his appeals had expired, he would be put to death by lethal injection. For the time being, however, Jeremy Jones felt that his circumstances had improved considerably when he made the transfer from the Mobile Metro Jail to Holman Correctional Facility.

Jones might not have realized that in Alabama, death row prisoners are not permitted to be interviewed by news media representatives under Alabama Code 15-18-81, and that his days of gabbing freely to the media had now ended. Jones had gotten accustomed to contacting the press at will, but those days were over, once he got to death row. He had bragged earlier that several writers and/or agents were clamoring to pay big bucks for his life story, and that those large amounts of money would then be funneled, via his attorney, to his mother and half brother, but those statements were obviously more of his legendary falsehoods. The law strictly forbade him from profiting in any way from his crime, and it was highly unlikely that Habib Yazdi, or any other attorney who hoped to continue practicing law, would have considered aiding Jones in directing any such payments to his family.

A big change was on its way in the many alleged cases attributed to Jeremy Jones, even while he was getting settled into his new cell at Holman. And in one way or another, it would affect almost all the murders or disappearances in which he was being considered as a likely suspect. On December 6, only a week after Jones received his death sentence and was transferred to the state prison, an unexpected event in Georgia would throw the investigations of all his many confessions into turmoil and cast a shadow of doubt on every claim of murder he had made.

Chapter 40

The members of the congregation at the Lebanon Baptist Church in southwestern Dawson County, Georgia, were looking forward to enjoying the new fellowship hall that church member Elbert Clark was building. Clark, along with his son, Andy, and others from his company, Clark Homebuilders, were working as quickly as they could to finish their construction of the fellowship hall so that it could be used to hold the church's annual Christmas celebration. The building was almost finished; the light fixtures were ready to install, and aside from a few other minor interior details and the cleanup of a little bit of construction debris still lying around inside the building and out in the yard, the job would soon be done.

When Elbert and the others stopped for lunch at noon that day, Tuesday, December 6, 2005, they noticed a group of vultures wheeling overhead, with some of the birds lighting in the trees and landing on the nearby ground. Elbert, an avid outdoorsman and deer hunter, knew that the birds usually circled in that manner over areas where they scented carrion and were planning to feed. He assumed that the vultures had found a dead deer in the forest and had been eating it. Elbert knew that someone had shot at a deer during a deer hunt that had been held in the woods adjacent to the church just a few days earlier. He thought that the deer might have been hit and had later died somewhere nearby, in the heavily wooded area that lay at the bottom of a ravine behind the church.

Elbert and Andy decided to go take a look to see what the vultures had found, and they walked back into the woods and down the hill into the ravine to see what was happening. They found that the birds were, indeed, in the process of eating a dead deer. With their curiosity satisfied, the two men turned around and headed back toward the church. Only a few feet away from the deer carcass, however, Elbert Clark glanced to the side of the path and noticed something that stopped him cold in his tracks. Lying on a thick bed of fallen leaves was what looked to be a human skull, along with a scattering of other bones, plainly visible, shining white in the midday sun.

Elbert asked his son, "Is that what I think it is? Do you see it?"

The two men moved closer for a better look, and it was obvious that Elbert had not been mistaken. Judging by the size and delicacy of the bones and skull, Elbert immediately assumed they were those of a child or a small woman.

"Don't touch anything; let's back off," he told his son. "We've got to get out of here now and call somebody."

Being very careful not to disturb anything as they quickly backed away from the scattered bones and left the area, the men hurried back up the hill to the church and Elbert called the Dawson County Sheriff's Office to report what he and his son had found in the woods. Then they paced back and forth in the parking lot, waiting for the officers to arrive. They didn't have to wait for long.

The first deputy to make it to the church's parking lot, arriving within minutes of receiving the call, was a sheriff's lieutenant, Brandy Branson. Other patrol cars followed, and when Elbert took the officers down into the ravine to the spot in the woods where the bones lay on a thick carpet of fallen leaves, it was as obvious to them as it had been to Clark that the bones were most likely the remains of a female. Police radios began buzzing with activity, calls for assistance were made to other agencies, the GBI was notified, and the area was quickly cordoned off with yellow tape. The woods behind the Lebanon Baptist Church had just become a crime scene.

Elbert Clark told the officers that he probably wouldn't have noticed the skull and bones lying there on the ground if not for some heavy rains that had fallen recently in the area. The layer of fallen leaves had been packed down by the moisture, he said, and that had made the remains more clearly visible.

"As soon as I realized what it was," Elbert said, "I got everybody out of the area and called the law."

With a large area of the woods behind the church sectioned off with yellow crime-scene tape, officers from Dawson County and Forsyth County and GBI agents carefully conducted their initial search of the area and collected the skull, some leg bones, and a pelvis. They were immediately taken to the GBI Crime Lab in Decatur, Georgia, where they would be identified and analyzed by GBI forensic anthropologist Dr. Rick Snow, who came to the scene on Tuesday and would be returning on the following day. The large number of searchers gathered in the church's parking lot were given instructions on how to proceed; then they began combing methodically through the surrounding area of the woods in an intense effort to find the rest of the bones. They also looked for other items, such as clothing or jewelry, that might help as a means of identification, as well as any possible clues as to the cause of death. No evidence of that type was found, however, during the initial search.

Many of the vehicles parked at the church remained on the scene overnight as work continued, and the search area was closely guarded. But television news crews had gotten wind of the grim discovery made in the woods about a hundred yards behind the rural church on Kelly Bridge Road. One station quickly went on-air with a report that, according to an unnamed source, the remains were believed to be those of Patrice Tamber Endres, missing since April 2004, and claimed by Jeremy Jones as being one of his many victims.

Chapter 41

The following morning, a hastily called eleven o'clock news conference was held in the church parking lot, with Dawson County sheriff Billy Carlisle, Forsyth County sheriff Ted Paxton, Dawson sheriff's sergeant Tony Wooten, and GBI special agent in charge John Cagle. They, along with several other authorities, were ready to answer questions from the host of reporters and camera crews from throughout the region. The parking lot was filled with satellite trucks from television stations, patrol cars, crime scene vans, and a score of reporters' cars and trucks.

Sheriff Carlisle made the first statement of the press conference and cut straight to the crucial information that confirmed what everyone had been waiting to hear.

"Yesterday afternoon, at approximately twelve-thirty P.M., our officers received a call about some skeletal remains that had been discovered behind the Lebanon Baptist Church on Kelly Bridge Road by members of the church.

"We came out and investigated those remains, and this morning, we were able to positively identify these remains as those of Patrice Endres, who was abducted last year out of Forsyth County."

Carlisle went on to give an account of how the partial skeleton had been discovered.

"The skeletal remains were located approximately one hundred yards behind the church building. We have confirmed the identity using dental records, known medical records, and other sources."

Special Agent Cagle told the reporters, "Some of the remains were taken to the crime lab and examined and compared to the records that had been obtained by the Forsyth County Sheriff's Office during their investigation. We were able to do that very early this morning."

One of the reporters asked if the authorities were speculating that Patrice had been murdered.

"We are classifying this as a homicide," Carlisle answered, "because of the known circumstances of the abduction of the victim."

Questions then turned to potential suspects in the case, Jeremy Jones in particular, since he had confessed to killing Patrice and said that he had left her body in a location that turned out to be almost sixty miles away from where she had been found. Sheriff Paxton told the reporters, "I can't comment on some of the aspects of this case; however, we have not ruled out Jones as a possible suspect. The discovery of the remains of Patrice Endres, right now, doesn't change that. He is still a suspect and there are no other suspects at this time."

Paxton said that his department hadn't had any direct contact with Jones for around six to eight months. When authorities had questioned him in Mobile, Jones had given information at that time that indicated he had firsthand knowledge of Patrice's disappearance and murder, including some information that had not been disclosed to the public. However, the sheriff said that some of the details that Jones had told the investigators during his confession would have been common knowledge to anyone who had closely followed the widespread media coverage of the case.

"We'd be very cautious once again about accepting what he told us," Paxton said, adding that the only conclusion his department was making at that point in time was that Patrice was the victim of a homicide.

"Up until now, we were still not sure," he said. "She was just missing."

Special Agent Cagle told the reporters that a team would continue to search the area, literally on their hands and knees, to try to recover the rest of Patrice's remains. An aerial search would also be conducted, he said.

"There are probably thirty-eight to forty officers participating in that now," he said. "We are trying to discover as many of the remains as we can to try to help in determining the cause of death. We have recovered some, and we are going to continue trying to find as many as we can this afternoon."

Freezing rain had been forecast for the following day, Cagle said, and the searchers were going to work as quickly and thoroughly as possible in order to beat the oncoming bad weather.

Paxton said that authorities from Dawson County, Forsyth County, and the GBI would be working together on the case. It had started in Forsyth County with Patrice's disappearance, he said, and Dawson County now would have primary jurisdiction of the homicide investigation because of the remains having been discovered in that county.

There were more questions dealing with possible motives, evidence, and condition of the remains, but the sheriffs were finished. They did not comment any further, telling the reporters that it was too early in the investigation to draw any further conclusions. Then the press conference, the first of many, concluded at around 11:30 A.M., which seemed to be far too soon for the media, which continued to clamor for more details about the unexpected discovery of the remains. After almost two years, the body of Patrice Endres had been found—not where Jeremy Jones had said he had dumped it into Sweetwater Creek in Douglas County, Georgia, but only eight miles away from Tamber's Trim-n-Tan hair salon, the location where she had been abducted.

Chapter 42

All of the big-city news media had flocked to Dawson County to be on hand for the press conference announcing that the remains of Patrice Endres had been found, but some of the best reporting on the case was being done by a reporter for one of the smallest local newspapers, the *Dawson Community News*.

At such small papers, the reporters also serve as photographers, proofreaders, and more, usually ending up doing a little bit of everything involved with publication of the newspaper, from laying out pages to answering phones. This was the case with George Herrera, jack-of-all-trades for the *Dawson Community News*, and one of the first reporters to arrive on the scene, camera in hand, at the Lebanon Baptist Church as soon as news of the discovery had begun to spread on Tuesday afternoon.

Herrera photographed much of the recovery of the remains as the operation began in the church's parking lot, where searchers were initially gathered together to hear their instructions before heading into the woods. As the officers and technicians filed down the slope and into the ravine, they fanned out around the location where Patrice's bones had been found.

Herrera kept taking pictures and making notes, describing the scene as the searchers began slowly walking a grid, careful not to miss a single detail. As the crime scene investigators came and went from their specially equipped vehicles to the ravine in the woods below the church, Herrera continued photographing the search and getting the correct names and titles of all the persons involved in the recovery operation.

The next morning, George Herrera was one of the first arrivals at the press conference, once again carefully documenting all the details of those proceedings with his camera and notebook. Then later, when there were very few media personnel remaining behind in the church parking lot after the press conference concluded, Herrera gradually eased down into the woods himself to get a few more pictures of the area where the remains had been found.

A short time later, when officers discovered the reporter had made his way to the scene and was photographing the search areas, they immediately sent him packing, but not in an overly hostile manner; after all, he was a local fellow with whom they had a good working relationship. But he was shooed out of the woods nonetheless, with orders not to come back into the area while the search was still taking place.

Before he was discovered and dismissed from the woods, George Herrera had managed to assemble one of the most complete photographic records of a forensic operation that had ever been compiled in the Dawson County area. His work would be viewed on the Internet and shown in other, larger publications as thousands of people around the nation searched for information on the discovery of the body of Patrice Endres.

When Herrera wrote his follow-up to the initial story of the events as they occurred behind the Lebanon Baptist Church, he called the Endres case "one of the most convoluted cases in recent local memory." This, he said, was due to the many twists and turns involving false witnesses, Jones's recanted confessions, and the massive publicity campaign that had initially surrounded Patrice's disappearance. Because her remains had been recovered in Dawson County, the investigation became the primary responsibility of the authorities there, and George Herrera continued with his meticulous coverage for the readers of the *Dawson Community News,* keeping them informed of ongoing developments with his accurate, careful reporting.

As was often the case, the local man with the inside track— who had gotten there the earliest, worked the hardest, and stuck around the longest—was able to scoop the larger papers thoroughly.

Chapter 43

When Patrice Endres's remains were discovered more than an hour's drive away from the place where Jeremy Jones had claimed that he had disposed of her body after kidnapping and killing her, that discovery cast immediate doubt on all of Jones's many other confessions. Now the authorities were left to wonder just how much of the details of his other claims of guilt were true, and how much he had fabricated. One of the first to weigh in with comments on the many discrepancies of the details he had given in the Endres case was Jeremy Jones, who told reporters that he hadn't murdered anyone in Georgia.

"I made up that crap," he bragged, going on to claim that he hadn't confessed to any murders whatsoever and hadn't ever killed anyone, not even Lisa Marie Nichols, despite receiving a death sentence in her case only a week before Patrice Endres's remains had been discovered.

Forsyth County sheriff Ted Paxton commented to the media about the ramifications of having found the partial skeleton around sixty miles from where Jones had indicated. This made it apparent that his claims about the location where he allegedly dumped Patrice's body were "clearly a lie, but that's the only thing we can say with certainty right now."

There were quite a few problems with Jones's confession, Paxton said, for he had told the investigators quite a lot of things that anyone who had followed the case would have known, and some of the other things that he told them could just as easily have been good guesses on Jones's part. But Paxton stressed that those problems, nonetheless, didn't over-rule the fact that Jones had also given some crucial details of the case that were more than enough to keep him first in line as a person of interest.

Trace evidence from the Jeep Cherokee that Jones drove had been collected for analysis, but Paxton held out little hope it would provide any usable evidence. Anything that might be found in the vehicle would have long since been contaminated between the time of Patrice's disappearance and Jones's Mobile arrest and subsequent string of confessions.

Investigator Mitch McRae told reporters that Jones had given quite a few conflicting statements in his story of Patrice's abduction and murder.

"He's been lying from the start," McRae said, expressing some doubt about Jones's guilt in that case, but adding that he was certain that Jones was responsible for other killings. After endless hours of interviews, McRae said, Jones had begun changing some of the details of his story, and McRae felt that it was obvious that he was guessing about descriptions of what Patrice had been wearing that day, and whether or not she had tan lines. Jones had also said that when he dropped Patrice's body off a bridge, he didn't hear a splash. And his claim of being stopped later that day by a Georgia game warden proved to be false when the investigators confirmed that the game warden who had been on duty in that area didn't remember ever stopping Jones at all.

Trying to get straight answers out of Jeremy Jones had proved to be extremely difficult, McRae said, with Jones jumping frantically from one topic to the next during questioning sessions. When Jones made his confessions of guilt in the series of murders he claimed responsibility for, McRae said there was always some little detail that prevented the investigators from confirming his statements. Jones would answer their questions at random, interspersing those answers with talk of fishing and hunting. Then he would effortlessly jump back to the subjects of kidnapping, murder, and rape.

"I have no doubt he's playing games with us," McRae told reporters.

Back in Alabama, when Assistant Attorney General Will Dill learned that Patrice Endres's skeletal remains had been discovered far from where Jones had said that they could be found, Dill said that he wasn't at all surprised that Jones had evidently lied. He told the press that lying seemed to always be a part of any statements Jeremy Jones might make.

"You have to pick through" what Jones might claim, Dill said, in order to find any truths that could be sufficiently corroborated with actual physical evidence.

Detective Paul Burch, lead investigator in the Lisa Nichols murder case, held a different opinion about Jones's confession in the Endres case than his partner Mitch McRae. From the conversations he'd had with Jeremy Jones over the course of his stint in the Mobile Metro Jail, Burch had no doubt that Jones had, indeed, killed Patrice Endres. Burch said he thought that Jones had intentionally given the wrong location when he said where her body had been dumped, hoping that the wrong information would sidetrack the search and confuse the police.

"In my opinion," Burch told reporters, "he killed her."

Chapter 44

Even though doubt had been cast on Jeremy Jones as the prime suspect in Patrice Endres's murder, Sheriff Ted Paxton continued to refer to him as the "only suspect." Paxton, however, admitted to having some doubts of his own. Some of Jones's statements were blatantly false; others were ringing true. Paxton called Jones a "pathological liar" who, because of his death sentence for the murder of Lisa Nichols, now had nothing to lose by giving bogus information that left the authorities running around in circles.

Since he had already received the death penalty, Paxton said, Jones had "nothing left but this game he is playing," and said that Jones was obviously delighted with all the attention he was getting from the media. Jones and his attorneys, Paxton said, were playing "legal games" with the many confessions that Jones had made, then subsequently denied. He said Jones's lawyer was "trying to grab onto whatever he can."

The investigation into Patrice Endres's abduction and murder was far from over, Paxton said. Patrice had always had a continuous stream of appointments at her busy hair salon, with people coming and going regularly all day. On the day she disappeared, Patrice had only a twenty-minute gap between appointments, at lunchtime, and Paxton said he had a hard time believing that Jeremy Jones had just accidentally happened to stumble upon the hair salon at such an opportune time.

"From the beginning, we've believed that she was targeted," Paxton told reporters. He said that he had always believed Patrice had been stalked or closely watched, and someone had known when she could be caught alone in the shop. That person, investigators believed, had loaded Patrice into a vehicle and had taken her into the woods behind the Lebanon Baptist Church. But whether she was alive when she was taken into those woods, or whether she was already dead at the time, had not yet been determined, and might never be. Finding out how Patrice died, with nothing but skeletal remains to go on, wouldn't be easy, Paxton said. Less than half of the remains had been recovered initially, and around 90 percent would eventually be found. Sweeps of the area with cadaver dogs and metal detectors continued.

Forensic anthropologist Dr. Rick Snow told reporters that the GBI Crime Lab would be looking for anything that might provide a clue, like cut marks on the bones, which would be an indication that Patrice had been stabbed, and also for any signs of bullet wounds or any sort of blunt-force trauma or skeletal damage. He and Dr. Mark Koponen, deputy chief medical examiner, would be working to find any marks or damage on the reassembled skeleton. Other than that, there would be very little for the technicians to examine that might indicate how Patrice had died.

GBI spokesman John Bankhead told reporters that since two years had passed since the murder, there had been animal activity and exposure to the elements, which would make the cause of death far more difficult to determine. Each individual bone would have to be inspected closely for anything that might indicate foul play or anything else that might have led to Patrice's death.

A few days later, Bankhead released a statement saying that the examination of Patrice's remains had been completed, but the cause of death would be withheld for investigative reasons. That information could possibly be used as a means of verifying the statements of any present or future suspects in the case if it was not released publicly. Due to the wild-goose chases Jeremy Jones had sent the authorities on after claiming that he had dumped Patrice's body into a distant creek, any information that could be used to corroborate his confession, or the statements of other potential suspects, would be kept strictly confidential. Bankhead said that Patrice's death was obviously a homicide, but other than that, nothing further would be said.

Bankhead did tell reporters, however, one more significant piece of information; he made the statement that it was beginning to appear that Jeremy Jones very likely had no involvement in Patrice's disappearance or murder.

The case was now legally Dawson County's, due to the location of the body, but Dawson and Forsyth Counties planned to work very closely together, along with the GBI investigators and other authorities, according to Dawson County sheriff Billy Carlisle. Unless it could be proven that Patrice was killed at another location, then transported into Dawson County, the case would remain there. But Carlisle said that, with the extensive case files already assembled by Forsyth County and the technical resources available through the GBI, all the agencies would be collaborating, sharing information, and working together diligently to identify the person who could be proven to be Patrice's murderer.

Rob Endres, whose sixtieth birthday came on the day Patrice's body was found, had first learned of the shocking discovery of his wife's remains from reporters, not from law enforcement. Rob said initially that he still believed Jeremy Jones was the person who had murdered his wife. He told reporters that Jones knew many things about Patrice and about the layout of the hair salon that hadn't been disclosed in the media. The fact that Patrice had been found far from the location Jones had named didn't necessarily mean that he wasn't guilty, Rob Endres said, and therefore, he thought that Jones shouldn't be eliminated yet as a suspect. His goal, Rob said, was to see Jones prosecuted and convicted, now that he could no longer hold out hope that Patrice might still be alive.

"I guess this means we won't find her in Italy, then," he said tearfully when told of his wife's remains being found, referring to some earlier rumors speculating that Patrice might have run away and gone abroad. Rob said that, despite remaining hopeful for Patrice's safe return for the entire 602 days since she had disappeared, he had also been realistic enough to realize that such a thing wasn't likely to happen. He told reporters now that Patrice's remains had been found his plan was to cremate them so that Patrice could then accompany him wherever he went. The engraving on the inside of the couple's wedding rings had read: "Patrice and Rob Forever." But, sadly, the message that she had written in a note she had left for him, on the day of her disappearance, would never come to pass.

"The best is yet to come," it read.

Chapter 45

The family of Patrice Endres had been dissatisfied all along with several aspects of the investigation into Patrice's disappearance, and on quite a few occasions they had been critical of law enforcement and made it apparent they were still suspicious of Patrice's husband, Rob Endres. Despite his claims of love for his wife and his continual and lengthy statements to the media about the search for her, Patrice's family remained convinced that Rob Endres might very well have been responsible in some way for Patrice's death.

Most vocal in her disapproval of the handling of the case, and her belief that Rob Endres might be the guilty party, was Patrice's sister, Kyleen Kramer. Kyleen and Patrice had always been close, even though Kyleen had been uncomfortable with some of the choices that Patrice had made in her earlier life. Kyleen told reporters that there were several years in the past when she and Patrice hadn't been in close contact with one another, at least not as much as usual. During that time, Kyleen said, Patrice was working as a dancer in clubs and partying quite a bit with her boyfriend at the time, who was twenty-four years older than Patrice.

When Patrice became a mother in 1988, Kyleen said, her

priorities shifted dramatically. She fell in love with and married Rob Endres, began working toward realizing her dream of a career as a hairdresser, and opened her own very successful salon. She and Rob Endres, who was twenty years her senior, had eventually planned to move to Florida after his retirement and operate a bed-and-breakfast there. In the meantime, though, they both worked toward their goal, putting in long hours—Patrice in her beauty salon, and Rob as a second-shift supervisor at a plant in Conyers, Georgia.

Kyleen told reporters that her sister's loss had been made even harder because Patrice had succeeded in turning her life around. Impatient with the progress of the investigation, Kyleen had gone out searching on her own for Patrice, combing through thick woods in the area around Sweetwater Creek, and had even contacted a psychic in the hope of getting even the smallest scrap of information about her sister's whereabouts that might help in the search. After the psychic sent her a sketch of an area that seemed to resemble an overgrown forest near Buford Dam, Kyleen and her young daughter, Brianne, had searched there on their own, combing through snake-infested briar thickets, with no results.

Kyleen and Patrice's other family members continued to feel that the authorities were not on the right track with the investigation, and they also thought that they were not being kept sufficiently informed of whatever progress was being made in the case. But Sheriff Paxton said that, even though he understood the family's position, Rob Endres was the person who was Patrice's legal next of kin, and the sheriff's obligation was to communicate first and foremost with him regarding the investigation. And Patrice's family and Rob Endres did not communicate well at all; as a result, they had received far less information about Patrice's disappearance than they would have liked to have.

Kyleen Kramer told reporters that the family still felt that Rob Endres, despite his extensive appearances in the media, was a suspect in Patrice's disappearance and death.

"In our hearts," she said, "we are confident about what happened to her."

Kyleen told reporters that Rob Endres had given everyone a very misleading account of her sister's marriage. Patrice visited her family and went on vacations with either Rob or with her son, Pistol, but never with both of them, together, at the same time. And when Patrice went missing, Rob Endres immediately sent Pistol to Birmingham, Alabama, to stay with Patrice's father, Richard Tamber, and her brother Rich. He worked at his job on the second shift, Rob Endres told reporters, and he was spending all his daytime hours searching for Patrice. And as a result, he did not have the time to take care of the fifteen-year-old boy. Pistol later chose to move back to Georgia and live with his biological father, Patrice's former boyfriend Don Black, and Don was granted the legitimation of his son. Don had also petitioned the superior court on Pistol's behalf for control of Patrice's assets, but he and Rob Endres reached a settlement in that matter and Rob was appointed the conservator of Patrice's estate.

Chapter 46

The developments in the Patrice Endres case had a great deal of significance to the many law enforcement agencies around the country that were investigating, or revisiting, all the unsolved crimes to which Jeremy Jones had confessed. So far, the Endres case was the only one of his many alleged confessions of the murder of a missing person in which a body had actually been recovered. It had also undermined all those confessions because of his obvious lies about the location of Patrice's body, along with some of the other details he had given that did not fit with the facts as they were already known. Police were left confused and doubtful, but the investigations continued in the hope that some of his many statements would actually turn out to be true.

On October 15, 2004, six months after Patrice's disappearance, a candlelight vigil had been held for her in the parking lot of the Coal Mountain Animal Hospital, where yellow ribbons were tied on the trees outside as a reminder that Patrice was still missing. The large stack of flyers about Patrice's disappearance had been taken off the animal hospital's front counter a few months earlier, but the ribbons would remain in place, the animal hospital staff said, until Patrice came home.

On Sunday, January 15, 2006, that homecoming finally occurred in the form of a memorial service, which had been
planned by Patrice's sister and brothers and was held at the
Coal Mountain Baptist Church in Forsyth County. The service, her family and friends said, was being held not to grieve
for their loss, but to celebrate Patrice's life and all that she had
meant to them and to the entire community.

Around a hundred people showed up for the service, including Patrice's mother, Charlene Prahl, who had come from
Texas, her father, Richard Tamber, and her siblings, Kyleen
Kramer and Rich and Brian Tamber. Rob Endres was there,
and Patrice's son, D. W. "Pistol" Black, attended the service
with his father, Don Black.

Most of Patrice's friends came to the service dressed in
purple, which had been widely known to be Patrice's favorite
color. Richard Tamber wore a purple shirt as he played "Bella
Notte" and "That's Amore" on the accordion for his beloved
daughter, one last time.

After the service, several of Patrice's friends spoke of how
much she had meant to them, and told about the many things
she had done that had impacted their lives. One woman,
Nancy Hunt, compared Patrice's hair salon to the one in *Steel
Magnolias,* and said that no matter what was being discussed,
"You always left there feeling better than when you went in."

Ashlee Vallis was one of several high-school girls who
skipped school on more than one occasion in order to take
part in the search for Patrice. She had earlier told reporters
that she felt nothing would be completely settled for those
who had loved Patrice until someone was convicted for the
murder. Ashlee and a girlfriend, Ramey Tucker, had both visited the hair salon regularly. The two girls said they had kept,
as mementos, the appointment reminder cards Patrice had
sent them before they had their hair styled for their prom.

Another friend told of Patrice's many contributions toward making the community a better place, saying that the hair salon was closed on Wednesdays because that was the day that Patrice always packed her Tahoe full of beauty supplies and went to the local nursing home. She had volunteered to style the hair of the ladies there, and they looked forward to her weekly visits with great anticipation. It boosted their self-esteem and their spirits, and Patrice's visits always left the nursing home seeming like a much brighter and happier place.

Judy Perrin, a salon visitor and a close friend, spoke of Patrice's love of people and said that even though the memorial service had provided some closure for Patrice's friends and family members, the important thing for them all to remember was that the murder remained unsolved. Judy said the investigators in Forsyth County were determined to solve the case and convict the person responsible, and they had posted Patrice's picture in their investigation headquarters to remind them every day of their goal. Judy said she thought the killer would eventually be brought to justice, saying that she felt sure there would be an "ultimate judgment" for Patrice's murderer, even if the crime went unsolved for many years.

Rob Endres said that he appreciated the friends who spoke so highly of Patrice at the memorial service. They adored Patrice, he said, as all those present did.

"They spoke from their hearts," he said. "I would just like having my beautiful, loving wife back," he added, "and that's never going to happen."

Another of Patrice's customers had written a letter to the editor of one of the local newspapers after Patrice was found, saying that everyone who ever stepped inside her hair salon was like a part of her family. On the day of the high-school prom, the woman said, the place was a madhouse, full of excited girls, and Patrice had greatly enjoyed helping the girls to look their very best for their big night.

The woman wrote that she had met Patrice shortly after she opened Tamber's Trim-n-Tan, she said, and instantly liked her. Even though she had not been in what she called Patrice's "inner circle of family and friends," she said that like everyone else who ever walked into the shop, she was always made to feel special.

The woman said that Patrice would never be forgotten, and she called on all the law enforcement agencies involved in investigating her death to "open their eyes and minds and let everyone be a suspect until the person responsible for this heinous act is caught."

Chapter 47

With the search for the bodies of Lauria Bible and Ashley Freeman failing to turn up any evidence, and prospects looking increasingly likely that Jeremy Jones had lied about murdering Patrice Endres, everything else he had told the investigators regarding his many confessions had now come into question. The only crimes prosecutors felt certain beyond any shadow of a doubt that Jones had been responsible for were the two for which he had already been officially charged, the deaths of Amanda Greenwell and Katherine Collins, and the murder of Lisa Marie Nichols, for which he had been convicted and sent to death row. Other than those three crimes, all else remained questionable. It was likely that the other cases would remain unsolved unless sufficient physical evidence could be found to corroborate Jones's many claims.

The reinvestigation of all those other cases still continued, but Alabama's attorney general had been hard at work in the meantime, preparing new legislation that he planned to propose—legislation that would permanently change Alabama trial law. The murder of Lisa Nichols had a great impact on all those in Attorney General Troy King's office who had worked on the prosecution and conviction of Jeremy Jones.

At the press conference officially announcing those many confessions that Jones had made, King had told reporters then of his intention to draft legislation that would allow juries to hear the no contest pleas that might have been previously entered by defendants in pertinent cases in other states. Before Jeremy Jones had been on death row for even as long as a month, King had completed drafting the bill he planned to introduce, and it was being sponsored by Senator Bradley Byrne, of Fairhope, Alabama. Byrne, a Republican from the state's Thirty-second District of Baldwin County, was also the sponsor of a number of other bills, many of which had gone toward making up some of the state's most effective legislation to be enacted during his time in office.

King's legislation was an important part of his efforts to close many of the current loopholes in Alabama law, including some much-needed changes to tighten the state's laws on the prosecution of pedophiles, upgrade identity theft to felony status, and aid drug-endangered children. One of the bills that the attorney general's office had worked on the hardest, and which had gotten a great deal of media attention and public support, was the protection of an unborn child bill. At one point, the *Brody Bill* had been threatened in the legislature and its passage looked as though it might be endangered, primarily due to partisan politics and governmental red tape. Some hard work on King's part put the bill back on track, and it successfully passed and became law. Alabama's children who were victims of crimes against their mothers were now fully protected, whether they were unborn or were already out in the world.

Now Troy King was determined that criminals like Jeremy Jones would no longer be able to sweep their prior offenses under the rug and hide them from juries because of an outdated point of trial law. King wanted to be sure that, during the trials of felony offenders, Alabama juries would be legally allowed to hear about their previous pertinent history in the courts of other states. Legislation was needed to enable juries to hear nolo contendere, or no contest, pleas that had been entered in other states by criminals on trial for similar criminal offenses in Alabama. With Senator Byrne's help, the *Lisa Marie Nichols Justice for Victims Act* had its first reading in committee on January 10, 2006.

In the synopsis of the bill, King said that under existing state law, a plea of nolo contendere, or no contest, cannot be used as a plea to a criminal charge. Also, under existing law, a criminal conviction from another state that is based upon a plea of nolo contendere is not admissible in Alabama, as are other criminal convictions.

This bill would provide that a conviction in another state based on a plea of nolo contendere, or no contest, would be admissible for impeachment purposes to the same extent as other criminal convictions. This bill would provide that a felony criminal conviction based on a plea of nolo contendere, or no contest, in another state would be used for sentence enhancement purposes under the *Habitual Offender Act*. The bill would also provide that a plea of nolo contendere, or no contest, for certain offenses in another state would be used as an aggravating circumstance upon a conviction of capital murder. The bill would specify that a plea of nolo contendere, or no contest, would not be available in Alabama to any person charged with a crime.

The *Lisa Marie Nichols Justice for Victims Act* had its second reading in committee on April 5, 2006, but the act did not make it onto the senate floor to be acted upon before the end of that session. King and the many other supporters of the act would be ready when the next senate session convened, and they were determined that the act would be signed into law.

There was little else that could have served as a more fitting tribute to the memory of Lisa Nichols. She had paid the ultimate price for stopping a vicious murderer, but because of her sacrifice, the world that her daughters and their families lived in would forever be a safer place. Now, thanks to the hard work and dedication of the Alabama attorney general and his staff, criminals like Jeremy Jones would no longer be able to hide their previous crimes in other states from Alabama juries if the legislation was voted into law. Attorney General Troy King wanted to be sure that the name and the lasting legacy of Lisa Marie Nichols would always be remembered.

Chapter 48

By the time Jeremy Jones received the death penalty and was taken from the Mobile Metro Jail to begin his residence at Holman prison for the remainder of his life, he had received a great measure of public notoriety. After being classified as a serial killer by the FBI's standards, Jones became one of the newest and most popular criminals, the "flavor of the month," on a countless number of Internet Web sites, message boards, and chat rooms dealing specifically with serial killers and their acts. Whether or not Jones realized the full extent of his Internet celebrity status, he knew that his many television and newspaper interviews had garnered him a great deal of attention, which he had obviously enjoyed. It is doubtful that he realized that serial killers have an enormous "fan following" in cyberspace. If not for his being thrust into that category by the FBI, Jeremy Jones would have more than likely been known only as a murderer of local and regional concern, instead of as a serial killer with hundreds of worldwide Internet search-engine hits.

The FBI's official definition of a serial killer requires the individual in question to have committed three or more separate murders, each followed by a "cooling off" period, which can vary greatly in length. Sometimes the kills come one after another in close succession, and at other times many years may pass between one murder and the next. Serial killers usually have several common traits, and beginning in the early 1950s, psychologists and psychiatrists began to speculate that their similar mind-sets and patterns of behavior might be used to identify "criminal personalities" and help to identify both the active serial killer, as well as those individuals who seemed to have an increased potential to become serial killers at some point in their lives.

The FBI established its Behavioral Sciences Unit (BSU) in the early 1970s, and profiling became a discipline that aided law enforcement greatly in the identifying and apprehending of serial killers, as well as other, less prolific murderers.

Profilers looked at crime scenes for details that might give them some insights into the killer's age, lifestyle, habits, and their motivation to kill. In many cases, FBI profilers could examine the details of a case and reasonably conclude that the killer was of a particular race and age, was socially maladjusted or sexually dysfunctional, and whether or not he selected and stalked his intended victims or murdered them simply by random choice.

Serial killers, on the average, are typically white males between the ages of eighteen and thirty-two, with a past history that nearly always includes either arson, bed-wetting, or animal abuse. The killer is likely to have been abused by relatives in some way, either physically or psychologically, at some point as a child. Usually, he acts alone. His victims, typically, are strangers that he has chosen at random. There are always exceptions to every rule, and there have been some serial killers who were well-treated by their families during what seemed to be a happy, normal childhood. Others had a partner or partners in killing; there were some who killed their family members or acquaintances; there have been some who were women, and some who were black. But the typical serial killer profile, as outlined, fits the vast majority of those who kill repeatedly.

Profilers didn't have the opportunity to make many predictions about Jeremy Jones; he was already in custody for the murder of Lisa Nichols by the time his involvement in the deaths of Katherine Collins and Amanda Greenwell was discovered, and he was officially classified as a serial killer. But as the investigators in all his confessed murder cases learned, there were countless characteristics that Jeremy Jones shared with other serial killers throughout history, from "Jack the Ripper" to the "BTK Killer."

Serial killers, as a rule, are not insane by the legal definition of the term, derived from the nineteenth-century McNaghten rules, based primarily on whether or not the offender understands the difference between right and wrong. When the offender tries to flee or cover up his crime, then he obviously knows that his actions have been wrong and fully realizes that they will have dire consequences if he is caught and charged. Jeremy Jones tried to cover up his murder of Lisa Nichols by using fire to destroy the evidence; then he fled from the area, vanishing from Mark Bentley's home without notice in an effort to get out of the Mobile area before he was tracked down by the authorities.

Another common characteristic of serial killers is their effort to assign the blame for their acts to childhood trauma, pornography, or the irresistible influence of someone or something else, an "evil twin" or alter ego. In Jeremy Jones's case, he placed the blame for all his crimes on his methamphetamine habit, an addiction that he alleged had caused him to be unable to control his impulses to rape and murder. Meth was, to him, an irresistible influence.

Many serial killers have claimed to have "split personalities," most notably the "Hillside Strangler," Kenneth Bianchi, who conveniently saw the movie *Sybil* a couple of days before he told his psychiatrists that his alter ego, "Steve Walker," was actually the one who was responsible for the murders that Bianchi had committed.

John Wayne Gacy created an alter ego named "Jack Hanley," a name he borrowed from an actual policeman who must have been mortified to have later learned that his name had been used in such a manner by a serial killer like Gacy. Gacy told his psychiatrists that he was overtaken by Jack when he'd had too much to drink; then he would feel compelled by his alter ego to kill a succession of young boys who he said "deserved to die," and then bury them in the crawl space under his home.

Jeremy Jones blamed his violent acts on the influence of methamphetamine, which he had used for years. He had allegedly been on a "meth binge" prior to the murders of Lisa Nichols, Amanda Greenwell, and Katherine Collins. His claims of heavy methamphetamine use also figured into his confessions of guilt in the Freeman/Bible case, the death of Justin Hutchings, his alleged killing of a number of unidentified prostitutes, and several of the other murders he told authorities he had committed. Jones claimed to have been "higher" than he'd ever been at the time of Lisa Nichols's death, and Vicki Freeman told the authorities that Jones had returned home from a days-long meth binge, covered with scratches, on the day of Amanda Greenwell's disappearance.

Studies have revealed that drug abusers, delinquents, and psychopaths all have a higher rate of sensation-seeking behavior and impulsivity, and Jeremy Jones was a long-term drug user with a history of impulsive and delinquent behavior dating back to his school days. It was easy for Jones to blame his crimes on methamphetamine, but it was equally easy for prosecutors to point out that Jones had made the conscious decision to use the drug. Therefore, he was responsible for the consequences of his actions during the times he was under its influence.

Serial killers often keep some sort of item as a "souvenir" of their crimes to enable them to relive the excitement that they experienced during a killing. A string of Mardi Gras beads was found in Jones's trailer after the murder of Katherine Collins, and the beads turned out to be instrumental in charging him with Collins's murder. Those beads might have been only a trinket that Jones brought back from New Orleans without necessarily having been kept as a souvenir of murder. However, Amanda Greenwell's ring, which was identified by Amanda's boyfriend after being found by the authorities while searching Jones's storage building, certainly must have been such a token.

Psychiatrists and psychologists claim that "stressors" are often the trigger event that sends the serial killer into murderous action. Those stressors can take the form of conflicts with women, parents, or the law; financial troubles or legal problems; the death of a loved one, or even the birth of a child. If Jeremy Jones began his series of rapes and murders following such a stressor in his life, it has not yet been determined. But the fact remains that many of his victims had long, dark hair and some, like Katherine Collins, were believed to be part Native American or had physical characteristics that resembled those of Native American women. Jones grew up in Oklahoma and must have attended school with a number of girls who were of Native American descent. Did he, at some time in his early life, have some sort of a stressful experience with a Native American girl with long, dark hair?

Another characteristic that Jones shared with others who

have been classified as serial killers was his claim to be responsible for the deaths of several prostitutes in the Atlanta and Mobile areas. Serial killers have always stalked their victims among prostitutes, drug addicts, runaways, the homeless, and others who live in the shadows of society, helpless and hopeless, vulnerable and easy prey for murderers and rapists. Jack the Ripper hunted and slaughtered London prostitutes, seemingly both attracted and repelled by the women who haunted the streets by night. Jeremy Jones also said that he had hunted and killed several victims from among the prostitutes of Atlanta and Mobile, and Katherine Collins was a New Orleans prostitute. Jones must have experienced a rush of extreme, violent anger at the time of Collins's murder, later telling the investigators that he had killed her because she "deserved to die." Following his confessions, authorities searched intently for any missing-persons reports or unidentified bodies in the areas where Jones said that he had made his kills of the Atlanta and Mobile prostitutes, but to this date, nothing has been found to prove his claims.

Media attention is a great attraction to many serial killers, who see themselves as celebrities, loving the fame and notoriety that they receive in the spotlight. Jeremy Jones clearly enjoyed his publicity, generating much of it himself, and saw himself as a larger-than-life personality. He bragged openly about his sexual prowess, saying that he could "talk the panties off a nun," and during his trial he said on the witness stand that he thought he was "very good-looking." In the documentary film *Crystal Death,* Jones described how he convinced younger girls, who were inexperienced with both sex and drugs, to try both with him. And after his conviction, Jones told reporters that he would file an appeal and win, and then said, "I'll write me a book, and laugh my ass off."

Alabama AG Troy King, Detective Paul Burch, and many of

the others who dealt with Jeremy Jones during his arrest, trial, conviction, and sentencing, described him as being totally without remorse for Lisa Nichols's murder. He was only concerned with himself and how his mother and girlfriend perceived him, they said. A psychopath, according to definition, has no regard for the rights of others and enjoys inflicting pain on others. Psychopaths feel no remorse for their deeds and have no conscience; they almost always have quite high opinions of themselves and their physical and mental abilities, and are unconcerned about the feelings of anyone else. Judging by his apparent conceit and his lack of regret for his actions and the effect they had on so many lives, Jeremy Jones would seem to fit the definition of a psychopath quite closely.

One of the most chilling attributes of most serial killers is their ability to blend into normal society, seamlessly presenting themselves to those around them as charming, likable, and responsible. Ted Bundy and the BTK Killer, Dennis Rader, are two of the best examples of serial killers who successfully hid their crimes behind carefully constructed facades.

Rader was one of those "exceptions to the rule" who had an average, normal upbringing, with no particular problems or trauma, and he had parents who treated him well and provided for all his needs. He served in the U.S. Air Force, spending some time overseas; then he came back home to marry a modest, respectable woman and have two children. Rader and his wife were married for over thirty years, during which time neither she nor their children ever had a single clue that their husband and father was a notorious serial murderer.

On one occasion, shortly before his arrest, Rader's wife, after seeing some of the earlier BTK notes and letters that had been reprinted in the newspaper, told her husband that he spelled "just like BTK," but she had no idea at the time just how true her comment was.

Rader also kept the knife that he had often used as a murder weapon stored in the family's kitchen cabinet, and he had a locked closet in his home where his bondage and pornography items were kept. His wife told the police that she had never looked in the closet; perhaps, subconsciously, she didn't want to find out what was inside, and then have to confront the truth about her husband.

Rader was a leader at the church that he had attended for thirty years, and he also served as a Boy Scout leader. But investigators learned that nearly all of his neighbors, coworkers, and acquaintances, as a rule, had not particularly liked him. They claimed that he was a control freak, and said he was arrogant, rude, and confrontational. But a few others said that they thought Rader was a nice, friendly, clean-cut guy. Even those who did not like him, however, would never have pegged him as being the notorious BTK Killer.

After Rader's arrest, he seemed to enjoy all the media attention.

"I feel like a star right now," he said.

Ted Bundy, one of the best-known of all serial killers, was, by all accounts, a very attractive and intelligent man, with a friendly, likable personality. Like Rader, neither Bundy's family nor his coworkers ever had any inkling that he was an extremely active serial killer. At the same time that Bundy was working at a rape crisis hotline as a kind and sympathetic counselor, he was also out trolling for his victims and luring them into his car by feigning an injury and asking them for their assistance. Sometimes he even used a leg cast or a cane as a prop to gain his victims' trust, and made quite a show of struggling to get into his car. With his good looks and his apparent need of help, girls almost always hurried to his aid, ready to give him a hand.

Bundy targeted college-age girls, attractive women with

long, dark hair, and the stressor that precipitated his long string of murders may have been the engagement that was broken off by his college girlfriend—an upper-class girl, beautiful, with long, dark hair.

Ted Bundy was so knowledgeable, personable, and well-spoken that at the end of his trial the judge told him that if his life had taken a different path, he would have been proud to see Bundy as an attorney, trying cases in his court, instead of standing before him receiving the death sentence for his crimes.

Jeremy Jones was also viewed as a personable, likable guy, not only by his friends and coworkers, but also by many of those who questioned him and heard his confessions of murder. Mobile County sheriff Jack Tillman described him as being a very pleasant fellow to talk with, coming across as a smart guy, seeming to be as nice a fellow as you could hope to meet. Like Ted Bundy, Jones never had any trouble attracting women. He charmed the women he met in the clubs and bars he frequented, and some of the women that he dated were higher-class professional women, according to the Mobile detectives, who were surprised at Jones's success as a ladies' man.

Photos taken of Jeremy Jones during his time in Georgia with Vicki Freeman, around the same time period when Amanda Greenwell and Katherine Collins were murdered and Patrice Endres disappeared, showed a clean-cut, smiling young man who would never be perceived by anyone as a threat of any kind, much less a serial killer and rapist. In the photos, Jones looked exactly as he had described himself so many times: a man's man, the guy next door, handsome and quite charming. In video footage taken during his trial and while he was in jail, Jones was quite well-spoken as he talked of his meth addiction and how it had affected his life. He looked clean-cut and sincere, and he was quite articulate. Like Rader, Bundy, and many more, Jeremy Jones wore the mask of normalcy very well.

The specter of child abuse in Jeremy Jones's background was raised like a red flag by Habib Yazdi during Jones's trial, with Yazdi even going so far as to claim that Jones had been raised in an atmosphere of physical and emotional abuse, drug and alcohol use, and sexual perversion. This may or may not have been the case, but Yazdi attempted to use Jones's early life and upbringing to generate sympathy from the judge and to help explain away his crimes.

Experts in criminal behavior acknowledge that child abuse, more often than not, can cause a child to turn to violence later in life as their reaction to any challenge. And serial killers' relationships with their mothers, in particular, seem to figure greatly in their backgrounds; whether the mothers were domineering or distant, uptight or uninhibited, they exercised an overpowering influence on their offspring. Many serial killers were exposed to their mothers' sexual activities when they were children, and others were taught by overprotective mothers that sex was a dirty act that would not go unpunished.

Serial killer Ed Kemper's mother was overbearing and frightening, locking him away in the cellar and abusing him continually in a countless number of ways. Despite this treatment, Kemper chose to go on living with his mother after he became an adult. But the effects of his horrifying ill-treatment at the hands of his mother had been building up over the years, and when Kemper eventually turned to violence, he got his revenge for a lifetime of abuse. He killed his mother, beheaded her, raped her headless body, and then was said to have displayed her head on the mantel in their home. And Henry Lee Lucas, the son of a very sadistic mother, followed suit by killing her near the start of his murderous career.

Many other well-known serial killers were exposed to their mother's sex lives while they were very young, impressionable children. Charles Manson's mother, a drug-using prostitute, handed her little son off to relatives, who were harsh and abusive toward the unwanted little boy. Henry Lee Lucas's mother was a bootlegging drunkard, and the mother of Bobby Jo Long entertained men in her young son's bedroom while the boy attempted to sleep.

Turbulent, abusive childhoods have not been present in the life of every serial killer; some, like Dennis Rader and Ted Bundy, were a part of relatively normal families and had average upbringings. But in the vast majority of cases, physical and psychological abuse, neglect, indifference, and overprotectiveness have planted childhood seeds of murder and mayhem that sprout and flourish in later years. To what extent this particular commonly shared characteristic of serial killers may have applied to Jeremy Jones is not known.

The facts are, however, that his family had some documented issues with drug involvement; his mother and stepbrother were arrested in Oklahoma on drug charges while Jones was in jail in Mobile awaiting his murder trial. And it was pointed out many times, by Habib Yazdi as well as by the many law officers who interviewed Jones, that the only thing that really seemed to matter to him was what his mother and Vicki Freeman thought of him.

That was the reason, authorities claimed, that Jeremy Jones freely and enthusiastically confessed to so many crimes during his questioning sessions with investigators, then did an about-face and roundly denied to the media that he had not confessed to anything and had never killed anyone.

He didn't want his mama to know.

Chapter 49

By all accounts, the mind and body of Jeremy Jones became completely dominated by the "Meth Monster" at an early age, mostly because he wanted above all else to fit in with a drug-using crowd at his school. High-school friends tell of a handsome, likable, fun guy, a good buddy whose personality gradually changed as he developed a drug habit that escalated rapidly and quickly took complete control over his life.

"It really scared me," one former girlfriend said, telling of a night after some time had passed and her relationship with Jeremy Jones had settled into a close friendship. Jones called her that night, strung out and panicky, telling her that he was dangerously high and asking her to come and help him. He begged her to come, and convinced the frightened girl that if he didn't have more drugs, he might die. He needed her, he said, to help him inject himself; he was so high that he was afraid he couldn't do it without help; he might accidentally kill himself, he told her.

He continued begging the girl to come and help him, and she said that she was torn between her fear that he would accidentally overdose on the drugs, and her Christian belief that drug use was not only illegal but terribly wrong. Finally she very reluctantly agreed to come over and do whatever she could to keep him from harming himself, because he had convinced her that something awful might happen to him if she didn't. The terrified girl held a tourniquet on Jones's arm while he injected the drugs, all the while mourning the loss of the boy she had adored as a young teenager, the boy who had been her first love. Thanks to the devastating consequences of methamphetamine use, that boy was now gone forever, a victim of the Meth Monster.

"I was a good kid," Jones told interviewers, "then I experimented with dope." After that, the "good kid" ceased to be.

Jones said that when he started "sticking that needle in my arm," he turned into an evil monster and did things he was ashamed of, things that he would always refuse to admit to having ever done. He knew, however, that he would someday be accountable for his acts, whether he admitted them or not. He might try to hide his crimes, "but God knows what I did," he said.

Almost all of the murders that have thus far been attributed to Jones were connected, in one way or another, with one of his many meth binges, and methamphetamine has been tied to many other rape/murder cases. A Las Vegas couple, Michael Thornton and Janeen Snyder, were captured, tried, and found guilty of murder after the 2001 homicide of a sixteen-year-old girl, Michelle Curran. The jury in that case, like the jurors in Jones's trial, recommended the death penalty for the couple. Thornton and Snyder had kidnapped and sexually assaulted at least two other teenage girls before they picked up Michelle Curran on her way to school one day. Thirteen days later, her ravaged body was found in Riverside County, California, over two hundred miles away from where Michelle had been initially taken. She had been tortured, raped, shot in the head, and left inside a horse trailer at a horse farm near a Riverside

County park, where her body was later discovered in the horse trailer by the horrified property owner.

During their trial, Thornton and Snyder's methamphetamine habits were credited by the prosecution with playing a large part in the couple's obsession with sex and young girls. They had both been previously arrested for false imprisonment and lewd acts with a child under fourteen years of age, but those charges had been dropped for lack of sufficient evidence. Drugs had played a major role in their lifestyle and figured largely in their appetites for sex and violence, which finally escalated to the point that their meth-fueled lust turned to brutal murder.

Another couple, from Oakland, California, James Anthony Daveggio and Michelle Lyn Michaud, were arrested for the murder of a twenty-two-year-old woman, Vanessa Lei Samson, in 1997. Authorities believed that the couple had raped and tortured at least six other women before Samson's murder, and prosecutors described the two of them as being heavy methamphetamine users. The couple, authorities alleged, had repeatedly raped Samson with curling irons while they drove to South Lake Tahoe, where her body was discovered dumped in Alpine County. The van they traveled in had been equipped with a number of torture devices, and inside the vehicle investigators found a book on serial killers and a pack of trading cards about serial killers.

Daveggio and Michaud, prosecutors claimed, had patterned their crimes on those of Gerald and Charlene Gallego, a pair of alleged serial killers from Sacramento, California, who were believed by authorities to have committed as many as ten murders in the late 1970s. Daveggio and Michaud were said to have idolized the Gallegos, and prosecutors claimed during their trial that they had tried to copy the Sacramento couple's methods of sexual torture and murder.

There are great numbers of similar instances where methamphetamine addiction has played a prominent role in sex-related crimes, and Jeremy Jones has claimed that on many occasions, during rape attempts prior to murders, he was so high that he didn't know where he was or what he was doing. Methamphetamine is perhaps the most harmful drug, both physically and psychologically, that has ever come onto the scene and into street use. Its systematic, total destruction of Jeremy Bryan Jones is only one example out of many hundreds of thousands. Because of the crimes he committed during meth-fueled sexual frenzies while in the grip of the drug, the media and prosecutors dubbed him a Meth Monster. But in reality, Jeremy Jones was, himself, yet another one of the Meth Monster's countless victims.

Chapter 50

Some very alarming statistics have shown that 25 percent of the people who are addicted to methamphetamines became addicted to the drug upon their very first use. That figure may seem staggering, but users verify its extreme ability to trap them, early on, into an uncontrollable craving for meth beyond everything else in life.

By these statistics, Jeremy Jones stood little chance of ever being able to break his methamphetamine habit on his own, even if he gave it his best effort, and when interviewed about his drug use, Jones agreed.

"Everybody gets wrapped up in it," he said about methamphetamine. "I don't see how you can't; it's so hard not to."

The drug is so powerful, experts say, that users are often compelled to continue getting high, even after their very first use. Nothing can deter them from taking that next hit.

"It becomes your universe," one meth addict said, when she was being interviewed while in treatment. "You and your friends think that you're just going to go on doing drugs forever, and everything is going to always be so perfect, and you'll be so full of energy."

Another recovering addict, a young girl from a well-to-do,

loving family, tried meth and was then trapped by it; she described how she and her girlfriends would find ways to get the drug they had all come to crave. She and her friends would steal checkbooks, usually from their own family members, who wouldn't press charges against them; then they would go to a store and buy merchandise with the checks. Later, they would return the items for cash refunds; then they would use that money to buy their methamphetamine. After her first round of rehab treatment, that particular young girl went back to using crystal meth again, almost immediately after she finished the program. Her second stint in rehab, however, seemed to have worked, which put her in a very small, elite group; the group of only 6 percent of meth users who go through rehab and are able to stay off methamphetamine afterward. A 6 percent success rate, like the estimated 25 percent rate of addiction upon first use, almost seems unbelievable, but users say that it is almost impossible for them to stay straight, the craving for the drug becomes so extreme and uncontrollable.

In the documentary *Crystal Death,* Jeremy Jones talked about how he would go about giving drugs to women, saying that he would first use meth in front of them; then he would encourage them to try it, too.

"I had women, eighteen or nineteen years old, they hadn't really messed with drugs, and maybe only had sex one or two times," he said. He would offer them methamphetamine to decrease their level of inhibition and, at the same time, rev up their sex drive.

"I'd say, here, smoke a little of this; here, this is how I do it"; then he would show the girls how he shot up the drug and attempt to persuade them to try it that way, too.

But once Jones had helped the Meth Monster to get a strong, unbreakable hold on a woman, the harmful physical effects she immediately began to experience from the drug use would start to show, causing her to become less and less desirable.

"They start losing weight," he said, describing lovemaking with meth-addicted women as being "like having sex with a skeleton with bones on it."

Jones said the drug "breaks women down." He also admitted that the drug had an effect on his sex drive that caused him to "get to where you want two or three women at a time." He had never watched pornography in his life, he claimed, until he became a meth user.

Methamphetamine and sex don't mix; they become intertwined with one another in an addict's mind and body. A user finds that meth leads, both mentally and physically, to an incredibly strong association with sex that is hard to break. But after its use for only a short time, the drug actually begins to affect brain cells, decreasing a user's ability to feel pleasure. That loss of feeling continues to downgrade quickly, causing a meth addict to need more and more of the drug in an attempt to feel "normal," much less to regain what he initially perceived as his heightened sexual powers.

Methamphetamine addiction often causes users to develop paranoia, imagining everything from perceived threats from family and friends to auditory and visual hallucinations that fuel their panic and suspicions. Users exhibit many of the same symptoms as schizophrenia, hearing voices and seeing hallucinations to such an extent that some meth addicts are mistakenly diagnosed as schizophrenics.

In *Crystal Death,* Jeremy Jones told of one occasion when he had stayed awake on a meth binge that lasted for fourteen days, and during that time, he said that he saw "everything from pink elephants to people ten feet tall."

Jones said that on another occasion, when he was at a house out in the country, the drug made him think that he was in some type of unspecified danger from some unknown source. He said he saw nothing unusual when he looked out into the woods during the daytime. However, as night began to fall, the hallucinations began coming on strong, right along with the increasing darkness.

"At night, I'd see people walking around out there," he said, and he'd get a gun and go outside and shoot at them. But the next morning, there would be nothing there except the spent cartridges from the previous night's gunfire, left lying on the ground. No one was there; no one had been there. The people Jones saw were hallucinations originating from his meth use.

"Whatever your scariest fear is," he said, "is what your brain will play on you. My biggest fear was getting busted."

Jones told about the relative ease of making methamphetamine, saying that it took the same amount of time for someone to cook up a whole pound of the drug as it took to produce just one gram. A person could cook up a "couple hundred grams in two or three hours," he said. He claimed the drugs would then sell for $100 a gram.

"For three hours of time," which it took to cook the batch of drugs, he said, "that's good money."

Although he would later deny ever having had hepatitis C, Jones initially claimed on many occasions that he had been diagnosed with both hepatitis A and C, and blamed it on his drug use.

"It's probably going to kill me before anything else will," he said of the liver disease. Meth addicts stand a far greater chance of contracting the illness because of their needle use, but they are far more interested in getting the drug than in the danger it presents.

"It won't happen to me, that's what everybody says," Jones told the documentary interviewers about needle-contracted diseases.

Jones said he had gone to drug rehab due to his methamphetamine addiction, "not to quit, though; just to make my family think I'd quit." When he spoke of the damage that meth had caused in his life, he said, "I had to get away from anyone who knew me." He said that if he could stay off methamphetamine, "I'd say, 'Let me out [of prison] today,' but there's just no guarantee that I'd be able to stay off.

"If I could go back in time," he said, "I'd never even have tried it."

Chapter 51

On taking a close look at methamphetamine, its effects on its users, and its unbelievably high rate of addiction on first use, it is easily understandable why so much violent crime is closely associated with use of the drug. Jeremy Jones has stated that if he had it to do over again, he would have never started using crystal meth. But, like millions of users worldwide, his good intentions might not have lasted very long, even knowing what he claimed to realize about the consequences of his drug use. The powerful hold that methamphetamine has on everyone who has ever used it, even the 6 percent of users who have successfully completed rehab and stayed clean, is a hold that is never really broken.

"Once you do it, you'll always go on wanting it," one recovering addict said.

Methamphetamine causes users to feel two overpowering sensations because of the chemicals it causes to be overproduced in the brain, adrenaline and dopamine. Adrenaline produces the rush, the instant burst of energy and alertness that the body recognizes as the "fight or flight" instinct. Dopamine causes the brain to feel pleasure and produces the highly addictive euphoric high. But at the same time the dopamine brings

such a pleasurable sensation to users, their brains are automat-
ically kicking into high gear, attacking and destroying the excess
dopamine cells. Pleasure without the drug gradually becomes
almost impossible and users are left caring about nothing in life
except doing whatever they must do to get more and more
methamphetamine.

Meth users are attracted to the drug initially because they
feel such increased energy and sexuality, along with a de-
creased need for food and sleep. But shortly after that first fatal
use, the brain begins to combat the drug, and those side effects
that at first felt so wonderful turn into extreme paranoia, hallucinations, violence, and binges of eating and sleeping.

Methamphetamine began as amphetamine, which first
came into being in Germany in the last years of the nineteenth
century. Its almost identical chemical twin, methamphetamine, was developed a few years later in Japan. Amphetamine was initially known in the United States as Benzedrine
and, starting in the 1930s, was used to treat depression, obe-
sity, and sleep disorders.

Military historians claim that Adolf Hitler was an amphetamine addict, and German and Japanese soldiers were given
the drug during World War II to enhance their ability to fight
indefinitely without need for food or sleep. Amphetamine use
was common among United States troops during the Vietnam
War, but when the *Controlled Substances Act* was passed in
1970, amphetamine became far more difficult to obtain
legally. Methamphetamine, with its relative ease of manufac-
ture, took its place, and its illegal production began to grow.

Biker gangs are credited with an initial surge of meth production, starting on the West Coast. Then, during the early
1990s, Hispanic drug organizations began taking over the majority of the meth trade. The most dangerous aspect of
methamphetamine production, however, is the fact that the

drug can be so easily and effectively produced in small home laboratories on the kitchen stove, in the basement, in a garage or outbuilding, or even in the back of a van or the trunk of a car. Meth is the easiest, cheapest drug for users to make for themselves, and at the start of the twenty-first century, it was ranked the number-one drug problem in most of the United States. Its use and its home production, especially in the Southeast, grew faster than statistics could be redrawn from one month to the next.

Darrell Collins, head of the DeKalb County, Alabama, Drug Task Force, said that the meth epidemic had struck northeastern Alabama full-force over the past decade, and told of the increasing numbers of home meth labs that were springing up around his jurisdiction. Collins said that in addition to all the inventive places meth users were hiding their labs, there had even been a few surprising developments.

"We've had people call us and tell us that their dogs have dragged up what we call backpack labs out of the woods," he said. He described the backpack labs as a means of transporting the equipment and materials for meth production back and forth from remote, secluded areas. Users would cram all the items into a backpack so that their trip into the woods would look like a simple hike, then find a good place to stop and cook off a batch of methamphetamine.

"The dogs would find it," he said of the backpacks full of materials left in the woods, "and come dragging it back up into the yard."

A task force officer from neighboring Jackson County, Alabama, another county being ravaged by the drug, said at a workshop on crystal meth that it would be practically impossible to find a spot in either county "where you could stand, and there wouldn't be an operating meth lab within a one-mile radius of wherever you were."

Jeremy Jones spoke of the destructive physical effects of the drug on its addicts, saying its use would "break a woman down." Both women and men are easily spotted as meth addicts after a short time of using the drug; along with the rapid weight loss that leaves them looking like skeletons, there are other very alarming physical indications of meth use. Tooth loss, skin lesions, and neglect of personal hygiene are only a few. When detectives from New Orleans interviewed Jeremy Jones in connection with the murder of Katherine Collins, they later described him as constantly picking at sores on his face during the questioning session. They were led to believe that the sores were from Jones's alleged case of hepatitis C, but it was later pointed out that such acnelike sores were not a common symptom of hepatitis. The sores were far more likely to be from Jones's meth use. According to medical authorities, methamphetamine causes addicts to scratch and pick at their skin, especially on their faces, because they begin to feel crawling, itchy sensations. Jones's Metro Jail mug shots clearly show such sores on his face, and he had admittedly been using the drug heavily for quite some time before Lisa Nichols's murder, which he claimed happened at a time when he was "higher" than he'd ever been.

The mental state of mind of meth users can change quickly, ranging from the initial state of euphoria and moving rapidly into paranoia, aggression, lying, and deception. Users disconnect from their families and friends, become remote and secretive, and show no interest in things that were of great importance to them in their lives prior to the start of their drug use. The symptoms of meth addiction mimic those of paranoid schizophrenia to such an extent that misdiagnoses of such mental illness are often made. In fact, if not for the extreme physical signs of meth use, the rate of misdiagnoses between paranoid schizophrenia and methamphetamine addiction might be far greater.

Addicts often are willing to turn to any means necessary to get more crystal meth as their need for the drug increases and it gets harder and harder to feel its effects. Meth addicts will steal from their loved ones, commit burglaries, armed robberies, and worse in order to get the drugs they crave, and there are also some potentially fatal dangers to be faced if users make their own methamphetamine in home labs. The chemicals that are used in the "cooking" process are toxic, corrosive, and highly flammable, and the production of meth sends vapors into the air, which condense and settle on walls, floors, furniture, clothing, and the skin. Rooms, and sometimes entire houses, that have been used as meth labs must be gutted if there is any hope of removing all the dangerous traces of the chemicals, and people who have been exposed to the meth labs must, for their own safety, be decontaminated, much as they would be after an industrial chemical accident. Few meth lab operators bother to take any precautions at all; safety measures are nonexistent, and the consequences are grave. Even greater danger exists from the flammability of the chemicals in use during meth production, and many a building has exploded and burned while being used as a meth lab, causing death and injury to those present. Emergency rooms have reported a rapid increase in the number of accidental burn cases they receive as a result of meth lab explosions, when the victim's face and hands have taken most of the damage. Deaths have also been reported as a result of operating meth labs exploding and burning, with the victims sometimes including innocent children whose drug-using parents had left them in the meth labs while they cooked their supply of the drug.

How could such a threatening drug have taken hold of millions so quickly and totally, and how many crimes, ranging from petty theft to multiple homicides, are due to methamphetamine addiction? Statistics can only answer these questions up to a point; as stated earlier, the problem is growing far more rapidly than the numbers can accurately reflect. Meth addicts, like Jeremy Jones, will continue to fill cells in the nation's jails and prisons, and the authorities will go on trying desperately to find a way to combat the deadly drug and decrease the number of victims claimed daily by the Meth Monster.

Chapter 52

Jeremy Jones had been on Holman Correctional Facility's death row for only a short time before he began taking part in one of the favorite occupations of death row inmates and other prisoners: the search, by way of the Internet, for pen pals.

Prisoner pen pal sites have become rampant in cyberspace, with countless numbers of Web sites and message boards listing contact information for death row inmates who are looking for contact with people on the outside. There have been efforts by prison officials in many states to eliminate or curb the use of such Web sites to generate mail to prisoners, and in several cases, inmates are forbidden to directly contact such Internet sites themselves. But prisoner advocates strongly object, saying that the inmates have the right to send and receive mail from whoever wishes to write to them. Inmates, always inventive, have found many sources willing to help them skirt direct contact with the pen pal Web sites and have their information listed. They use their mail and phone privileges to maintain a network of advocates, friends, and family members willing to help them into cyberspace.

Human rights groups, commercial pen pal Web sites, ministers, and others send prisoners' information to the pen pal sites on behalf of the inmates, acting as a go-between. On those sites, the prisoners usually beg for mail from the outside, saying they need mail to help them fill their many empty, lonely hours in the slammer. They often proclaim their innocence and say that they have been wrongfully imprisoned or sentenced to death. Many go on to ask their new pen pals to provide them with everything from stamps to large monetary deposits into their legal defense funds.

The Arizona Department of Corrections strongly objects to prison pen pal sites, largely due to an incident that happened at one of their prisons in 1997. A death row inmate's pen pal ended up marrying him while he was in prison; then the two concocted and staged a breakout plot, which got her and her incarcerated husband killed during the botched escape attempt. While the inmate was outdoors tending a prison vegetable garden, his wife showed up with an AK-47 assault rifle and began a shooting match with prison guards. She was killed, but before she died, she shot and killed her husband. Following that incident, the Arizona authorities became some of the first in the nation to seek strict restrictions on communication between inmates and prison pen pal Web sites.

Most prison authorities feel that a great deal of pen pal activity is a scam, with the inmates mainly out to get whatever they can from whomever they can con into providing it. Granted, there are countless numbers of prisoners who are having genuine, sincere correspondence with people on the outside who have become their friends, but in many other instances, the outside pen pal becomes just another victim.

There have been cases of people entering into mail relationships with prisoners who have ended up depositing thousands of dollars into inmates' alleged legal defense fund accounts, taking out mortgages on their property, and running their credit cards up to the limit. There are many, obviously very lonely, women from Belgium, England, Australia, and several other countries who have moved to the United States to be near their death row boyfriends after being manipulated into falling in love with them through pen pal communications. But despite the obvious scamming nature of much of the Internet pen pal activity, its advocates continue to defend the rights of prisoners to solicit such contacts, and the rights of people on the outside to become involved with the inmates. One woman, who runs an advocacy organization, said that she didn't think anyone had been coerced by inmates to give them money. People could determine for themselves, she said, whether or not they chose to send money to their prison pen pals.

"It's a personal decision," she claimed.

That personal decision has been very costly for some well-meaning people, including one woman who, investigators believed, had sold her condominium and then deposited $30,000 in one death row inmate's legal defense fund. Another of the same prisoner's pen pals was said to have taken out a $12,000 loan, which was given to the same defense fund. The Arizona Attorney General's Office said that the death row inmate, a triple killer, could possibly have collected many more thousands of dollars from a large number of other women he contacted via the Internet after he wrote to them, claiming that he loved them.

After settling into his cell on death row, Jeremy Jones wasted no time in getting his address and personal information posted on a Web site. His listing said that he was on death row and needed someone to talk to, a friend with whom he could share his "last days here on earth." He went on to say he felt alone and scared, and claimed that his life felt like "a bad dream or movie," and said that the American justice system had let him down.

Jones listed his age and date of birth, and described his personality, saying that he was a fun guy who loved to laugh and have a good time, and claiming that he was very open-minded. He listed the things he liked, which included camping, beaches, swimming, skiing, romantic walks on the beach, movies, dancing, horses, and, unbelievably, Mardi Gras. The authorities who viewed this listing on the pen pal Web site were astounded that Jones had listed Mardi Gras as one of his favorite things, considering the fact that Katherine Collins had been murdered during Jones's trip to Mardi Gras. The string of beads that were kept as a souvenir of that trip, and probably as a reminder of the killing that took place then, had contributed greatly to Jeremy Jones being charged with Katherine's death.

In recent years, several states followed Arizona's lead in attempting to curb prisoners' contact with Internet pen pal sites. Inmates normally had two or three pen pals on the average, prison officials said, but because of the Internet pen pal sites, that number had jumped, in some cases, from a few to hundreds. The prison mail rooms had been swamped under the increased volume of mail solicited on the pen pal sites, officials said, and they asked for regulations governing inmates' contact with the Web sites. The state enacted a law that would completely ban such contact, but that legislation was declared unconstitutional in U.S. District Court in 2003.

Other states tried different means to control the prison pen pal problem, with California attempting to prohibit inmates from receiving mail that contained Internet-generated information. That, too, was immediately challenged in court and was struck down in U.S. District Court, with the U.S. Circuit Court of Appeals upholding the ruling.

The Florida Department of Corrections prohibits inmates from "soliciting or commercially advertising for money, goods, or services," including advertising for pen pals or having ads posted with the assistance of another person. The regulation also bans correspondence or materials from persons or groups marketing pen pal advertising services. The regulations were challenged, but the law is being strictly enforced in the meantime.

The Alabama Department of Corrections ran into a particularly loathsome problem, courtesy of a death row inmate, Jack Trawick, who got his writings and artwork posted on the Internet on a Web site managed by a New Jersey man who claimed to be a pen pal of Trawick's. The Web site included Trawick's detailed descriptions of how he had murdered one of his victims, and his gruesome drawings of murdered and mutilated women. The mother of Trawick's victim filed a lawsuit against the inmate, the Alabama Department of Corrections, and the New Jersey man.

Alabama state senator Bill Armistead, who was at that time a member of the Alabama Prison Oversight Committee, decided that he'd had enough of death row prisoners freely having access to a convenient forum on the Internet, on which they could vent their spleen against the system and post their poems, writings, and what Armistead called "their so-called artwork."

Armistead named the Canadian Coalition Against the Death Penalty as one of the most prominent of the inmate Web sites, and said that inmates from Alabama's death row were, at the time, taking full advantage of the opportunity to be featured on the organization's site. Armistead said that Alabama inmates were being given Web pages and pen pal ads by the organization under the banner of free speech. But Armistead said he felt prisoners on death row had forfeited their right of free speech when they had committed their crimes.

The inmate Web sites that Armistead had viewed contained bloody and graphic art, he said, which could be viewed internationally by anyone of any age at any time. According to news reports, Armistead said, one of the death row inmates who was being given space on the Internet had been convicted as being one of four teenagers who committed an especially horrendous murder. He had been found guilty of stabbing a woman 180 times, cutting off her fingers and thumbs, breaking every bone in her face and skull, and cutting open her chest and removing one of her lungs before throwing her body over a cliff.

The prisoner had posted drawings of nude women with bloody swords and the bodies of their decapitated victims, and wrote about all that he knew turning "black with hate," saying death was his choice and that he would await his readers in Hell.

"How sick can you get?" Armistead asked, adding that he couldn't imagine the kind of feelings this so-called freedom of speech would bring to the murder victim's family if they viewed the horrific material on the Internet.

Armistead said that he had seen many of the online requests for pen pals, and he noted that most of the prisoners looking for correspondence showed no remorse for anything that they had done, blaming everything but their own actions for their situation.

There was no place in society, Armistead said, that he could see for death row inmates having the right to display their writings and artwork. He said that he planned to do everything in his power to keep Alabama's death row inmates from having the opportunity to take advantage of the Internet and call it "freedom of speech." As a member of the state senate and the Alabama Prison Oversight Committee, he said, he would work to see that prisoners' access to such forums would be curtailed.

Armistead also stressed that one organization, the Prison Fellowship Ministries, had his wholehearted support. That ministry allowed laymen as well as clergy to go into prisons, speaking and witnessing to the inmates, and the group had always been given high praise by prison officials and prisoners alike.

Jeremy Jones and thousands of other prison inmates might continue to solicit pen pals from the Internet, but their activities would be carefully monitored. There were countless numbers of people who would be watching closely, doing all they could do to keep the many inmate scam artists from preying on those well-intentioned people who wrote to them. There would also be a continuing effort by prisons to carefully monitor inmates' outgoing mail, preventing those prisoners from relaying harmful materials and statements about their victims that might later be posted for them on the Internet by an outside party.

Thanks to watchful prison authorities, legislators like Bill Armistead, and many others working to combat the growing problem, trolling by inmates on the Web was not going to be as easy in the future as it once had been.

Chapter 53

As Alabama approached its 2006 Election Day, there was a battle brewing for the office of attorney general between the incumbent, Troy King, and his opposition, Mobile County district attorney John Tyson, and that battle was becoming quite heated. There were several heavily contested races taking place in the state, including campaigns for the offices of governor, lieutenant governor, attorney general, and seats in the state senate and on the state supreme court. Candidates for all these offices were making news around the country because they were spending some of the highest amounts ever spent by candidates anywhere in the nation on their television campaign ads, and Tyson and King were waging a fiercely fought battle in the media. In late October 2006, that battle ratcheted up dramatically when a campaign ad for Troy King began airing, featuring Jennifer Murphy telling of what had happened in the prosecution of her mother's case and endorsing King's campaign for office.

Tyson, still keenly feeling the sting of having the Jeremy Jones case taken over by the state attorney general's office, immediately held a news conference and began demanding that King pull the commercial at once. Tyson said that King, both at the time of the trial and at the present, was "playing politics with capital murder prosecution."

King had taken prosecution of the Jones case away from Tyson at the request of Jennifer Murphy and Lisa Nichols's other family members, who felt that, seven months after Jeremy Jones's arrest, Tyson was not moving quickly enough to move the prosecution forward and bring Jones to trial. Tyson was infuriated that Murphy stated in the ad that he had stalled for seven months in prosecuting the case, and had told the family that it might be "years before we could get a trial. We asked Attorney General Troy King to intervene. Troy King got an indictment in four days."

Tyson took the opportunity to tell those in attendance at the press conference that he would promise the voters that he would "not rely on a convicted thief" as the spokesperson for his campaign. This remark referred to a 2003 theft case against Jennifer Murphy, who said that Tyson's statements left her feeling that the Mobile County district attorney had victimized her yet another time.

"I feel very confused," she said of Tyson's attack. "I thought his job was to protect crime victims, not attack them. Everyone makes a mistake from time to time in their life," she said. "This is how we learn. I made a mistake, I paid for it, and I learned from it. I'm a stronger person today for the mistakes that I have made."

Jennifer said she was horrified that Tyson would use an incident out of her past in such a manner.

"My background has nothing to do with the murder of my mother or the prosecution of Jeremy Jones," she said. "I will survive this horrible public attack by John Tyson, and I hope and pray that the next victim of a violent crime in Mobile will be treated better by Tyson than our family has been."

Tyson said at the news conference that he had not slacked

off on the case of Lisa Marie Nichols's murder. He claimed that he had personally surveyed the murder scene, and said that he had decided that when Jones was apprehended, he should be charged with capital murder for the crime. Tyson said that King's prosecutors had presented evidence to the same grand jury that he had already scheduled—in effect, stealing his thunder. He claimed that the case had gotten "top-drawer attention" from his office from the very start.

Tyson also accused Troy King of causing some of the other investigations involving Jeremy Jones to be stalled by his takeover of the case, and said that at the time, Jones had been talking with Tyson about his other crimes. Jones had stopped talking, he said, when King took over, but numerous other sources contended that Jones had continued to talk to anyone and everyone who showed up to interview him. Jones was continuing to talk from his prison cell, giving an interview only days before Tyson's press conference.

Tyson also claimed that Jones had been important in the investigation of a Mobile County meth lab that also involved another related murder. Tyson made the statement that Jones had supplied chemicals for production of meth at the lab and had sold the meth that had been made there. It is unclear when Jones had the time to do this on his most recent stint in Mobile, arriving in the city during a hurricane and leaving again only a couple of days later. Tyson could have been referring to an investigation that dated back years, to Jones's first period of residence in Mobile.

Both candidates for attorney general pulled out all the stops to win over the voters during the final days of the 2006 campaign, but the ad featuring Jennifer Murphy was, by far, one of the most compelling.

"Now Alabama has to choose between John Tyson and Troy

King," Jennifer said. "Take it from me. We need to keep Troy King on the job."

One man who viewed the commercial said that he felt it was sincere and straightforward, coming as it did from the daughter of a crime victim whose murder had sent Jeremy Jones to death row, courtesy of the prosecution conducted by the attorney general.

"With all the ridiculous campaign commercials that have been shown again and again on television this season," he said, "I think it's a good thing for the public to hear from a real person, someone who is speaking from their own personal experience with the candidate."

Attorney General Troy King handled the political mudslinging in the same manner that he had handled his duties since his term in office began—with calm confidence. The commercials featuring Jennifer Murphy continued to air, shown very frequently on all stations and in some of the most prominent airtime slots. They were featured during local and national evening news broadcasts, as well as at other peak viewing times. King, in his act of leaving the campaign ads on the air despite Tyson's attacks, once again stood behind Jennifer Murphy and her family, and his support was noticed and appreciated by many of the state's voters.

Chapter 54

In mid-October 2006, Jeremy Jones made another one of his announcements to the media from his cell on death row, relayed by a reporter with whom he was still in fairly regular contact. His appeal process was about to begin, he said, and he wanted to let the press know that his court-appointed attorney Habib Yazdi would no longer be representing him. Jones said that he and Yazdi had experienced what he called a failure to communicate, and he planned to use that lack of communication as an important part of his appeal.

Jones told reporters that he didn't "feel like me and him communicated right," so he had asked for Yazdi to be replaced, claiming that his conviction for the murder of Lisa Marie Nichols was due to Yazdi's poor representation, as well as the amount of publicity generated about the case prior to the trial. Judge Charles Graddick had pointed out to Jones and his attorneys, over and over again, that the lion's share of the pretrial publicity had been intentionally generated by Jones himself, and Graddick had refused to have the trial moved from the Mobile area for that reason. Jones still held out hope, however, that he could use the publicity as his get-out-of-jail-free card.

Habib Yazdi was replaced on Jones's legal team by a

Mobile criminal defense attorney, Al Pennington, who was highly experienced in appellate law. At the time of Jones's comments about his new representation, Pennington was in the process of filing a federal complaint that challenged the death penalty laws in Alabama on an array of points ranging from legal funding for indigent defendants to the level of competence and experience that was required by the state from court-appointed defense attorneys.

Pennington claimed in that complaint, which was filed on behalf of another death row prisoner set for execution within days of the filing date, that his client Larry Hutcherson had suffered a number of injustices at the hands of the state.

Hutcherson had been sentenced to death for the 1992 murder of an eight-nine-year-old Mobile woman, a particularly gruesome and violent crime that he had committed after drinking a great deal and taking Valium, then being discovered by the elderly homeowner while he was in the act of breaking into her house, with robbery in mind. Like Jeremy Jones, Hutcherson wasn't difficult to apprehend; he'd left his driver's license at the scene of the crime, and he came back to the scene of the murder the following day, intending to steal some additional items out of the home.

Hutcherson's civil rights had been violated, Pennington said, because his attorneys during the trial and subsequent appeals weren't trained well enough in death penalty cases and were not required by the state to have had such training.

Pennington also contended that once a direct appeal of a death sentence was made to the Alabama Supreme Court, there were not enough means in place to get a stay of execution while filing preparations were made to appeal to the United States Supreme Court.

Attorney General Troy King said that Hutcherson's appeals were exhausted, an execution date had been set, and there were no further stays available, nor any other legal matters to be dealt with prior to the execution. His office would review the complaint and respond, he said, but King maintained that the case had already gone through three levels of the appeals process and the death sentence had been consistently upheld by the courts. Pennington's tactics in filing the complaint were "nothing more than a delaying tactic," King said.

It must have been slightly unnerving to Jeremy Jones when his new attorney's other death row client, Larry Hutcherson, was executed by lethal injection on Thursday, October 26, 2006, at 6:00 P.M., in Holman's execution chamber. Hutcherson's final appeal, to the United States Supreme Court, had been rejected on Thursday afternoon, and Pennington told the press that Hutcherson didn't choose to ask Governor Bob Riley to grant him clemency. His client didn't want to beg, Pennington said, and had resigned himself to execution. After spending time with a large number of family members that afternoon, Hutcherson turned down any requests for a last meal, choosing instead to have food from the vending machines in the visiting area so that he could spend the time with his family. Later, Hutcherson became the 738th death row prisoner to be executed in the state of Alabama and was pronounced dead at 6:18 P.M.

The Hutcherson case was only one of many that Al Pennington had dealt with as a court-appointed appellate attorney, and despite the dismal outcome of Hutcherson's series of appeals, Jeremy Jones still had high hopes that Pennington's transfer to his legal team would increase his prospects of a successful appeal. In fact, Jones bragged to the press that he would win his appeal of the Lisa Nichols murder conviction and that the charges against him in Georgia and Louisiana would also be dropped.

When he was first transferred to Holman Correctional Facility from Mobile County's Metro Jail, Jones had high praise for the prison as opposed to the jail that he had just left. Prison was much more comfortable than the county jail, he said, and he was being treated far better at Holman than he had ever been in Mobile. But by the time the appeals process was about to start, Jones had flip-flopped and was calling his prison quarters "cruel and unusual punishment," and saying that his incarceration there was unconstitutional.

Al Pennington joined Jones's other court-appointed attorney, Greg Hughes, and a third attorney, Glen Davidson, to begin the mountain of legal paperwork for the lengthy appeals process that Jones would work his way through prior to his execution. That process, in Alabama, could continue on for years before the death penalty could be enacted, and in the meantime, Jones's new defense team would have plenty of time to search for loopholes and file for further appeals.

Pennington told the press that Jeremy Jones, like anyone else he had represented, was entitled to the best defense he could provide; Jones's crimes were not the issue, he said. He and the others on the team had a job to do, and would do it to the best of their abilities.

Jones's high hopes for an overturned conviction were not seen as much of a possibility by Jennifer Murphy and her family. Jennifer said that she was confident that Jones would eventually be put to death for her mother's murder. His conviction was so solid, she felt, that there was no way it would fail to hold up under the close scrutiny it would undergo during the series of automatic appeals. She firmly believed that someday she and others of Lisa Marie Nichols's family members would see Jones die by lethal injection in Holman Correctional Facility's execution chamber.

Jennifer said that when that day came, she planned on being present as a witness to Jones's execution.

Assistant Attorney General Will Dill, lead prosecutor in

Jones's trial, said the evidence against Jones at his murder trial had been so overwhelming that he felt there was absolutely no possibility of Jones's appellate attorneys being able to overturn the conviction. Dill said Jones's claims that he would be able to beat the death penalty were "preposterous," and said that Jones's guilt of committing such a horrible crime was beyond dispute.

There was, however, a strong possibility that Jeremy Jones would get to leave his cell on Holman's death row for at least a short time. It was beginning to look likely, authorities in Douglas County, Georgia, said, that Jones would be taken there to stand trial for the murder of Douglasville teenager Amanda Greenwell. That trip to Georgia might come in late 2006 or early 2007, according to Douglas County chief investigator Scott Cosper. Cosper told the press that there was a very strong case against Jones in Amanda's murder, and the investigation process had been continuing while the evidence against Jones continued to pile up.

Rick Greenwell, Amanda's father, was as certain as Jennifer Murphy had been that Jones would not be escaping the death penalty. Rick Greenwell had attended the trial, and he said he felt the case had been so solid against Jones that "there's no way he's going to win any appeal." Jones was behind bars to stay, Rick said, and would only leave the prison if he were to be taken out of state to stand trial on any of the other cases against him.

It was not looking likely, however, that one of those other cases would be the Oklahoma murders of Danny and Kathy Freeman and the disappearances of Ashley Freeman and Lauria Bible. Despite an intensive renewed search effort after Jones confessed to those crimes, no shred of proof had yet been found that could back up his claims of responsibility. The area where Jones said he'd dumped the bodies of the two girls had been combed through, one inch at a time, to no avail. Craig County sheriff Jimmie Sooter told the press that although he still personally believed that Jones had done the crimes, the search had ended and the disappointed authorities had given up and had closed the case. There was no proof, other than Jones's word, that he was guilty of the crimes. And that word, Sooter knew, was no good whatsoever.

Another exhaustive search had taken place in Mobile County for the bodies of the several prostitutes that Jones said he had killed and then dumped into a swamp in the Chickasaw area, but there, as in Oklahoma, no bodies had yet been found. The murder case against Jones in Louisiana for the death of Katherine Collins was in the hands of the Orleans Parish District Attorney's Office, but it didn't seem likely that Jones would be taken there to stand trial very soon. The entire legal system in New Orleans, since the onslaught of Hurricanes Katrina and Rita, had gotten backlogged almost beyond remedy, and since Jones was already on death row and wouldn't be going anywhere, his prosecution in New Orleans might be back-burnered indefinitely.

Attorney Al Pennington—with appeals to handle and, possibly, out-of-state cases to deal with—would have his hands full dealing with his new client. Pennington had told the press that the nature of Jones's crimes, and whether or not he was guilty of them, was not an issue. He had dealt with so many defendants, he said, and his job was to represent Jones to the best of his ability. But it was unlikely that Pennington had ever dealt with a client who was even remotely like Jeremy Bryan Jones. Jones was not necessarily going to follow his new attorney's advice or recommendations, and he would probably continue with his habit of contacting the press at will, saying anything and everything he chose to say, without the consent or the presence of counsel. Pennington was very likely going to have his work cut out for him during the time that he represented Jeremy Jones.

Habib Yazdi could have told him so.

Chapter 55

Alabama's death row has, for some time, been the subject of a great deal of interest among groups around the nation, and even worldwide, that are in favor of abolition of the death penalty. In addition to helping its inmates to find pen pals on the Internet, many of the countless Web sites of those groups, constantly lobbying to abolish the death penalty, also keep close tabs on the goings-on at Holman Correctional Facility. The groups and individuals who maintain those sites and post entries on their message boards stay in constant touch with each other, and their hope is that the state's death penalty will be abolished before Jeremy Jones, or anyone else, is executed in the state of Alabama. This might seem like a tall order, with the goal of doing away with the death penalty in a state where it is favored by a large majority of the residents, but it would seem that the abolitionists have gained at least one extremely powerful ally.

In April 2006, the state's largest newspaper, the *Birmingham News,* was informed that a series of columns, which had been written earlier by their editorial board, was one of the three finalists in its category for the Pulitzer Prize. The subject of the series? The paper's opposition to the death penalty in Alabama.

The newspaper fully realized, when going into the series, that their position might not be a popular one among the majority of Alabamians. According to one study, current polls indicated that over 70 percent of people in the state were in favor of the death penalty. However, the same poll also stated that even more, 80 percent, thought that the present legal system in place regarding the death penalty and its application could lead to an innocent person being wrongfully sentenced to death. Less than half of those in the poll thought the death sentence was applied fairly in the state, and slightly more than half thought that the death penalty should be suspended temporarily while its use could be studied and possibly changed for the better.

The *Birmingham News,* in its series of editorials, stressed the real possibility of an innocent person being executed in Alabama; five innocent people had been exonerated and freed from death row, and the newspaper posed the question that if there were more such innocent people slated for execution, what were the odds that they would have an opportunity to prove that innocence in time?

The newspaper's editorial board stated that even though the paper had supported the death penalty for years, they could no longer continue that support. Their decision was based on their opinion that Alabama's capital punishment system was at fault, but their belief in a "culture of life" was their foremost reason for their change in policy.

"We believe it's up to God to say when a life has no more purpose on this Earth," one of the editorials stated.

The alternative to execution, the paper said, was to sentence criminals to life without the possibility of parole, ensuring that they would never again be free to walk the streets and have an opportunity to commit further crimes.

One of the most compelling reasons to abolish the death

penalty, the editorials said, was a study that showed an alarming number of conviction reversals in Alabama because of such errors as biased judges and jurors, incompetent defense attorneys, and suppression of evidence by prosecutors. The state's former attorney general, Bill Pryor, claimed that during the five years following the study period, 1995 to 2000, error rates had been far less than those prior to 1995, but the *News* still held to their position.

"When possibly innocent lives are at stake," the newspaper said, "even Pryor's figures are too high."

In 2002, the most recent change in the state's death penalty was enacted when lethal injection became the state's official method of execution and the state's electric chair, the notorious Yellow Mama, was permanently retired. The *News* said that even though the method of execution had been changed to one that was considered to be more humane, any form of execution was still the taking of the life of a human being and, therefore, was wrong. And because of the potential shortcomings in Alabama's criminal justice system, an innocent man or woman might still run the risk of wrongful execution.

Committees of the Alabama legislature have passed some proposed bills that would prevent judges from overriding the recommendation of juries and imposing death sentences against their wishes, and to prevent the execution of inmates whose crimes were committed before they reached the age of eighteen. None of those bills have yet made it to the floor and been passed by the full legislature, but their proponents intend to keep them active, hoping for eventual passage.

Some of the reforms in Alabama's execution laws that the *Birmingham News* has recommended would involve several changes in the state's current system. Those changes included the establishment of a defense system for lower-income defendants that would ensure their court-appointed attorneys were capable to serve their clients throughout their prosecution, sentencing, and appeals. Before taking on death penalty clients, those attorneys would be required to receive an adequate amount of training in the specialized areas of capital trials and the lengthy and complicated automatic appeals process.

Another recommended change would eliminate the ability of judges to overrule a jury's recommended sentence of life in prison without parole. Alabama is one of only a few states where judges have the power to impose the death penalty despite the jury's recommendation, and the *News* believed that such a power should be eliminated. As previously mentioned, legislators in favor of that power being rescinded had gotten bills to that effect through committee, but they had yet to be passed.

A system should be established, the editorials said, to set up a process of review that would help prosecutors in deciding when to seek the death penalty in murder cases, and those prosecutors, they said, should be required to disclose every piece of evidence in capital cases. This process, called open-file discovery, is already a law in other states, and the *News* felt Alabama should follow suit, especially in cases where the death penalty could come into application.

The number of crimes qualifying for capital punishment in the state should be reduced, the *News* said; currently the death penalty is allowable for eighteen different types of murder in Alabama. Also, definite guidelines should be put into place, the editorials stated, defining mental retardation, since the United States Supreme Court has banned executions of the retarded. At present, the definition of mental retardation where murder defendants are concerned is not always as clear-cut as it should be, and guidelines were needed, the editorials said.

The *Birmingham News* also advocated the enacting of safeguards that would regulate and improve such things as the credibility of police or prison informants and lineup identifications, and recommended one process that had already been adopted as a required practice in the Mobile County Sheriff's Office before the time of Jeremy Jones's arrest. During homicide questioning sessions or confessions, the newspaper said, audiotapes or videotapes should always be made, and should be required by law. Several of the tapes of Jeremy Jones's interrogations and confessions were heard as evidence in court by the jurors during his trial. Those tapes played a very large part in Jones's conviction for the murder of Lisa Marie Nichols, and the Mobile investigators had known that even though they were not yet required to be taped or filmed, their sessions with him would have to be indisputably well-documented for presentation in court.

Another area of concern for death penalty abolitionists was the fact that since 1976, the state of Alabama had executed twenty-two prisoners for murders they committed when they were juveniles. A U.S. Supreme Court ruling deemed it a violation of the Eighth and Fourteenth Amendments to execute persons who were under eighteen years of age at the time their crimes were committed. Alabama had set its age limit previously as sixteen years of age for a person to be considered a juvenile, and the Supreme Court ruling overthrowing that state age limit affected the sentences of fourteen death row inmates, who will probably be resentenced, as a result, at some point in the future.

In its editorial series, the *Birmingham News* claimed it was likely that some of the state's death row inmates didn't receive fair trials or get a proper defense, and there could be some who might not even be guilty of the crimes for which they had been sentenced to die. The *News* said it was in favor of the state halting executions altogether, because "the system is broken, and because we believe in the sanctity of life." Knowing such a halt was unlikely, however, the paper called for a temporary cessation of executions, pending a reform of the state's death penalty practices, for three years at the very least. The death penalty, the editorial series said, should be imposed only after a thorough review of the legal processes that ensured fairness, and should be applied only to those who were found to be fully responsible for their crimes.

The *Birmingham News* was well aware that a large percentage of its readers would not agree with the paper's position on the death penalty, and chief among those who immediately disagreed were the members of an organization called Victims of Crime and Leniency, or VOCAL, which was founded by Miriam Shehane. Shehane's daughter was murdered in 1976, and her killer was not executed until more than thirteen years after the crime. Shehane started VOCAL to serve as an advocacy group for others whose loved ones had been murdered. Shehane felt that the *Birmingham News* was bent on protecting murderers while ignoring the grieving families of their victims. Shehane agreed that some people on Alabama's death row might have been wrongfully convicted, but she said that she felt it was unlikely anyone who was truly innocent would be executed. Appeals in the state are automatic, she said, and often lasted for fifteen years or more, allowing for ample time and opportunity for an innocent inmate to be exonerated and freed during the appeals process.

AG Troy King said that his belief was that certain crimes were so heinous that the death penalty was the only suitable punishment. In answer to the claims of death penalty opponents that defending life did not justify taking life, King said he didn't view the death penalty as so much a deterrent to crime as he considered it to be an exacting of justice for the victim.

"The death penalty is a strong statement that we value life,"

King told the press, adding that he believed it cheapened life when a victim's life was taken and the killer didn't get the sentence that was deserved. Carrying out justice in such instances, he said, meant that the killer's life was required to be forfeited.

The *Birmingham News* said it had fully expected opposition to its new position against the death penalty, but that the initial reaction by the readers had been positive. Speaking out against the death penalty had earned the paper much criticism, along with an even greater amount of praise from abolitionist organizations. The editorial board acknowledged that they realized it might be decades before any reform of the state's death penalty laws might be enacted, and in the meantime, inmates like Larry Hutcherson, whose appeals had been exhausted, would likely continue to be executed. Death penalty opponents would keep on aiming the nation's attention to Alabama's death row population, and Jeremy Jones and the other inmates imprisoned there would continue to hope for changes in the law that might save them from their fate.

And the families of Lisa Nichols, Amanda Greenwell, and Katherine Collins, along with all those other victims who had been robbed of their lives by someone who currently sat on death row, would continue their long wait for justice. The execution of their loved ones' killers would never bring back that person who had been taken from them, but for most, the death penalty's enactment would at least bring them some small measure of closure.

Chapter 56

Jennifer Murphy felt that she finally had everything that she had ever wanted out of life. She was happily married to a wonderful man, they had two children, who were the center of their world, and their lives were moving right along, just as Jennifer had always hoped and planned. But on September 18, 2004, her happy, well-ordered life changed forever in a heartbeat.

"I found my mother, Lisa Marie Nichols, murdered in her own home," Jennifer said.

Even after the trauma of her mother's tragic death, the arrest of Jeremy Jones for the murder, and his subsequent trial and conviction, Jennifer was still left without complete closure. There were a great many questions that she needed answers for, and like so many other loved ones of crime victims, she felt tortured by survivor's guilt. Often she found herself asking, "Why did this happen? What could I have done that was so wrong?"

Eventually the closure and acceptance slowly began to come. Jennifer realized that although some of her questions might have remained unanswered for the time being, she believed that eventually she would somehow find those answers through her faith, inner strength, and determination.

"We cannot question God; He has our lives planned for us at the moment of conception," Jennifer said. "There are so many questions we ask ourselves when we suffer a violent crime, and one of the first questions is 'How do I survive?'"

Jennifer learned from her experiences that for those left behind—the families and friends of the victims of violent crime—just learning how to survive from one day to the next is the first, most important goal.

"We cannot let the criminal take us also," Jennifer said. "We cannot shut ourselves out from the outside world. We must become stronger than we ever thought we could. We must speak out for our loved ones, who were taken too early. We must be a survivor."

Jennifer said that the first year after Lisa's death had been the hardest, but she had known what she had to do. It was up to her, and to all the other loved ones of Lisa Marie Nichols, to stand together in their resolve that Lisa would have justice.

"Every morning, I would wake up and look right up into the ceiling of my bedroom, and start talking," Jennifer said. "I'd say things like, 'I really don't want to get out of bed,' but then I could hear something coming from deep inside, saying to me, 'Get up, Jennifer, and take care of your family,' so I did. And the fight for justice began."

Jennifer had always firmly believed that people came into the lives of others for a reason. In the months after Lisa's death, she found that there would be countless numbers of people entering her life, people who would be giving her their help through difficult times and providing the support and guidance that she so badly needed.

"I met many people on the way along the road to justice,"

she said. "The detectives, the media, the prosecutors, the jurors, and the judge."

Jennifer believed that each and every one of those people had been handpicked, sent to help and support her and Lisa's other survivors.

"We could not have received justice for my mother if any one of these people had been absent from the equation," she said. They would always have her undying gratitude and admiration, she added, and they would never, ever be forgotten.

"After the trial, I found myself wondering what I should do next. It was clear to me that I wanted to continue speaking out, doing everything I could to help other crime victims' families. There were so many who could not bring themselves out of the dark walls of depression without someone there to give them the same kind of support and encouragement that I and my family had gotten from all those who had helped us."

During the months between her mother's death and the end of Jeremy Jones's trial, Jennifer spent countless hours on the Internet and the telephone, contacting the survivors of Jones's other victims to let them know that they weren't alone in their grief. She became a very proactive victims' advocate, reaching out to scores of people who desperately needed to know that there was someone else out there who understood how they felt and cared about what they were going through.

"I encourage victims to grieve for their lost loved ones, to cry their tears, but to let those tears lead to laughter as they remember the memories that were made with their loved ones over the years. And, most importantly, I tell them to remember that, although the body of the person they have lost is no longer with us, their spirit will always remain around us."

The hopes and dreams that Jennifer once had just didn't seem that important to her anymore. They were forever changed by the death of her mother and everything else that followed.

"I don't dream about having a big house overlooking a horse pasture anymore," she said, "or a new car that cost more than the house that I live in now."

Jennifer's new goal in life is for a time to come when she can become financially able to leave her current job and become a full-time victims' advocate.

"I want to help people," she said. "I want to help other victims get justice for their loved ones. I want to be that person that they can call on when they just need to talk. I want to be there for them, too, when they need just a little thing, like a soda during a trial or a parole hearing.

"I want to help fight for victims' rights."

And so, out of the terrible tragedy of her mother's murder, something good has come. Jennifer Murphy's life goal has changed. Her experience, her empathy, and her determination to help other people has grown even stronger since her mother's killer received the death penalty, and she now feels a calling to share what she has learned with others who are in such great need of help—the special kind of help that only another survivor can give. Jennifer Murphy is determined to help them past their grief and make a difference in their lives, the same sort of difference that was made in hers.

The spirit of Lisa Marie Nichols must be smiling down from Heaven.

Afterword

When I started gathering information for this book, Jeremy Jones had already been arrested and was an inmate at the Mobile Metro Jail, awaiting his trial for the murder of Lisa Marie Nichols. Authorities all around the country were contacting the Mobile County investigators and hurriedly going through all their cold cases that fit the pattern of the crimes he claimed to have committed. A formal announcement about Jones's confessions would not be made until after his conviction, but word had been spreading for months in news reports and on the Internet that he was being considered "the next big serial killer" and "the redneck Ted Bundy." It was common knowledge that Jeremy Bryan Jones was believed to have been responsible for a large number of murders, and he was getting enormous amounts of press coverage.

Some highly technical search efforts were taking place in Oklahoma and Kansas for the bodies of Ashley Freeman and Lauria Bible, and cadaver dogs were being led along creek banks in Georgia, searching for any trace of the body of Patrice Endres. Arrest warrants were served on Jones for the murders of Amanda Greenwell and Katherine Collins, and as

time passed, more and more information about his many alleged confessions and denials appeared.

Following his capital murder conviction, I began writing,
while I continued to collect every scrap of information I
could find about Jeremy Jones, his crimes, his victims, and
his continual manipulation of the media. I was amazed at the
way he had managed, from his jail cell, to pull the wool over
the eyes of otherwise sensible and experienced reporters.
Jones was able to get them to pass along his every word to the
public, taking his announcements, claims, and presumptions
and putting them into print or onto the six o'clock newscast,
just like he wanted.

After Jones was sent to Holman Correctional Facility's
death row, I decided that, in the interest of fairness, I would
contact him and at least give him an opportunity to say, in his
own words in this book, whatever he wanted to say to his
friends, family, or the authorities. I saw the offer as a chance
for him to offer a sincere apology for the terrible crimes he had
committed. Instead, he thought he saw another easy mark
coming, thinking that he was going to get yet another chance
to continue on with his endless chain of lies and manipulation.

I don't know why I ever expected anything else.

I had hoped that Jeremy Jones was feeling even a little bit of
remorse for the things he had done, and that he would use the
opportunity I offered him as a means to communicate that remorse to all of the many people whose lives he had shattered.
But no, all he wanted was another forum from which to proclaim his innocence, shift the blame for his actions, and make
accusations about the officials who had put him behind bars.

He started, in his first letter, by claiming that I didn't want
the truth from him; no matter what he told me, he said, I'd
never print the real truth. I'd write a book totally based on the
court transcripts, and that wasn't the truth at all, he claimed.

Jones then informed me that if I really wanted him to give me his whole life story, and the truth, "then get my trust."

I didn't plan to write the Jeremy Jones life story; the book is about his crimes, not his entire past history. And, as far as I was concerned, getting the trust of a killer on death row wasn't really an issue.

"There is no way you got all the research to do a good book on me," he proclaimed in his letter. "You haven't even scratched the surface."

He would send me a list of all his old friends and their phone numbers, he said, his real close friends, "not a bunch of bullshit police reports."

Then he asked, "Do you want to see it thru [*sic*] my eyes, yes or no."

That far into the first letter from Jones, I saw that I could expect to end up in the same boat with Paul Burch and Mitch McRae, listening to an endless stream of deception, demands, and deceit. But I continued reading, just to see if anything even slightly sincere might appear somewhere among Jones's boasts and claims of innocence.

He told me that he'd kept a journal since the time of his arrest, and said that he had already put together four hundred pages of his life, having gotten, at that time, from his birth to when he had reached the age of twenty-five.

"I'm saving the best for last," he bragged, claiming he was also keeping a daily journal of prison life.

Jones told me he'd had a few editors write to him and ask to write his life story, but he claimed he'd already written 80 percent of it. He had put nothing in his account but the truth. Then, in the next sentence, he jumped to another subject.

"Fuck an appeal," he said, "I say I got something better."

One of the witnesses at the trial, he said, a woman who had testified against him, had later supposedly gone to his lawyers and told them that she had lied on the stand, saying that Scooter Coleman had told her the truth.

"See, all you people out there," he said, "watch your TVs and your computer screens and pretend that's the real world.

"Wake up," he said, advising me to "put my do's (dues?) in, put some miles on them feet," and travel to Oklahoma to meet his family and friends, and the people with whom he worked.

Then he told me, "I played Paul Burch like a fiddle."

I might not have done enough research to uncover the whole, unabridged life story of Jeremy Jones, but I had already learned enough about the police officers involved in the case to assure me that Paul Burch wasn't a man who would be easily played. But Jones seemed to believe that he'd had Burch and the other investigators jumping through hoops at his command.

And after Habib Yazdi's courtroom descriptions of Jones's family, which pegged them as drunks, drug users, and child-abusing sexual perverts, I didn't think "them feet" of mine were going to be logging any mileage in the direction of Oklahoma.

That first letter closed with four numbered statements.

First, Jones said he had one question for me: who put me under contract?

Then he would help me "fill in the blanks," he claimed.

His next question was on the topic that obviously interested him the most.

"Who makes the profit off of this?" Jones asked. He had obviously not yet become familiar with the *Son of Sam Law*. And when he asked about profit from the book, his question reminded me of a story I'd heard at a tiny café in the little Alabama town where I live. One man was complaining to another about his unfaithful wife, saying that she'd slept with "every man in the whole town." His easygoing friend told him that he ought not to be too mad at her—the goods couldn't have been damaged that much.

"Aw, hell, buddy, it ain't hurt nothing," he said to the cuckolded husband. "This ain't that big of a town."

And I could have told Jones that as far as profit is concerned, "this ain't that big of a book."

Jones's fourth statement, at the end of the letter, asked me if I wanted the "good stuff" or not.

There were evidently several afterthoughts that Jones had after sealing the envelope, so he wrote them on the outside. They were more demands than afterthoughts, actually; he ordered me to write him back as soon as possible, and said for me to call the prison and set up a visit "so you can hear the truth from me and not some dam [*sic*] cop." Jones told me to talk to the warden and tell him I was writing a book, then finished that set of marching orders with some encouraging words: "Where there's a will there's a way. Don't give up."

One of the last items on my priority list would have been traveling for hours in order to spend a few minutes face-to-face with someone whose only intention was to maneuver me into doing whatever he wanted. No sir, not me. Been there, done that. Wouldn't have heard one word of truth the entire time. And then came his final, most preposterous demand, at least to a writer:

"I want to see your rough draft."

When I answered that first letter, I told Jones that I wouldn't be calling the warden, didn't plan on coming down to visit, and that there was no such thing as a "rough draft" when I wrote, so he wouldn't be seeing anything. But I did tell him that I would be glad to get in touch with anyone whose address he sent to me, and that if there were any photos of him in his earlier years, I'd like to include them in the book's photo section so that he'd be shown in something other than mug shots.

After a couple of weeks, I got another letter from Jones apologizing for not writing back sooner. He'd been going through a bad depression period, he said, but he was glad I wanted to find out more about him besides just a court transcript.

"Let's get one thing straight, OK," he said, "I'm not a killer."

Jones told me that he had played with the police "cause they made it so easy," and said that he was still playing with them. In return, he said, he got three-way calls that would usually cost him $27.50 per call, out of state. Then he acknowledged that he'd done a lot of things, "with drugs or whatever," and had been involved with the wrong women, who, he said, also had used dope.

"All the women who say negative stuff are all known dopers, OK?" he said; then he listed the names of several of the women in his life that he thought had fit into that category. Then he made yet another attempt at manipulation, saying that he wasn't going to waste his pen and paper defending himself to me, because he believed that I had already judged him. That, very obviously, was my cue to assure him, when I answered his letter, that no, I hadn't judged him at all, and that I was giving credence to his claims of innocence.

I didn't take the bait.

What he was going to do, he said as he continued his letter, was to give me some addresses of his friends or old girlfriends, "who will give you their side." He had pictures of himself fishing, hunting, at the beach, skydiving, deep-sea fishing, and big-game hunting in Idaho, he said, and his friends could send them to me. He was very much an outdoorsman, he said: "My middle name is sport."

On the back side of the page, he listed the names and addresses of five women, to whom I immediately wrote. Out of the five, I got phone calls from two, and a letter from another girl, someone who was not on the list, who said that she'd known Jones for twenty years. The two women who called me were both very nice, and they both had good things to say about the Jeremy Jones they had known when they were young. But the young Jeremy apparently bore little resemblance to the man who now sat on death row, convicted of murder. The women said that Jones had been a charming boyfriend, a fun guy to hang out with, and someone that their mothers had doted on when he spent time at their homes. But one of the women described what had happened to Jones as time passed.

"Jeremy got into drugs," she said, "and it started changing him. It really scared me."

Both the women told me how they had gradually drifted apart from Jones as he became more involved with a rougher crowd, a crowd that was into drugs, motorcycles, and some occasional juvenile delinquency. Jones had wanted to fit in with his new friends, and the women said he had joined in enthusiastically with the things his new crowd was doing. After that, his old girlfriends said, they didn't see very much of him anymore.

One of the women talked to me for quite a while, telling me about how her life had gone in the years since she and Jeremy Jones had been high-school sweethearts. Her life had been very hard at times, but she had worked her way through some very rough spots and apparently had come out stronger. Jeremy Jones would always have a place in her heart, she said, no matter what he had done, but she had moved on. She'd had to work very hard for the life she had now, she said. It had not been easy, but her strong Christian faith had brought her a measure of peace. She couldn't afford to risk that peace by getting too deeply involved with Jones again, she said, but she planned to at least get in touch with him in the hope of sharing her beliefs with him and maybe helping him to find some of the same peace she had found in God.

The other woman, who'd had a much more casual relationship with Jones during their high-school years, said they had been friends for a long time, and she told me how likable he'd always been and how much fun they'd had together. She, too, said she intended to write to him and try to be a friend to him once again, but didn't want to get too deeply involved with him in his current situation.

There was one thing that I heard, several times from both women, during our phone conversations.

"I know that he must have done what they say that he did," each of them told me, "but it's still just so hard for me to believe it."

None of the others on Jones's list got back in touch with me after I wrote to them, and none of Jones's family or friends bothered to send any photos of Jones that had been taken in some of his earlier, better days. Even though I carefully explained to them that I wanted to show him as a real person with friends and family during happy times, they never replied.

At the end of Jones's list of names and addresses, he added a PS, which said he had lots more people that I should contact, then added, "I really think we need to talk on the phone or in person." Then, along the side of the page, another note was added asking if I'd been in contact with the Mobile reporter who had befriended him and had served as his best conduit to the media, or if I'd contacted his off-again, on-again girlfriend, Vicki Freeman.

"I need to know, OK?" he said.

Then another tantalizing addition was added, written in the margins across the other side of the page:

"Check into the suicide of Scooter Coleman, that's where a lot of answers are."

Poor Scooter Coleman, he was still being promoted as the villain in the scenario. His untimely death—which was confirmed to have been by accident, not by his own hand—had left him continuing to serve as the perfect stooge, someone to lay the blame on, who was no longer able to defend himself.

As it happened, the reporter Jones asked about had written to me, saying that Jones had given him my name and address, and said that Jones had asked him to contact me. At this point, he said, Jones didn't trust me. When I called the reporter as requested, I made it very clear to him that, as I said earlier, earning the trust of a death row killer wasn't an issue, as far as I was concerned. If Jones wanted to talk to me truthfully, he would; if not, and he wasted both our time with his endless lies and manipulation attempts, then that was his choice.

In his third letter to me, Jones thanked me for writing back to him, and said that he hoped some of the people on the list he had sent me had been able to send pictures and tell me good things about him. He sent me another woman's address, saying that he had lived with her in Mobile for almost a year. She was his roommate, he said, and a good friend. "We even shared a bed sometimes, you understand," he said. She would explain everything to me, he told me, and he said that she had been questioned by Mobile police. She might also have some pictures of the two of them together.

She never wrote back to me.

Jones then switched into high fibbing gear, making what was, to me, a quite obvious attempt to win sympathy. He had tried, he said, to give me what he could so that I could write an honest book about him. Then the lies kicked into action.

"In my eyes, I look at myself as a hero," he said, going on to claim that he had given those many confessions to the authorities because he had been protecting his family and Vicki Freeman from the dreaded Scooter Coleman and all his cousins, including Mark Bentley. Poor Scooter, getting used as a scapegoat, blamed yet again and unable to defend himself from Jones's accusations.

"I confessed to protect my family," Jones claimed.

He went on to admit that he did change his name to John Paul Chapman, and said that he did have a past in Oklahoma, "but I can explain all that."

Then came more preposterous statements, with Jones saying that the police, Paul Burch and Mitch McRae, had used him "for promotions, and to cover their asses." Jones said that Mobile County was very corrupt, and asked me to please "check all this out before you print me as a monster, cause I am a loving caring man, just ask my friends, OK?"

Jones ended that letter with a request that I send him a book of stamps. I was expecting that; from previous experience writing to prison inmates, I knew that it was only a matter of time until I was asked for something of the sort. For that reason, I had been sending Jones stamped, self-addressed envelopes to use if he wrote back to me. I had no intention of funding his correspondence with dozens of those people who write to "prison pen pals," the chief form of entertainment of many death row prisoners, and there would be no stamps coming from me to be used for anything other than letters to me.

When the next letter arrived from prison, Jones was rather miffed at me, and his writing took on a slightly different tone. I had told him that I was getting no cooperation from most of the people he'd told me to contact, more than likely because they didn't want to get involved, and he had a ready answer. What the problem was, he said, was that no one trusted me.

"My family don't think anyone should profit off of me except my own family," he said. He repeated that he had over four hundred pages, front and back, of his life, and of "adventures, of people and places I have been," and also over two hundred pages of his daily journal, kept from the time of his arrest.

"You seem smart," he said, "you should know you get more flys [*sic*] with honey."

Yes, I knew that, and I was also smart enough to know that honey will draw a buzzing horde of yellow jackets, too.

Jones told me that he'd gotten three more book offers since I'd contacted him, "and they're willing to make a deal with my lawyer, and put the money in a family member's name, or a good friend."

Well, there's that *Son of Sam Law* coming into play once again. And Jones must not have been paying attention in court when Judge Graddick issued his order that if any money was ever paid to Jones or his family for such purposes, it would immediately be seized by the court and given to Lisa Nichols's family. Habib Yazdi and Greg Hughes were listening to the judge's order, I was certain, and they surely would not risk the consequences of violating it.

Until I really talked to him on the phone or in person, Jones said, all I had were court transcripts and police reports. He would like to talk to me, he said, "and let us print the truth, and let me express my ideas on the book too, with you."

Jones then griped that he had asked me several times for a book of stamps, but all I ever sent was an envelope addressed back to me.

"How am I supposed to write my friends and family and give them my permission to talk to you?" he asked.

His family was all about respect, he said, and without his permission, "you might as well be talking to a rock. Quit being so dam [*sic*] CHEAP yes CHEAP."

Jones then claimed that he didn't trust the reporter who had befriended him, and to whom he'd told so many tales during the time since his arrest.

"Him and another woman from Oklahoma is putting a book together of their own," he told me. "They even offered my family $10,000 for information. So wake up, there's more people than just you."

Then he said that there was yet another reporter in California who was also offering money for his story.

"If you want more of my help," he said, "get off your DUFF."

I'd been around in the newspaper business for quite a while, and I knew just about what sort of income most reporters make, which, unfortunately, is not nearly as much as most of them deserve. I feel certain that those three people whom Jones named to me, claiming that they had offered him such huge sums of money, would be horrified to know that he was making such outlandish statements about them and their intentions. They, like Yazdi and Hughes, certainly would not want to risk the consequences of violating Judge Graddick's order, even if they did have that kind of money to spend on what would likely turn out to be a lot of totally useless falsehoods.

Jones ended his letter as usual, dropping an interesting bit of information. In a previous letter to him, I had asked if his health was any better as far as his case of hepatitis C was concerned. He informed me that he didn't have hepatitis at all. "I was trying to escape from the jail if they took me to the hospital," he admitted. He said there were no medical records to even say that he'd ever had the disease.

"I lied," he said. "Open your eyes."

That was the last letter I had from Jeremy Jones. There would have been no point in writing to him any further; he was only interested in using me, however he could, and his friends and relatives clearly weren't going to do anything on his behalf. And since I had no intention of bankrolling his jailhouse correspondence with anyone other than myself, I didn't write back.

During the time I worked on this book, so many people involved with his cases had told me that Jones was an incredibly manipulative con artist and a compulsive liar. I'd believed them at the time. And after I'd had some personal experience of my own with him, I could clearly see what they said about him was all too true. I knew with certainty that the only information I'd have ever gotten from Jeremy Jones would have been an unending string of useless, self-serving falsehoods.

Epilogue

Even though Jeremy Jones has been tried, convicted, and sent to death row for the murder of Lisa Nichols, the other cases that he has been charged with, and those in which he is considered to be the prime suspect, are still very far from being over. Jones may be tangled up in the legal systems of several states for years to come. Some of the families of those he has confessed to murdering may never really know with any kind of certainty whether or not he was telling the truth. The questions surrounding the deaths of their loved ones may never be answered unless bodies are found, sufficient evidence is collected to file charges against Jones, and the authorities in the jurisdictions involved will then make an effort to bring him to trial in their states.

The likelihood of these things happening is not great; Jones might stand trial in Georgia for the murder of Amanda Greenwell, but other prosecutors may consider his current death sentence to be sufficient punishment in their cases.

"You can't execute him more than once," one prosecutor said.

Until his round of court appearances begins as he starts Alabama's automatic appeals process, Jeremy Jones sits in his cell on Holman Correctional Facility's death row, occupying himself in whatever ways he can devise. If he has been skillful enough to wrangle a large group of pen pals, there are many letters for him to answer and many plots to hatch as to what he can get those pen pals to do for him. There will be legal papers to read, and entries to make in his journal of prison life, and more pages to add to his life story. But all those things won't magically transport him out of the situation he is in, and there is no escaping the knowledge that once his appeals process is exhausted, he will be brought before a judge far more mighty than any he has faced before. The final justice for Jeremy Jones, when that time comes, will be swift and terrible.

The families of Jennifer Judd, Justin Hutchings, and the others that Jones claimed as his victims still continue to hope, each and every day, for some sort of solid information. Will York will never resign himself to giving up on his nephew's murder, and will continue to demand justice for Justin. Since his career change after Justin's death, when York decided to go into the field of law enforcement, he has kept feelers out for any scrap of information that might pertain to the case. With his determination, maybe he and his family will be able to eventually to find what is needed for a positive ID of Justin's killer.

Jennifer Judd's family wants justice for her, but only if there is positive proof of guilt. If Jeremy Jones is not the person who murdered Jennifer, they don't want to run the risk of letting the real killer go free and unpunished. Jennifer's family wants desperately to see her killer identified and prosecuted, but if Jeremy Jones wasn't responsible for the murder, as he has claimed, the authorities must continue their investigation until there is, finally, justice for Jennifer.

Lauria Bible's family, and the relatives of Danny, Kathy,

and Ashley Freeman, have been left in an agonizing limbo, with the second major search effort for the bodies of Lauria and Ashley officially canceled. The investigation into the disappearance of the two girls will still continue intermittently, when and if any new leads come in, but with each day, month, and year that passes, prospects of finding the girls grow dimmer.

The outcome of the fruitless searches that took place following Jones's claims of responsibility has been an extreme disappointment to Sheriff Jimmie Sooter. Because he knew the two girls during his time as a teacher, he had a very personal involvement and concern with the case, and he was disheartened to have to announce that the search had officially been discontinued. Sheriff Sooter, who left a career in education to go into law enforcement, is a good role model and a man who takes his duties seriously. If he should ever decide to become a teacher again, he'd be a great asset to any school lucky enough to have him.

Despite the fact that no bodies of prostitutes were ever found in the Mobile area after Jones claimed to have murdered several of them there, Paul Burch and Mitch McRae continue to keep a close eye on all the missing persons reports and the unidentified bodies found anywhere near the area. They, like so many families of Jones's alleged victims, have been left without resolution in so many of the cases they dealt with, and they will never stop looking for evidence in those cases. Both men are still with the Mobile County Sheriff's Office, and they remain in close touch with many of the other agencies that they worked with during Jones's time in their custody.

Mobile County sheriff Jack Tillman, who served as sheriff during the time of Jeremy Jones's arrest, trial, and conviction, retired from law enforcement shortly after Jones was convicted and sentenced. Tillman spent a great deal of time working with the Jones case and its many other connections around the country, and he remembered Jeremy Jones as being a very personable and pleasant fellow who was easy to talk with. But he also said, in his opinion, that Jones is a true sociopath and a compulsive liar, someone that was unique in his experience, and one criminal that he was never going to forget.

Before becoming sheriff, Tillman had worked on a long investigation of several cases involving the use of steroids by high-school athletes. During that time, he gathered a wealth of information about the dangers of steroid use; information that every school athlete, coach, and parent should know. The riveting stories Tillman has to tell about the many cases that he worked during that investigation are stories that need to be made public. He hopes to put them into book form someday, now that he's retired, and his book will be a good one.

Tina Mayberry's family still hopes for a break in Tina's case, something that will either point to Jeremy Jones as her killer, or prove that some other person is responsible. Jones was able to give so many details of the crime, including the fact that Tina supposedly fought him furiously for her life, but the assault occurred at a place that he patronized on a very regular basis. He could very well have learned enough details about Tina's assault from his conversations with other patrons of the bar and restaurant to piece together a believable confession. The authorities in Douglas County, Georgia, will continue searching for evidence, and Tina's killer will be positively identified someday.

The family of Patrice Endres still waits for further developments in her murder case, but if any clues have been found that point to a suspect, those clues have not been released by the authorities. The case remains unsolved, and it is essential for the public to remember that if Jeremy Jones didn't kill her, as he claimed, then someone else did. That person is walking free, unpunished for her death, and must not be allowed to escape justice.

Patrice's father, Richard Tamber, is a good man, a kind man. You can hear it in his voice. But even those who have only spoken with him on the phone can hear the sadness that is there. If Patrice receives justice, perhaps some of that sadness will be relieved. But even if Patrice's killer is brought down and punished to the fullest extent of the law, the pain of losing his beautiful daughter will never leave Richard Tamber's broken heart.

With all the flood of publicity that Patrice's disappearance generated, surely there is someone out there who has the information necessary to break the case. If that person called the Georgia Bureau of Investigation and gave them what they need to identify Patrice's killer, a grieving family, along with Patrice's friends and her entire community, would have a measure of peace.

The phone number for the GBI, along with the other agencies involved in the Jones cases, is listed at the end of this book. If you know something—anything—that can help, use that number. You could make a difference.

In New Orleans, Sergeant Jeffrey Walls and Investigator Armando Asaro are still haunted by the murder of Katherine Collins. They managed to break the case and successfully bring charges against Jeremy Jones, but whether or not he will ever be tried for Katherine's murder remains to be seen. New Orleans suffered such tremendous devastation during Hurricanes Katrina and Rita, and its legal system is still in such a shambles, that Walls and Asaro may never see Jeremy Jones standing in front of a judge in their jurisdiction. They have the satisfaction of knowing that he has received the death penalty in Alabama, but they will always remember their trip to Mobile to question him and his blood-chilling statement: "The bitch deserved it." And they will always hope that, someday, Jones will have to answer in court for his crime in their city.

Of all those whose loved ones may have been taken by Jeremy Jones, Rick Greenwell and his family have the greatest chance of seeing Jones stand trial for the murder of young Amanda, the beautiful teenager he has been charged with killing. Even before this book reaches the shelves, Jones may have been extradited to Georgia for trial in Amanda's death. Of all those he has claimed to have killed, only the cases of Amanda and Katherine Collins have resulted in formal charges, and Amanda's is the most likely of all to actually end up in court. That will be some measure of comfort for her family, but Rick Greenwell has said that Jones took everything from him that he cared for, and that can't ever be undone. At least justice for Amanda looks to be a good possibility, and one that her family can continue to hope for and await.

Jennifer Murphy, Amber McKerchie, and the other relatives and friends of Lisa Marie Nichols have tried as best they could to move on with their lives, but it hasn't been easy. The trial, the conviction, and the sentencing, and Jones's continuing statements from prison, have kept Lisa's murder always in the forefront of their minds, but they have had more closure than the other families touched by Jones, knowing that he is slated to face execution eventually for their mother's murder.

Jennifer and Amber will never have another holiday or special occasion without being keenly aware of the empty space, in the room or at the table, where Lisa should have been, but she will always be in their hearts and minds. Her presence is felt every day, and her daughters try to remember all the good times with their mother, not the horror they faced on the night they discovered that she was gone. They realize that their mother would want them to move on with their lives, and remember all their good times together, and that's what they are trying to do.

Jennifer's determination to serve as a victims' advocate will be a lasting tribute to Lisa, and every time she is able to comfort a grieving family and help them make it through an experience like the one she has endured, Lisa will be remembered and honored.

Attorney General Troy King, who was returned to office by Alabama's voters, has planted the seeds of a lasting memorial, the *Lisa Marie Nichols Justice for Victims Act.*

King, along with Will Dill, Don Valeska, and Corey Maze, put every ounce of their effort into winning a conviction in the Jeremy Jones trial. Thanks to the excellent, careful collection of evidence by Paul Burch, Mitch McRae, and the other officers of the Mobile County Sheriff's Office who worked the case, the attorney general's team of prosecutors had everything they needed to bring about a successful conviction. All these gentlemen have the most sincere thanks of Lisa Nichols's family, as well as the respect of all those from other states who worked closely with them in an attempt to determine which of their own unsolved cases might have a connection to Jeremy Jones.

George Herrera, the small-town reporter who did such a thorough job reporting on the discovery of Patrice Endres' remains, has moved on to another job, and odds are that he will do that job with the dedication and attention to detail that he showed in his work on the Endres case. George provided proof positive that sometimes the little guys win.

As for me, I hope never to have to write about another case where so many victims' families are with as many loose ends and unfinished business as the Jeremy Jones story has left. So many people have had their hopes raised, then dashed, by Jones and his innumerable claims and denials of murder. I urge everyone who reads this book to remember—please remember—all those unsolved cases. They must not be forgotten. If Jeremy Jones was the person responsible for those many deaths, as he has alleged, then the authorities have a duty to the loved ones of his victims to resume active investigating and not allow the many deaths to remain as cold cases.

If the proof is there, it must be found. And if Jeremy Jones was not guilty in any of the cases, then someone else was. Those persons are out there, walking free and feeling smug, believing that they have gotten away with murder. This must not be allowed to happen. The authorities, in all the jurisdictions where unsolved cases remain, must be urged and encouraged to continue their work. It is their duty and their obligation to bring about justice for all those many people whose lives have been devastated by the countless confessions and denials of Jeremy Bryan Jones.

The following agencies may be contacted by anyone who is able to provide information on any of the cases included in this book:

Carroll County, Georgia, Sheriff	(770) 830-5888
Dawson County, Georgia, Sheriff	(706) 344-3535
Douglas County, Georgia, Sheriff	(770) 920-5104
Forsyth County, Georgia, Sheriff	(770) 781-3056
Georgia Bureau of Investigation	(404) 244-2600
Kansas Bureau of Investigation	(785) 296-8200
Craig County, Oklahoma, Sheriff	(918) 256-6466
Oklahoma Bureau of Investigation	(800) 522-8017